4-4·74

POLITICS
AND THE
HOUSING CRISIS
SINCE 1930

POLITICS AND THE HOUSING CRISIS SINCE 1930

Nathaniel S. Keith

UNIVERSE BOOKS

New York

Published in the United States of America in 1973
by Universe Books
381 Park Avenue South, New York, N.Y. 10016

Library of Congress Catalog Card Number: 73-85852

Cloth edition: ISBN 0-87663-201-0
Paperback edition: ISBN 0-87663-912-0

Printed in the United States of America

Contents

1799436

The prostration of the construction industry—the housing bond scandals—the disappearance of credit—foreclosures rampant—the Hoover Conference—legislative palliatives. The focus of the New Deal and Congress—jobs and housing—rescuing the middle-class homeowners and the lenders—enticement of the bankers and builders through the FHA—the emergence of the housing professionals and the education of the politicos —"One-third of a nation ill-housed"—the fight over public housing and the Housing Act of 1937—the opposition and the real estate lobby—the New Deal and labor—the shadow of World War II.

Housing in the war economy—population immigration and growth and their impact on the Administration, Congress, and localities—emergence of local power centers through city halls, the housing authorities, and labor—vista of the future: the Taft hearings, postwar preparations in the Administration, the Senate hearings, the Wagner-Ellender-Taft bill.

pact of Newark and Detroit riots on LBJ and big capital—Congress again takes the housing initiative—LBJ's
final push on housing: 26 million houses in 10 years—
the Housing and Urban Development Act of 1968—
the dangers of continuing contrasts between promises
and accomplishments—housing and the 1968 elections.

Acknowledgments

This book has been on my agenda for a number of years. That it has now been written I credit largely to support and constructive criticism from my wife Marjorie. I also received great stimulus from Robert N. Butler, and valued professional guidance from my old friend Hiram Haydn.

I enjoyed the enthusiastic backing of Laurine ("Winnie") Winlack, veteran of many a housing legislative battle. Charles Ascher gave me helpful background information on the early years of housing organizations. The late Warren Jay Vinton, "Mr. Public Housing," critically and sympathetically read a number of key chapters. William L. Slayton, now the executive vice president of the American Institute of Architects, was an encouraging reader of early chapters. The late B. T. Fitzpatrick, the former general counsel of the top housing agencies and drafter of much of the basic legislation, examined much of my manuscript with insight and sophistication.

For the important work of typing and proof-reading I am indebted to Charlotte Hoeglund, Mrs. Cary Tremblay, Barbara McCracken, Gloria Forrester, Paulette Moorhead, and Susan Appelbaum.

Throughout my writing of the book I benefited from the sympathetic interest of my friends in the National Housing Conference and on Capitol Hill.

Introduction

The housing problem, its role in the crisis of the cities, and its relation to riots and urban unrest represent a central issue in the contemporary American scene of turmoil, tension, and pressures for change.

This current focus on the housing problem reflects an intensification and crystallization of pressures which have been evolving since the great depression of the early Thirties. Since 1933, there has scarcely been a session of Congress without controversy and debate on the housing problem. And, in the communities, there has been continuing conflict on what housing to build for whom—and where. In the background increasingly is the race issue.

Out of this controversy, there has developed over the years a substantial national housing policy and national housing program. Yet the absolute accomplishment of these efforts in meeting the housing crisis are amazingly small when measured against the dimensions of the need, aggravated by massive population growth and massive migration of poor whites and poor Negroes from rural areas to the cities. In the depresson era of the mid-Thirties, Franklin D. Roosevelt raised the slogan: "One-third of a nation ill-housed." Today, in a national economy surpassing the trillion-dollar a year level, the best that can be said is that only one-fifth of the nation is ill-housed. And that one-fifth is in the ghettoes, the urban blighted areas, and the rural pockets of poverty.

This book appraises the political forces which, on the one hand,

11

have forged the nation's housing policy as far as it has evolved and, on the other hand, have opposed and inhibited the carrying out of that policy. It includes not only the votes and debates in Congress but also information about the social and economic pressures in the society and in the localities which shape those votes.

What are the political forces which, on the one hand, have forged the nation's housing policy as far as it has evolved and, on the other hand, have opposed and inhibited the carrying out of that policy? For it is a basic premise of this book that it is the alignment of political forces, not the availability of material and financial resources, which has primarily determined the rate of progress over the past 40 years, or lack of progress, in housing in the United States as in other essential human enterprises in the modern era.

Since shelter involves the largest immediate capital cost of any personal commodity except for the very rich, the potential supporters of effective government housing programs might seem to comprise all households. But events have shown that there are likely to be political differences between those households which can readily afford that capital cost and those which cannot. Similarly, there is likely to be political division between those households which have relative freedom of choice as to the location and character of their home and those which do not, for economic or racial reasons. There also are relics of American folklore which can still evoke positive or negative political responses in relation to housing—the tradition of making your own way and the Puritan ethic that the poor deserve only poor housing are examples. These have also been translated at times into political slogans that Federal intervention in housing is "socialistic," a threat to "the American way of life," and also a threat to "the American free enterprise system."

In the time-span of four decades covered by this book, progress in housing legislation has generally been a response to crisis conditions. Until the catastrophic depression of the Thirties, housing was considered a matter of total Federal unconcern. Private enterprise built the tenements and workers' housing in industrial centers to shelter the successive waves of immigrants required for the nation's industrial expansion. (Today, much of this housing is still in use but now occupied predominantly by Negroes and Puerto Ricans.) There was some concern about the sanitary conditions in the tenements, some corrective state legislation, and a few eleemosynary attempts by the wealthy to develop better housing for the poor. During the boom of the Twenties, the burgeoning middle class built homes in the suburbs, financing them with first, second, and third mortgages for short terms. But these were not matters which were considered to demand Federal involvement.

All this was changed by the collapse of the early Thirties. By the time that the first Roosevelt Administration took office in March, 1933, homes were being foreclosed at a rate over one thousand per day, the foreclosing financial institutions (banks, building and loan associations, insurance companies) were closing their own doors or were threatened with insolvency, building construction was at a standstill, and the unemployment rate of one-third combined with underemployment of most of the balance of the population had paralyzed purchasing power. President Hoover had stubbornly and calamitously refused to intervene in this or other sectors of the private economy.

Franklin D. Roosevelt did intervene and on a massive scale. However, it is important to distinguish that this intervention was primarily an emergency action rather than the assumption by the Federal Government of responsibility for the housing welfare of the American people. The acute emergency thus was the rationale for refinancing with Federal funds home mortgages facing foreclosure, thereby rescuing both the homeowners and the mortgage holders. While the establishment of the FHA mortgage insurance program had some reform aspects from the standpoint of correcting the mortgage abuses of the Twenties, it was primarily sold politically as a program to unfreeze the home-building industry and thereby stimulate employment and the economy. Even the first venture into direct Federal financing of housing in 1934 was presented more as a public works program to provide jobs and consume materials than as a program to improve the housing conditions of the poor. FDR later was to embrace public housing as part of the New Deal crusade but this also was accompanied by a bow to the impact of public housing on increased construction employment.

The onset of World War II brought a halt to almost all construction except for war purposes. However, the resulting postwar housing shortage, intensified by the housing demands of returning veterans, provided much of the political pressure that ultimately resulted in the passage of the Housing Act of 1949 in which for the first time

Congress and the Executive Branch formally established a national goal of decent housing for all Americans.

After the lull during the Eisenhower years in the White House, the pressure for housing received impetus from the mounting urban tensions and the increasing demands from the cities for Federal aid. This was reflected in the significant housing legislation enacted in 1961, 1965, 1966, 1968, 1969, and 1970. The serious riots in 1966 and 1967 played a significant role, in part by penetrating the calm of the big corporations and by frightening the top power structure. Previously, the big corporations had generally ignored these tensions as no affair of theirs and had not participated in the production or financing of housing aside from manufacturing the materials and equipment used in construction.

Throughout this period since the early Thirties, the political alignment on housing issues has followed what have become familiar lines. The Northern Democrats in Congress have generally supported strong housing legislation; most Republicans and most Southern Democrats have generally opposed. There have been exceptions, of course: the late Senator Robert Taft of Ohio, the epitome of Republican conservatism on most issues, was, as a sincere gesture of capitalist *noblesse oblige,* a strong advocate of Federal aid for public housing, urban development, education, and health. Other outstanding exceptions are the two Alabama Democrats—Senator John Sparkman and former Representative Albert Rains—who have been consistent, imaginative, and progressive legislative leaders in the field of housing.

However, the liberals of both parties have tended to cluster in the legislative committees and have been largely responsible for the major housing and community development legislation which has been enacted. On the other hand, the conservatives have tended to cluster in the Appropriations Committees of the two Houses where control over the purse-strings has largely determined what can actually be accomplished under the legislative mandates.

Thus far, notwithstanding the mounting pressures for decisive Federal action to relieve the physical and financial crisis of the cities, there has not yet developed the political power consensus essential for achieving this decisive action. I refer to the political power consensus responsible for the massive appropriations achieved by the military-industrial complex, by the interstate highway program, by the space program, by the farm lobby, and by the health and education movements.

The ensuing chapters of this book describe and analyze the varying political fortunes of the movement for decent housing over the past four decades. They also undertake to appraise the prospects for reaching the political consensus needed to accomplish the nation's formal goals.

CHAPTER 1

Collapse and Depression, 1930-33 Rescue and Recovery, 1933-39

Housing development was the bellwether of the great depression. After the sharp but short-lived post-World War I economic crisis in 1921, residential construction was a leading factor in the development of the boom of the Twenties. But house-building peaked in 1925, four years before the tell-tale signs of the weakening in the general economy which appeared just prior to the Wall Street crash in the fall of 1929.

In 1925, 937,000 housing units were built, more than double the amount in 1921. By 1929, residential construction had dropped 46 percent to 509,000 units. In dollars, this meant a decline from $4.5 billion in 1925 to $2.45 billion in 1929.

The significance of this sharp retraction in a major segment of the national economy was largely ignored at the time. Retrospective studies attributed it largely to the imbalance in the segment of the total housing market served by the private housing industry; it was estimated that three-fourths of the housing production in the Twenties was marketed to the top one-third of the household income spectrum and that there was no production for the bottom one-third. In short, the narrow market for new housing was increasingly being saturated. A related important factor, especially in 1929, was the unprecedented diversion of bank and other credit to speculation in the securities markets. In any event, the recession in house-building was a portent of the drastic pressures which faced the United States economy as a whole.

The housing segment of that economy was in a weak position to withstand those pressures. Single-family homes, increasingly concentrated in the suburbs, were typically financed through an unsound patchwork of first, second, and even third mortgages, generally of short terms and without any built-in orderly system for repayment of principle. As unemployment deepened and personal incomes dropped, many of these mortgages were sitting ducks for defaults and foreclosures.

A second basic weakness was the imbalance of the housing economy previously referred to. With the onset of the depression, the sources of credit for speculative apartment building dried up even more rapidly and drastically than the financing resources for new single-family homes. The impact of this on housing production as a whole was further accentuated by the fact that, alone among the developed Western nations, the United States had no government-supported housing program for low- and moderate-income families. Hence there was no public effort to pick up the slack of declining private housing production, to say nothing of improving the lot of the families living in slums or other substandard shelter. By contrast, in Western Europe and particularly in Great Britain, since the end of World War I governments had been deeply involved in the production of workers' housing through subsidies and other financial support.

This second weakness was, of course, only one further illustration of the predominant economic and political philosophy in the United States during the boom of the Twenties: the supremacy of private enterprise and the cult of rugged individualism. During the 1928 Presidential campaign, Herbert Hoover synthesized this philosophy;

> The poor-house is vanishing from among us. We have not yet reached the goal, but given a chance to go forward with the policies of the last eight years, we shall soon with the help of God be in sight of the day when poverty will be banished from this nation.

There was a vanguard, primarily in the large metropolitan areas, which recognized the drastic limitations of the national housing economy and attempted to organize remedial action. In 1926, New York State had enacted a housing law granting twenty-year tax exemption to limited dividend companies developing housing projects. There was increased interest in workers' housing cooperatives and in garden communities like Radburn and Sunnyside in the New

York area and Chatham Gardens in Pittsburgh. These were pioneering and influential experiments but their combined impact was small as to total volume and as to significance to low-income families.

The severity of the advancing depression was sufficient to frustrate even these experiments, in the absence of government support. In 1930, total housing production receded to a point 60 percent below the 1922-28 average; by 1931 the rate had descended 69 percent below that average. Foreclosures of home mortgages were mounting rapidly in the path of sharply rising unemployment and wage and salary cuts. In 1932, foreclosures reached the disastrous level of 250,000 homes. With purchasing power drastically curtailed, these foreclosed homes became a drug on the market for the foreclosing institutions and jeopardized their solvency. The blows of the depression also hit the housing status of the formerly affluent. There were widespread real estate bond scandals and failures resulting in the loss of higher priced apartments which had been marketed at inflated prices during the late Twenties. There was a similar collapse in the higher-priced housing cooperatives which had become popular and and fashionable during the same period, especially in the larger cities. (A later study by the Twentieth Century Fund was to characterize this latter mode of financing as follows: "Probably no form of real estate was so exploited by unscrupulous promoters. As a result values were inflated to untenable levels and the resultant thin equities left no margin when rentals declined. Failures were consequently widespread.")

During those critical years, the main political focus was on the collapsing stock market, the beginnings of bank failures, spreading unemployment, and sharply rising relief rolls. Throughout 1930-31, the Hoover Administration stubbornly refused to intervene with the financial resources of the Federal Government on the grounds that prosperity was just around the corner. While not equally in the limelight with these hallmarks of the depression, the housing problem had become sufficiently acute to prompt President Hoover to call a President's Conference on Home Building and Home Ownership. The Conference was convened in Washington on December 2-4, 1931, with 3,700 registered participants under the joint chairmanship of Robert P. Lamont, the Secretary of Commerce, and Ray Lyman Wilbur, the Secretary of the Interior.

The Conference brought together substantially all the leadership and expertise which then existed in the fields of housing production, design, management, and finance and the related fields of planning, zoning, and code enforcement. The participants naturally represented a wide range of political, economic, and social points of view as well as a widely varying degree of realism in recognizing the critical nature of the housing crisis.

The Conference produced a series of well-informed reports which were to be useful as guidelines in future years. These reports covered such matters as the development in communities of building programs meeting local needs; improved planning and zoning; better homes at lower costs through improved technology; broadening of home ownership; adequate systems of home credit for better protection of home owners and lending institutions; rehabilitation of old homes; elimination of slums and blight through municipal and State action; facilitating large-scale housing operations; modernization and simplification of local building regulations, and so forth.

These recommendations were all well and good for the long haul under so-called normal conditions. But they clearly were not pertinent to the housing crisis existing and growing in December, 1931, and to the necessity for massive Federal intervention to cure that crisis. This lack of pertinence no doubt was to be expected under the prevailing philosophy of Federal non-responsibility for such matters. Secretary of the Interior Wilbur edged close to the recognition that public subsidies would be required to solve the housing problem of low-income slum dwellers. Addressing himself to "those who look upon government operations in housing construction with abhorrence," he warned in a foreword to one of the conference's reports:

> If business, financial and industrial groups fail to take the task in hand and apply the large sums of capital required and the utmost of planning genius and engineering skill to the problem, it seems likely that American cities will be forced to turn to European methods of solution of this problem, through subsidization by State and municipal treasuries and probably through actual ownership and operation of housing projects by municipal authority.

It should be noted that Wilbur's statement did not refer to the Federal Treasury as a potential source for such subsidies.

The Conference's Committee on Negro Housing followed the same general line: "If it is not feasible to build low-priced apartments as business investments, we recommend that consideration be given to use intervention by public funds either through tax relief or through direct subsidies as has been done by Vienna and other European cities." Even as dynamic a progressive as Louis Brownlow did not identify a Federal role in providing decent housing for the poor even though recognizing the essentiality of "government" subsidy for this purpose.

In fact, the only recourse to the Federal Government recommended by the Conference was to provide capital for the establishment of 12 regional Federal home loan banks under a Federal Home Loan Bank Board. These regional banks were to make advances of credit to the sorely-pressed savings and loan assocations on the security of first mortgages. Legislation carrying out this recommendation was enacted on July 22, 1932. While the Federal Home Loan Bank system ultimately became a major factor in private residential finance, in 1932 the depression was too far advanced to permit the new banks to carry out a rescue operation at that time. A later analysis by the Twentieth Century Fund commented: ". . . the housing situation at the time called for more drastic treatment. Measures that might have helped to forestall a collapse, if enacted a decade before, were powerless to stem the tide of urban foreclosures."

With the depression constantly deepening and with the 1932 Presidential campaign in the offing, President Hoover finally did relax his strict position against Federal financial involvement in measures to relieve the collapse. But this relaxation was not for the relief of the unemployed or of the insolvent home-owner. Instead, he requested and approved legislation in January, 1932, establishing the Reconstruction Finance Corporation (RFC), with paid-in Federal capital of $500 million and authority to sell debentures in the amount of $1.5 billion. Under its original statute, the RFC was limited to making loans to banks, insurance companies, and railroads. Responding to the pressures stimulated by these limitations, Congress broadened the legislation to increase the RFC's lending authority to $3.5 billion and to expand its purposes to include loans for productive purposes. After first being vetoed, the amendments were finally approved by President Hoover in July, 1932 as the Emergency Relief and Construction Act. Under this legislation, RFC was authorized to make self-liquidating loans for the construction of housing for low-income families or for the reconstruction of slum areas. Only one such loan was made for urban housing, in the amount of slightly over $8 million for the Knickerbocker Village development in New York City.

These belated and limited moves were too little and too late to stem the collapse. They also were too little and too late to stem the national political revulsion against the Hoover Administration. During the 1932 Presidential campaign, it was enough for Franklin D. Roosevelt to exude confidence and charm and to promise action to cure the depression through a then vaguely defined New Deal. President Hoover's absurd prophecy that "grass will grow in the streets of 100 cities, 1,000 towns" if his opponent were elected only added to the tide for Roosevelt. His landslide victory, with 59 percent of the popular vote, could have surprised only the most hidebound Republicans.

During the grim and archaic lame-duck interregnum between the November election and Roosevelt's inauguration on March 4, 1933, the nation's collapse approached its nadir. By early 1933, unemployment was estimated variously at from 12 million to 17 million persons or from one-fourth to one-third of the national work force (there were no accurate statistics). Many of those still employed were working only part-time at reduced wages. National income and total industrial production had been cut in half since 1929. Again, the collapse in construction led the depression cycle. In 1932, only 134,000 dwellings had been built in a nation of 120 million persons; this was a decline of 84 percent from the 1922-28 average. There were increasing runs on the banks and increasing hoarding of currency and gold.

With all banks closed throughout the country, with farmers in quasi-revolt over foreclosures and disastrous price declines, and with huge relief lines in all the cities, the nation was on the brink of violent upheaval. General Hugh S. Johnson, who was to lead the National Industrial Recovery program for FDR, was quoted later as remarking that no one would never know "how close we were to collapse and revolution. We could have got a dictator a lot easier than Germany got Hitler." And Rexford Tugwell, one of FDR's original "brain trust," declared: "I do not think it too much to say that on March 4 we were confronted with a choice between an orderly revolution—a peaceful and rapid departure from the past concepts—

and a violent and disorderly overthrow of the whole capitalist structure."

In these circumstances, the crucial priorities facing the New Deal Administration were to get the banks reopened on a reasonably sound basis, to check the flight from the dollar, and to meet the relief crisis. Under the panic psychology of the spring of 1933 and with the emergence of FDR's strong national leadership, these measures were enacted into law with remarkable speed. This was the first segment of what came to be known as "the hundred days."

Nevertheless, the national economy remained largely prostrated in terms of production, employment, and purchasing power. There also were the persistent and critical credit problems involving home and farm foreclosures. It was within this complex of pressing issues that the first steps toward the establishment of a national housing policy began to emerge.

In the United States Senate, strong pressure was developing for a major public works program to stimulate recovery in the acutely depressed construction industry and likewise to expand direct construction employment. The principal figures in this movement were Senator Robert F. Wagner of New York (who was to author much of the New Deal social legislation), Senator Edward Costigan of Colorado, and Senator Robert M. La Follette, Jr. of Wisconsin. Within the New Deal Administration, the principal public works supporters at that time were Mrs. Frances Perkins, the Secretary of Labor; Harold L. Ickes, the old-time Bull Moose Progressive who was Secretary of the Interior, and Rexford Tugwell.

This interest in public works with Federal financing provided an opening for a group of housing professionals, largely centered in New York City, to seek the inclusion of public housing both to produce construction jobs and, for the first time, to provide good housing for low-income families through Federal funds. This group—which included such persons as Clarence Stein, the eminent planner; Edith Elmer Wood, Mrs. Mary Simkhovitch, director of Greenwich House in New York City; and Father John O'Grady of the National Conference of Catholic Charities—had access to Mrs. Eleanor Roosevelt as well as to Senator Wagner.

It was through this combination of emergency circumstances that the National Industrial Recovery Act, enacted June 16, 1933, authorized the use of part of its $3.3-billion public works appropriation to finance the construction of low-cost housing and slum clearance projects as well as subsistence homesteads and Greenbelt towns. Ultimately, 21,600 housing units in 50 projects in 37 cities were developed under this authorization, which was the forerunner of the present low-rent public housing program. In addition, 15,000 units were built in resettlement projects and the three Greenbelt towns.

Simultaneously with the initiation of the public works program, the Roosevelt Administration and Congress enacted legislation to rescue the beleaguered home-owners from foreclosure. During the early months of 1933, homes were being foreclosed at an average rate of about one thousand per day. The new law established the Home Owners' Loan Corporation (HOLC), financed by Federal capital and bonds, to purchase defaulted home mortgages from holders who could carry them no longer and to refinance the loans to the occupant, including delinquent real estate taxes and deferred repairs. The refinanced loans carried a moderate interest rate and were repayable in monthly installments over a long period of years. During its first three years, the HOLC refinanced over one million homes with mortgage loans in the amount of $3.1 billion. This was equivalent to one out of five of all mortgages on owner-occupied homes in the non-farm areas of the nation. The average borrower was delinquent two years on his old mortgage and was in arrears almost three years on real estate taxes.

The HOLC operation also prevented a total collapse in home financing and, by freeing funds frozen in defaulted mortgages, permitted lending institutions to begin to resume making new mortgages. The repayment pattern set by HOLC on its refinanced mortgages was also of great influence in modernizing mortgage lending practices, in contrast to the crazy-quilt of multiple short-term loans which had largely prevailed during the Twenties. Arthur M. Schlesinger, Jr. was later to comment: ". . . by enabling thousands of Americans to save their homes, it strengthened their stake both in the existing order and in the New Deal. Probably no single measure consolidated so much middle-class support for the administration." *

In 1934, there was a related effort to stimulate the revival of the private residential construction industry through Federal legislation.

* *The Coming of the New Deal* (Boston: Houghton Mifflin Company, 1959).

The HOLC program, confined entirely to the refinancing of existing homes, was under the administrative control of the Federal Home Loan Bank Board, established belatedly in 1932 by the Hoover Administration and rejuvenated by the New Deal. The primary direct function of the Home Loan Bank Board was to make advances of credit to its member institutions on the security of home mortgages, a function somewhat similar to that performed by the Federal Reserve System in the case of commercial banks. However, by reason of the provisions of the Home Loan Bank Act, the members of the Home Loan Bank System were limited almost exclusively to savings and loan associations.

Consequently, significant support developed for establishing a companion system of Federal assistance for residential financing by other types of institutions, primarily the commercial banks and life insurance companies. There was also support of this approach from the still acutely depressed building materials and equipment industries and from the surviving remnants of the home builders themselves. The underlying pressure for this further action stemmed from the sheer fact that the residential construction industry remained at a level of almost complete prostration during 1933; the total housing units started amounted to only 93,000 compared with 134,000 in the crisis year 1932. In 1934, there was only modest improvement.

This was the setting for the enactment on June 27, 1934, of the National Housing Act, creating the Federal Housing Administration (FHA). The new FHA program, unlike the public housing program under the Public Works Act and the HOLC operation, involved no direct expenditure of Federal funds aside from a small capital contribution for initial reserves. The FHA principle was to stimulate recovery in private mortgage lending and home building by a system of mortgage insurance protecting the lender against loss in the event of default by the home buyer. In such event, the FHA would acquire the mortgage in return for its debentures covering the entire unpaid balance. These debentures had an ultimate full guarantee from the Federal Treasury as to principle and interest, although throughout the extensive history of FHA it has never been necessary to fall back on this guarantee.

The cost of the FHA program was met by a small mortgage insurance premium paid by the home-buyer as part of his monthly mortgage payment. In return for this protection, the mortgage lender made a long-term mortgage (initially twenty years) at a high percentage of the cost of the home to the buyer (initially 80 percent). The mortgage interest rate was required to be within a ceiling set by FHA. The FHA thus contributed further to the reform in mortgage lending practices which had been initiated by HOLC. It also had ancillary benefits ultimately by improving the standards of construction, especially for lower-priced homes, and also by raising the quality of subdivision site planning, primarily in the suburbs.

The National Housing Act also provided insurance for short-term installment loans to finance home improvements and repairs upon better terms than were prevalent for installment credit at that time; this program was popular with consumers, commercial banks, and building materials and equipment suppliers. In another section, the Act established the Federal Savings and Loan Insurance Corporation to protect savings in savings and loan institutions on a basis generally comparable to Federal bank deposit insurance.

These were the programs which made up the substance of the New Deal's housing effort. While the establishment of each of these programs had been justified in large degree as emergency measures to help overcome the great depression, their basic long-range significance lay in the tacit recognition that solutions to national housing problems required intervention by the Federal Government. Within the space of two years, there had been a complete reversal of the long-established and generally unquestioned principle in the United States that housing was the responsibility of private enterprise exclusively, except for minor actions by State and local governments, and in no sense should be considered a matter for Federal responsibility. The new principle of Federal intervention and responsibility in housing survived not only the depression and the years of partial recovery but also the crisis of World War II and the vagaries of the post-war period. It survives today.

The business of getting these new concepts into effective action in 1933 and 1934 involved varying problems. In the case of the HOLC, with hundreds of thousands of distressed home-owners clamoring for assistance and with ample Federal funds available, the problem was essentially one of assembling and training a staff adequate to process the applications. This was done with remarkable speed and, on balance, with highly satisfactory results. To a lesser extent, the Federal Home Loan Bank Board also had a built-in clientele of savings and loan associations, especially after their solvency had been at least partially restored by the HOLC program.

The problem of developing the Federal Housing Administration as an effective force in the financing and production of housing was much more complex. The FHA had no Federal funds to disburse as such. It faced the necessity of developing an entirely new system of credit insurance in an untested field and of persuading innately cautious bankers and insurance executives that this system was sound, acceptable, and helpful. In these circumstances, it was not surprising that FHA did not achieve a significant volume of mortgage insurance until 1936. From then on, its role in private residential financing and home building became increasingly influential.

The difficulties of launching a public housing program under the public works program were even more complex. This was a field in which there was no Federal experience (aside from the small World War I war housing program) nor was there any State experience which could be tapped. The Federal law was extremely general if not vague as to the specifics of the direction which the program should take. From the outset, there were also serious legal questions. Harold L. Ickes, who was in overall charge of public works, at first attempted to set up a $100-million housing corporation but was blocked from securing the necessary Federal funds by the conservative Controller General who contended that such a corporation would be unconstitutional. Ickes also experimented with direct loans to limited dividend private housing corporations at 4 percent interest, covering 85 percent of the total cost of a housing project, to be repaid over twenty-five to thirty-five years. This approach drew more than 500 applications totaling over $1 billion. However, after scrutiny by Ickes' Housing Division, only seven of these applications, involving about $11 million and 3,065 housing units, were finally approved and built. In February, 1934, the limited dividend program was terminated as to future projects. The limitations on this program were twofold: first, the difficulties in securing the substantial equity capital investments required by the formula, and, second, the fact that the formula produced rents sharply above the amounts which low-income families in the depression era could afford to pay. This, in turn, reflected the lack of any direct housing subsidy.

The next venture to achieve sizable production of public housing was through direct construction and financing by the Housing Division of the Public Works Administration (PWA). This was started in the spring of 1934. Under this approach, the Federal agency acquired the land, let contracts for the construction of the housing, and owned and operated the project. Of the total cost of the housing, 45 percent was considered an outright grant (in short, a capital subsidy) and the balance of 55 percent was considered to be a loan at 3 percent interest to be repaid out of the earnings of the project over sixty years. This plan had the advantage of the substantial Federal capital subsidy which made it possible to achieve rents more in line with the needs of low-income families living in the slums. The plan also had some innate disadvantages stemming from the fact that it was in essence a program of direct Federal intervention in local communities for the production and operation of housing as distinguished from Federal financial assistance for locally-sponsored housing development. There was a serious related legal question as to whether the Federal courts, as then constituted, would find that the use of Federal condemnation powers to acquire private property for housing use represented a valid "public purpose" under the welfare clause of the Constitution.

In fact, this issue was tested in a case argued before the Federal District Court in Louisville in January, 1935, which resulted in a ruling of unconstitutionality. This ruling was later upheld by the United States Court of Appeals. The Louisville case did not stop the development of public housing under the public works program. But it did compel the PWA Division of Housing to rely primarily on the negotiated purchase of its project sites rather than on condemnation. And the case gave further strong impetus to seeking the establishment of a system for transmitting Federal aid for low-rent housing which would avoid the constitutional issue and also foster local responsibility. Such a system would involve Federal loans and grants to local housing authorities, established under State laws.

The problem here was that the principle of public responsibility for housing, even at the State or local level, was so novel that not a single State or municipal government had the legal authority to engage in slum clearance or low-rent housing development when the New Deal took office in 1933. By the end of 1934, only seven states had enacted legislation authorizing the establishment of local housing authorities. In December of that year, at the urging of Harold Ickes, President Roosevelt wrote the Governors urging the enactment of such state legislation. Extensive missionary work was still required by the PWA to persuade Governors and state legislatures to move in this direction. When the PWA Housing Division wound up its activities in late 1937, 29 states had passed enabling legislation and 46 local housing authorities had actually been established.

While the New Deal housing programs were going through these growing pains, an alignment of political and economic forces on housing was in the process of development; this alignment would persist with little basic change for the next three decades. In a broad sense, this reflected the adjustment in political attitudes toward the New Deal which was occurring nationally. The fervent endorsement of FDR and his policies by conservative economic interests which was so prevalent during the first months of the New Deal was short-lived. With the abatement of the acute crisis psychology of the spring and summer of 1933, many of these interests began to revert to political type. This even led to wishful thinking that the off-year Congressional elections in 1934 would show that the New Deal was only a temporary political phenomenon and would begin a return to Republican "normalcy." Instead, despite heavy support for the Republican candidates from important business interests, the Democrats increased their top-heavy majority in the House of Representatives to 322 out of 432 seats from 313 and won 26 out of 35 Senate contests.

In the narrower field of housing, the polarization of political positions centered around the new issue of public housing. This was viewed as a dangerous threat to private enterprise in real estate by four organizations which were to lead the opposition to public housing until the 1960's. These were the Chamber of Commerce of the United States, the National Association of Real Estate Boards, the United States Savings and Loan League, and the National Association of Retail Lumber Dealers. Three of the four principal individuals involved were also to be in the van of this opposition for many years: F. Stuart Fitzpatrick, the secretary of the Construction and Civic Development Department of the Chamber of Commerce; Herbert U. Nelson, executive vice president of the Real Estate Boards; and Morton Bodfish, executive vice president of the Savings and Loan League. The ideological opposition of these groups to Federal intervention in housing did not extend to the entities formed to support private enterprise—the FHA and the Federal Home Loan Bank System. On the contrary, these organizations had played a role in the enactment of the legislation establishing FHA and the Home Loan Bank Board. But they viewed public housing as an entering wedge for the eventual socialization of residential real estate. This polarization was mirrored within the New Deal Administration itself. The PWA public housing program was, of course, under the jurisdiction of Harold L. Ickes. The "old curmudgeon" was a staunch defender of any activity within his responsibility even though he was always careful to keep a discreet public silence on matters involving Administration policy. On the other hand, the clientele of FHA was primarily the large commercial banks, mortgage banks, insurance companies, building material suppliers, and private builders. These groups were beginning to organize in opposition to public housing. As the first administrator of FHA, President Roosevelt had appointed James A. Moffett, a wealthy oil man whose father had been president of Standard Oil of New Jersey. Moffett felt himself obligated by his position to act as spokesman for private housing within the Administration and was soon being quoted in the press in support of private housing and in opposition to public housing. This was played in the press as a major dispute between Ickes and Moffett. Eventually, President Roosevelt had to intervene personally and to emphasize that FHA and the PWA Housing Division were in two separate and distinct fields—FHA to stimulate the private housing market and the Housing Division to build homes for those unable to afford the product of the private market. While Moffett himself did not long remain as head of FHA, the attitudes he expressed persisted within that organization for many years. There was also covert opposition to public housing within the Federal Home Loan Bank Board but this was controlled much more adroitly by its astute chairman, John A. Fahey, who was also the head of HOLC.

During this same period of polarization on housing, there was also increasing activity on the part of groups pressing for a long-range permanent program of Federal aid for low-rent public housing. Here again, many of the individuals in the forefront of this movement in the early New Deal days were prominent on the liberal side of the housing issue for many years. The first organization specifically formed to press for a long-range public housing program was the National Public Housing Conference (NPHC) founded in New York City in 1931. (This organization is the principal liberal lobbying force in housing today under the title of the National Housing Conference.) The leading figures in the formation of this organization were Mrs. Mary K. Simkhovitch, director of Greenwich House; Ira Robbins and Louis Pink, then legal advisers to the New York State Board of Housing; and Helen Alfred, a social worker. Others prominent in the organization were Mrs. Edith Elmer Wood, a noted housing expert; Father John P. O'Grady of the National Conference of Catholic Charities, Harry W. Laidler of the League for Industrial Democracy, Judge Charles Poletti, Loula D. Lasker of *Survey* magazine, and Irving Brant of the *St. Louis Star-Times*.

With the beginning of the efforts for public housing development under the PWA program, another significant development was the formation in November, 1933, of the National Association of Housing Officials (NAHO) as a professional organization to provide technical assistance to the developing housing movement. (This continues to be today the principal professional organization in housing under the title of the National Association of Housing and Redevelopment Officials.) NAHO was formed under the sponsorship of the Public Administration Clearing House, headed by Louis Brownlow, and was financed by grants from the Spellman Fund of the Rockefeller family. A principal figure in the formation of NAHO was Ernest J. Bohn, a resourceful and energetic Republican from Cleveland, Ohio, who became its first president. Bohn went on to a distinguished career in public housing as executive director of the Cleveland Housing Authority while continuing an influential role in national housing affairs. The first executive director of NAHO was Charles Ascher, a public administration expert; he was succeeded in the summer of 1934 by Coleman Woodbury, a specialist in the economics of housing.

The supporters of a long-term public housing program soon gained an important political sponsor in Senator Wagner of New York who introduced the first draft of such legislation in January, 1935, which had been prepared by the National Public Housing Conference. However, before significant momentum was achieved for such legislation, it was necessary that there be crystalization of support both within the New Deal and among the public at large. One important gap was closed in October, 1935, when the American Federation of Labor, previously lukewarm on housing, got behind the legislation and threw its support to the Labor Housing Conference. This was a group formed in 1934 by John Edelman, a leader in the textile workers union, and by other labor leaders in Philadelphia and New Jersey. It was directed by Catherine Bauer, a brilliant young writer and researcher in the field of architecture and housing. The objective of the conference was to stimulate interest in housing by local labor unions. Boris Shishkin, a prominent labor economist, was assigned to work with this group.

A year previously, in November, 1934, there had been a significant conference in Baltimore which assembled the 75 principal professionals and operators in the publicly-oriented housing field. The occasion was the presentation of a report by three European housing experts—Sir Raymond Unwin and Alice Samuels of England and Ernest Kahn of Frankfurt—of their study of housing problems and potential solutions in 14 of the principal cities in the United States. Their tour had been sponsored by NAHO and financed by the Rockefeller Foundation. The purpose of the Baltimore meeting was to seek a consensus on a housing program for the United States which could meet the needs of low-income families in a context of local responsibility, sound urban planning, and necessary Federal financial support and subsidies. This consensus was accomplished. Through the auspices of Mrs. Eleanor Roosevelt, the President was personally exposed to the findings of the European experts and the report of the Baltimore conference. The recommendations of the conference also proved to be influential in building support for a long-range program among city governments.

With organized labor finally a strong ally for the legislation and with growing support from the mayors, Senator Wagner decided that 1936 was the year for a major push for its enactment. This also had the political advantage of being a presidential election year. In preparation for this push, Wagner also established the political line to counter the opposition of the private organizations on the right. In a speech before the National Public Housing Conference in December, 1935, he said:

> The object of public housing, in a nutshell, is not to invade the field of home building for the middle class or the well-to-do which has been the only profitable area for private enterprise in the past. Nor is it even to exclude private enterprise from major participation in a low-cost housing program. It is merely to supplement what private industry will do, by subsidies which will make up the

difference between what the poor can afford to pay and what is necessary to assure decent living quarters.

By contrast, the opposition stressed the sanctity of private ownership of housing under the American system, regardless of the financial problems of poor families. Walter S. Schmidt of Cincinnati, then the president of the National Association of Real Estate Boards, expressed the position in this manner:

> Housing should remain a matter of private enterprise and private ownership. It is contrary to the genius of the American people and the ideals they have established that government become landlord to its citizens. . . . There is sound logic in the continuance of the practice under which those who have initiative and the will to save acquire better living facilities and yield their former quarters at modest rents to the group below . . .

On April 3, 1936, Senator Wagner introduced the United States Housing Act. The bill had been drafted by Leon Keyserling, the brilliant young Harvard Law School graduate who was Wagner's legislative assistant (11 years later Keyserling was to become the chairman of the President's Council of Economic Advisers). The legislation generally reflected the views of NPHC, the Labor Housing Conference, and NAHO. It also had had technical advice from Warren J. Vinton, the research director of the Resettlement Administration, and David L. Krooth of the PWA Housing Division legal staff, among others in the Administration. A companion bill was introduced by Representative Henry Ellenbogen of Pennsylvania in the House where it faced an uncertain future because of the known hostility to public housing on the part of Chairman Henry Steagall of Alabama, the chairman of the Banking and Currency Committee which had legislative jurisdiction.

The fate of the measure even in the Senate was cloudy because of uncertainty as to the position of President Roosevelt. In view of the divided opinions within the Administration and the absence of any final decision by the President, Senator Wagner had introduced the bill on his own without waiting for a formal White House blessing. With his campaign for reelection in the immediate offing, FDR was carefully balancing all political factors. At his press conference on May 4, the President said he favored the Wagner bill in principle and hoped it would pass, subject to certain unspecified amendments. But he declined to attach to it the magic label of "must" legislation. This proved to be the death-knell of the bill in the 1936 session of Congress. The implication was that FDR concluded that the backers of the legislation were bound to support him in the election in any event but that an all-out push for the Wagner bill might further solidify his conservative opposition, especially in the South.

It was only through his great personal prestige and political strength that Senator Wagner was able to penetrate the rush to adjourn prior to the Democratic convention in late June and to bring his bill to a vote on the floor of the Senate, after agreeing to various amendments sought by the White House. It passed the Senate on June 16 by a vote of 42 to 24. In the House of Representatives, the lack of the "must" label was fatal. Chairman Steagall was widely reported as expressing his personal opposition to the bill as socialistic but as also expressing his willingness to get the bill out of committee if the "chief" really wanted it. The Congress adjourned on June 20 without any action by the committee.

Notwithstanding this setback, the Democratic Convention adopted a platform plank drafted by Senator Wagner expressing a general commitment to housing for low-income families:

> We maintain that our people are entitled to decent, adequate housing at a price they can afford. In the last three years the Federal Government, having saved more than two million homes from foreclosure, has taken the first steps in our country to provide decent housing for people of meager incomes. We believe every encouragement should be given to the building of new homes by private enterprise; and that the Government should steadily extend its housing program toward the goal of adequate housing for those forced by economic necessities to live in unhealthy and slum conditions.

Public housing legislation was not a major issue in the 1936 Presidential campaign. But FDR's landslide victory over Governor Alfred M. Landon of Kansas, in which he carried every state except Maine and Vermont, clearly set a favorable backdrop for legislation of this type. Senator Wagner lost no time after the election in pressing his case with the President for support of his bill at a White House meeting on November 17. And the Executive Council of the American

Federation of Labor, at its November convention, declared: "The United States Housing Bill, unchanged in any important respect except for a larger appropriation of funds and greater bond-raising power, can and must be passed this coming winter."

President Roosevelt himself delivered his strongest personal commitment to the cause of housing in his second inaugural address on January 20, 1937. This contained the now familiar peroration:

1799436

But here is the challenge to our democracy: in this nation I see tens of millions of its citizens—a substantial part of its whole population—who at this very moment are denied the greater part of what the very lowest standards of today call the necessities of life . . . I see one-third of a nation ill-housed, ill-clad, ill-nourished . . .

The prospects that the Wagner Bill would be enacted in 1937 were enhanced when Chairman Steagall of the House Banking and Currency Committee introduced the Senate-passed 1936 bill when Congress convened in January, notwithstanding his personal opposition to public housing. This implied that Congressman Steagall had read the election returns. Again, when Senator Wagner introduced his own revised bill in the Senate on February 24, Steagall filed the identical measure in the House on the same day.

If Congressman Steagall had read the election returns in this light, this did not appear to be the case with the main opponents of the legislation. The National Association of Real Estate Boards reiterated its opposition to the Wagner bill, declaring among other things that in no case should local governments undertake to build or operate new housing facilities. This position continued to be shared by NAREB's principal allies—The Chamber of Commerce of the United States, the U.S. Savings and Loan League, and the National Association of Retail Lumber Dealers.

The main delays and problems encountered in 1937 by Senator Wagner derived not so much from the conservative opponents of the legislation as from divisions within the Administration and among the general supporters of the legislation. Because of his inability to get agreement from the various factions within the Administration, Senator Wagner again had introduced his bill without getting final clearance from the White House. There ensued a power struggle, largely over the issue of jurisdiction over the public housing program within the Federal Government. The Treasury Department under Secretary Henry Morgenthau pressed for a conservative financing system under Treasury control which the supporters of public housing contended would seriously hamper the program. Harold L. Ickes sought to have the administration of the program lodged within the Department of the Interior and secured the support of the NPHC. The Labor Housing Conference and NAHO favored an independent agency and gained the support of Senator Wagner himself. There were also basic policy differences, principally concerning whether public housing should be built on cleared slum sites or on vacant land as a method for increasing the housing supply, and whether the Federal subsidy should take the form of capital grants as in the PWA housing program or annual contributions geared to the annual needs of the local housing authorities.

While these disputes resulted in protracted delays, there was a ground-swell of support for the legislation generated mainly by organized labor and the Labor Housing Conference, by the NPHC, and by the Housing Legislation Information Service, organized in Washington by Ernest J. Bohn. Senator Wagner persistently wove his way through these difficulties and on July 23 his bill was finally reported favorably by the Senate Education and Labor Committee. On August 6, it passed the Senate by a vote of 64 to 16, including a number of restrictive amendments which later were largely resolved in conference. Of equal importance to the ultimate fate of the measure, in late July it received the blessing of President Roosevelt who then pressed Chairman Steagall to hold prompt hearings in the House. The House passed a modified version on August 18 by a vote of 275 to 86, and the compromise conference bill was signed into law by the President on September 1.

The passage of the United States Housing Act of 1937 was the high water mark for the tide of New Deal liberalism in housing. The concept of annual Federal subsidies to local housing authorities to provide housing for the poor at rents geared to their ability to pay was to survive over the coming decades, notwithstanding many vicissitudes and bitter political controversies. The new public housing program started with great verve. While Harold L. Ickes had won his point by having the administrative jurisdiction of the new United States Housing Authority lodged within the Department of the In-

terior this proved to be a Pyrrhic victory. Without consulting Ickes, FDR at Senator Wagner's urging nominated Nathan Straus, a wealthy New Yorker, to be the Administrator of USHA. Ickes characterized Straus as a "dilettante" an̄ ̄ ̄rsonally objectionable to him; he therefore washed hiᵉ ̇ ̣ole in the new agency. But many of the persoᴨ⸍ ̇ in the struggle to secure the enactmᵉ̣ ̣is's staff. Leon Keyserling beᵣ⸍ oth took a prominent legal ̣of research. Lee F. Johnson, ̣, first as legislative repre-
Catherine Bauer became

which proceeded ener-
the passage of state
̣ng authorities, and
ι ̣: housing projects.
A̤ ̣using units were
put ̣he number pro-
duceᵥ ̣ears of opera-
tions.
The ̣ ̣ᴜ with controversy from
the outse ̣gnt was only intensified by its
early succᵤ ̣ nurdle in Congress was surmounted
without diff. ̣when additional authorizations for annual
subsidies weɪ ̣ᵤ. With the overwhelming New Deal majorities carried over fᵤᴏm the 1936 landslide, this was passed in June by votes of 60 to 10 in the Senate and 297 to 70 in the House.

The conservative forces in the housing field continued to focus their political opposition on the growing low-rent public housing program. With the gradual revival in private home building, the now familiar conservative quartet—the Chamber of Commerce of the United States, the National Association of Real Estate Boards, the United States Savings and Loan League, and the National Association of Retail Lumber Dealers—ultimately became a quintet with the advent of the National Association of Home Builders. This organization was comprised primarily of small private builders of individual homes. Its members had been drastically buffeted by the depression and were easily susceptible to charges that public housing, even though limited to poor families well outside the potential market for new private homes, represented "socialistic" government competition with private enterprise.

This opposition rested on two basic premises: first, an ideological opposition to any form of public ownership of residential property even for the poor, and, second, the more practical concern that public housing was in fact in competition with privately-owned slum dwellings. This dual reasoning is illustrated by these excerpts from the confidential weekly newsletters of the National Association of Real Estate Boards during 1939:

> USHA projects now under way are undiluted socialism . . . Opinion is growing that any plan of operation which would put housing and building permanently into private hands is preferable to the present program of local and Federal ownership of housing projects . . .
> If the Federal Government is going to give subsidies, let it subsidize people and not brick and mortar. Let the Federal Government go directly to its objective instead of going into the real estate business and elaborating grandiose plans which often seem to fail of their purpose.

The political climate in Congress, and especially in the House of Representatives, became somewhat more responsive to these arguments in 1939 and 1940. In the broad background was the reaction to FDR's unsuccessful attempt to enlarge the Supreme Court in order to secure a majority on the Court sympathetic to New Deal policies, and the reaction against his equally unsuccessful attempt to purge the Congressional opponents of his court legislation in the 1938 elections. Along with the disappointing pace of the national economy in 1938, this resulted in the net loss of 72 Democratic House seats in the 1938 Congressional elections, although a Democratic majority of 261 to 164 was still retained.

In this setting, the increasing pressure from the conservative lobbies produced a legislative setback for the low-rent public housing program in 1939. A contributing factor was the personal antagonism felt toward Nathan Straus by a number of influential House Democrats, notably Albert Gore of Tennessee. In an unusual action, the House of Representatives by a vote of 191 to 169 refused to take up a bill proposing major extensions to the USHA law. The bill had previously passed the Senate by a margin of 48 to 16. On this House vote, 55 Democrats, mainly from the South, joined with 136 Republicans to defeat the bill.

From an overall standpoint, the New Deal housing programs were contributing to a steady recovery in the total volume of housing production. By 1939, starts of new dwellings had recovered to about the 1929 level but with the help of 56,000 publicly financed units which were unheard of in 1929. In 1940, there was a further expansion of 16 percent to 603,000 dwellings, including 73,000 publicly financed units. The FHA program was playing an increasing role in the development of privately financed housing during this period. By 1940, about 40 percent of all private housing starts were under the umbrella of the FHA mortgage insurance system.

But looming in the background after September, 1939, was the shadow of World War II. The transition to a wartime economy in the United States began in 1940, even though under the pseudonym of "defense." This transition of necessity also marked the beginning of the end of New Deal reforms and social and economic advances.

Housing inevitably and promptly felt the impact of this transition. On June 28, 1940, the United States Housing Act of 1937 was amended to authorize the use of its loan and subsidy provisions for housing defense workers during the emergency. Ultimately, almost 30 percent of the housing units financed under the 1937 Act were developed for this purpose. On July 21, 1940, an Office of Defense Housing Coordinator was established in the Council of National Defense to plan and carry out defense housing programs. On September 9, 1940, $100 million was appropriated for the erection of defense housing by the War and Navy Departments. On October 14, 1940, the so-called Lanham Act, the basic defense housing law, was passed, involving direct Federal financing and construction.

Also in 1940, the United States for the first time conducted a Census of Housing, including the condition of housing. This disclosed that more than 17 million dwelling units, or 49 percent of the total national housing stock, was structurally substandard or lacked a private bath. But the correction of these deplorable conditions had to go on the shelf for the duration of the war—and for too long thereafter.

CHAPTER 2

The Crisis of War and a Vista of the Future, 1940-45

The transition to a full war economy was not complete until after Pearl Harbor. In housing, a total of 715,000 dwellings was built in 1941; much of this production was still for the general civilian market. But there was a growing shortage of building materials in reflection of the diversion of materials to the armament industries and the beginning of a priority system for defense activities.

In January, 1941, the President established the Division of Defense Housing Coordination and broadened the responsibility of the Defense Housing Coordinator to include the programming of housing for defense plants. He had appointed to that post Charles F. Palmer of Atlanta, who had had early experience in public housing. But Palmer's charter did not include direct authority over the 16 Federal offices which had functions in one way or another in the production or financing of defense housing. In bureaucratic fashion, these offices were jealous of their prerogatives and resisted coordination by an outsider. The result was extensive confusion.

The disaster at Pearl Harbor completed the cycle to war. Among the many steps taken to place the nation on a total war footing, President Roosevelt on February 24, 1942, used his war powers to consolidate all Federal housing functions into a new National Housing Agency (NHA) under a single administrator with full powers. The explanatory statement by the White House, after referring to the 16 offices previously involved, commented: "There have been duplication, conflict, disputes and overlapping among these public ageencies themselves and also between them and the private building agencies."

John B. Blandford, Jr., was appointed by the President to be the Administrator of the new wartime agency. Blandford, then 45, had had no direct housing experience but had a successful record as a skillful public administrator. Since the fall of 1939, he had been Assistant Director of the Bureau of the Budget; during that period he had developed close relations with the White House staff and had gained the confidence of FDR himself. From 1933 until 1939 he had been coordinator and the General Manager of the Tennessee Valley Authority. He had threaded his way through the internal conflicts in the three-man board of the TVA and had played an effective leading role in the success of the TVA experiment. Blandford thus began his new post with strong White House backing but with no personal commitments to the various vested interests in the housing field.

Under the reorganization, all publicly financed housing functions were consolidated in a Federal Public Housing Authority (FPHA), built around the nucleus of the United States Housing Authority. Nathan Straus, who had become increasingly controversial as the head of USHA, had resigned prior to the reorganization. To head the new FPHA, Blandford appointed Herbert Emmerich, also a professional public administrator; Emmerich had been active in the influential "garden city" development in the New York City area during the Twenties. The Federal Housing Administration and the Federal Home Loan Bank System retained their identities and functions but with a wartime focus.

Under the sweeping provisions of the executive order establishing the National Housing Agency, Blandford had clear directive powers over the policies and operations of these three so-called "constituent units." He exercised these powers firmly insofar as wartime activities were concerned. But he was cautious about intervening directly in the internal bureaucratic structure of these agencies. This was especially true of the FHA and the Home Loan Bank System. Blandford's caution reflected his recognition of the economic and political strength of the built-in clientele of these agencies—the private builders, the banks and insurance companies, and the savings and loan associations. In the case of FHA, he did install Earle S. Draper, a professional planner and former TVA colleague, as assistant commissioner for war housing and more or less as his personal representative and watchdog.

For his own top staff, with crucial authority for the programming of war housing, Blandford recruited an effective, youngish group. He appointed Coleman Woodbury, the executive director of the National Association of Housing Officials, as assistant administrator for programming. Leon Keyserling became general counsel. To head up field operations, Blandford named Philip M. Klutznick, an energetic and forceful attorney from Omaha. Lyman Moore, another professional public administrator, became the top official for internal administration and control. For director of public information, Blandford selected Howard F. Vickery, a professional newspaperman of the *Denver Post* variety and a man of intense personal loyalties. In my own case, I was recruited as Blandford's principal speech writer and to handle special policy correspondence (after eleven years as a reporter for the *Wall Street Journal* in New York and Washington, I had joined the FHA public relations staff in 1940). Later, I became Blandford's special assistant for Congressional relations.

The harsh realities of World War II quickly forced a drastic readjustment in the housing field. The tremendous requirements for materials and manpower for the unprecedented expansion in production of articles of war dried up the civilian supply for all except the basic necessities of life. A rigorous system of materials priorities and allocations was established and enforced by the War Production Board in order to channel the distribution and use of critical materials, including those needed for housing construction, for war production and related purposes. At the same time, the massive expansion in the armed forces was draining off manpower in the 18-to-37-year-old age brackets. Enrollment in the armed forces increased from 1.6 million in 1941 to almost 4 million in 1942, 9 million in 1943, and over 11.4 million in 1944 and 1945. Furthermore, the remaining civilian workforce was not necessarily living where the needs for war production workers were the greatest. This disparity was augmented by the large development of new war factories, mostly financed directly by the Federal Government, built to meet production requirements which could not be met through conversion of existing industrial plants. The result was a large migration of industrial workers to the centers of civilian war employment. This was officially estimated at 3 million war workers during the first year and a half alone of the U.S. involvement in World War II. This migration represented a total population shift of 8 to 10 million people; there undoubtedly was an accompanying sizable additional migration not directly related to war production jobs as such.

John Blandford guided the National Housing Agency through this complex situation with great skill. Because of his standing at the White House, he was invited to attend Cabinet meetings regularly, which heightened his prestige with the wartime establishment in Washington. He established close relations with the War Production Board and the War Manpower Commission and gained their recognition that the provision of housing for in-migrant industrial war workers was essential to the achievement of war production schedules. As a result, the NHA became the official claimant for critical materials to be allocated for construction of war housing. In return, Blandford agreed that such materials would be used exclusively for housing for in-migrant war workers and only for that portion of the in-migrant housing need which could not be met through the use of existing or converted buildings. In short, none of the materials could be used for the general civilian housing market, no matter how acute the need.

Of the 3 million migrant war workers who moved during the first year and a half of the war, approximately 1.7 million were housed in existing buildings and 1.3 million in new structures. Blandford also had to make some difficult decisions as to the distribution of the development of new war housing between private and public financing. His final decision was to authorize private construction wherever there was reasonable expectation of continued economic need for the housing after the war and wherever private builders could meet the wartime restrictions on size, location and occupancy. Otherwise, he authorized publicly financed war housing which was soon limited almost entirely to temporary housing intended to be dismantled after the war. Of the 1.3 million new war housing units referred to, about half were privately financed, mostly under a special FHA mortgage insurance program for privately built war housing, and the balance was publicly financed.

As was common throughout American society during the war, the adjustment to tough wartime policies on housing did not occur without strain, tensions, and dissatisfactions. In addition to complaints against wartime restrictions generally, pressures were generated by the influx of migrant workers into settled, previously stable communities which sometimes felt their way of life was threatened, especially when the migrants were rural whites or blacks from the south.

In March, 1943, John Blandford commented on these pressures in a policy statement on the war housing program (on which I assisted):

> There have been and probably always will be, conflicting views on the need for housing during this war period. Many communities opposed any war housing; many still oppose it, with the very real fear that over-building will end in a collapse of all real estate values after the war. Many groups in many communities felt war workers should be housed in barracks, opposed all family accommodations on the theory that men should be willing to leave their families as if they were going into the armed services.
>
> Other groups wanted to build as usual, even after the war began. They opposed the limitations on cost and the use of materials. Still other groups, knowing that thousands of people were living under unsatisfactory conditions, wanted at least part of the peacetime housing program to be continued to provide better living standards for those people. Still others, opposed to the expenditure of public funds for any type of housing, advocate private financing regardless of the danger of over-building in many communities. . . .
>
> Too much emphasis cannot be placed on the fact that the decisions controlling war housing—nationally or locally—must be based on the needs of the war program and cannot be predicated on a peacetime program of improving community housing conditions or on supplying a continued volume of business during wartime. Even when the market, the need, and the building capacity are available when judged by peace-time standards, new construction cannot be authorized unless necessitated by imperative war requirements. That hard fact is not unique to the housing industry but is common throughout our war economy. It is not the product of anyone's arbitrary will but is part of the price we have to pay to win the war.

While the primary focus of the National Housing Agency's activities at that time was necessarily on the war housing program, this emphasis did not preclude attention to the postwar housing scene. On the contrary, from the outset Blandford's top staff, reflecting their past experience and future objectives, were thinking in postwar program terms, to the extent that time permitted. This became a paramount issue with John Blandford too, once he had successfully consolidated and rationalized the war housing program and especially when, in 1943, it appeared the tide of the war was turning in favor of the United States and its allies. Postwar thinking also was in process within the "constituent units" of NHA although not necessarily in identical terms, especially in the case of FHA and the Federal Home Loan Bank Administration.

In his own immediate office, Blandford delegated the principal responsibility for postwar planning to Coleman Woodbury. Leon Keyserling also played a leading role, as did B. T. Fitzpatrick, the associate general counsel of NHA. Also, Jacob Crane, a professional planner who had held a top position in USHA in its early days and had been Deputy Defense Housing Coordinator, was detached from any war housing responsibility and placed in charge of a small urban studies office working entirely on postwar problems. Under Blandford's guidance, the prime direction of this thinking about the postwar years soon became clear. This was that solutions to the problems of housing and urban development needed to be approached as parts of a comprehensive whole. It followed that from the standpoint of Federal responsibility for assisting in these solutions, there would be a central point of administrative authority, like the NHA. This last principle was not a self-serving argument to perpetuate wartime jobs; I can testify that it represented a deep conviction. Ultimately, after many trials and tribulations, this principle prevailed in the postwar period.

John Blandford's first major public thrust on this approach occurred in September, 1943. He had cultivated good relations with Howard Myers, the editor of the *Architectural Forum,* which was widely read not only by architects but also by major builders and contractors, materials producers, financial institutions and public groups. Howard Myers was well informed, sophisticated, and broadgauged in his points of view; he also had relative freedom of policy under the Time-Life-Fortune umbrella. He arranged a major interview in which Blandford responded in depth to nine questions dealing with the postwar scene. The interview was prominently displayed, with a full page photograph of Blandford, in the September issue of the *Forum.* The foreword to the article stated:

Whether homebuilding actually realizes the brilliant postwar future so many have predicted depends not on one man but on many men. But more than any other, it will depend upon the National Housing

Administrator. What John Blandford thinks about postwar housing is important to private home builders and public housers, to real estate men and architects, to material manufacturers and bankers. It is important because of his official position as head of NHA, the coordinating agency which directs the broad policies of the Federal Housing Administration, the Federal Public Housing Authority and the Federal Home Loan Bank Administration. It is doubly important in view of his personal reputation as a student of public affairs, and his brief but concentrated experience at the center of the war housing effort. . . . While the wartime job of housing war workers continues to have first call on the National Housing Agency, a full discussion of postwar housing is desirable and increasing study should be given to postwar housing considerations.

While most of the questions posed by the *Forum* to Blandford were related to short-term transitional problems from wartime to peacetime conditions in the housing field, on two questions he was able to chart a broader course of action. To a question as to the desirability of continuing a consolidated housing agency on a permanent basis in the postwar period, Blandford responded:

> In my judgment, the advantages secured in wartime from a unified approach to housing apply with equal force to the postwar period, if we are to achieve a really adequate postwar housing program. There is increasing realization that housing is one, broad, interrelated problem, rather than a series of unrelated problems which can be neatly segregated into separate compartments. This realization is a reflection partly of the experience we have all gained through a unified attack on war housing; it also reflects broader recognition by all groups of the realities of the housing program. I therefore believe that teamwork and a unified approach to housing should be preserved in the postwar period.

To a direct question whether Federal assistance for new low-rent public housing should be resumed after the war, Blandford purposely hedged:

> Our broad longterm objective for postwar housing must be a maximum program to provide good housing for all American families. Within that framework, the challenge to private enterprise is to do as much of the job as possible. The area for privately financed operations will be limited only to the extent that private capital

does not meet adequately the needs of the low-income groups. To determine the extent to which direct Federal financial assistance will be required for acquisition of land and construction in postwar housing, we must have first some early indication of what part of the total need for housing can be met by private enterprise, either unaided or with only indirect assistance of insurance and secondary credit. This determination must be made by the communities themselves, operating through local housing authorities, local planning commissions, the building industry, and lending institutions.

Blandford was well aware that an objective analysis of local housing needs would demonstrate that the private housing industry could not meet the needs of low-income families and that a resumption of the low-rent public housing program would be essential if all postwar housing needs were to be met. His cautious hedge on this key question was his response to a complex political situation in the housing field and to his hope (which turned out to be ill-founded) that wartime experiences had caused enough sophistication among private housing leaders to bring their support or acceptance of the unified approach to postwar housing which he was advocating. Blandford had cultivated good relations with the leaders of the private housing and financing fields, including the National Association of Home Builders. His war housing policies, while geared to the war effort, had had the effect of keeping an important nucleus of the private housing industry in business during the war, as distinguished, say, from the automobile industry which was converted almost entirely to the production of war material. Consequently, his policies gained the support of those leaders. But it developed that this support, springing from pragmatic motivations of survival in wartime, was quite a different kettle of fish than support for Blandford's broad-gauged postwar housing proposals.

There also was a sensitive political situation on housing questions in Congress. In his reelection in 1940 for an unprecedented third term in the White House, FDR had strengthened somewhat the control of the Democrats over both houses of Congress. But, in the Congressional elections of 1942, the tensions and dissatisfactions generated by the war caused a substantial resurgence of Republican strength. In the Senate, the Republicans gained 11 seats, although the Democrats retained a comfortable majority of 19 seats. However, in the House of Representatives the Republicans made a net gain of 47 seats, reducing the Democratic majority to only 13. This was by far the narrowest Democratic margin since before the New Deal landslide in 1932. These events strengthened the political hand of the conservative opponents of liberal programs, including housing.

On the other hand, there was increasing pressure from organized labor and other liberal groups for the early development of a blueprint for an aggressive and comprehensive postwar housing and urban development program, with major emphasis on public financing. These organizations were generally favorable to the National Housing Agency and to the postwar proposals which it was gradually putting together. There was, however, some criticism from this sector on the predominant role afforded to the private building industry in developing permanent housing under the war program, the relegation of public war housing entirely to temporary facilities, and the delay in the unveiling of the NHA's postwar program.

In this setting, Blandford proceeded with the development of his postwar proposals, with the tacit blessing of the White House. Preparatory activities were also started in Congress. The essential support of Senator Robert F. Wagner was assured through Leon Keyserling, his long-time legislative assistant during the early New Deal days. Blandford himself spent considerable time nurturing the confidence of Senator Robert A. Taft of Ohio, eldest son of the late President and Chief Justice of the Supreme Court, who had been elected to the Senate in 1938. Senator Taft, who was extremely conservative on most issues, had developed an enlightened attitude on housing and related urban issues, largely under the tutelage of Ernest J. Bohn, the resourceful Republican director of the Cleveland Housing Authority. Senator Allen J. Ellender of Louisiana, who was a liberal on public housing, also was cultivated.

I was given the assignment of establishing good relations with a number of the key members of the House of Representatives. These included Brent Spence, the venerable Representative from Covington, Kentucky, who had become chairman of the Banking and Currency Committee, and Wright Patman, the East Texas populist who was ultimately to succeed Spence in that post. They also included several rising youngish Democrats who were later to achieve influential roles in the Senate: John Sparkman of Alabama, Warren Magnuson of Washington, Mike Monroney of Oklahoma, and Estes Kefauver and Albert Gore of Tennessee.

Blandford decided to unveil the main facets of the NHA postwar housing proposals in a major address on "Housing Principles for America" before the National Committee on Housing on March 9, 1944. The committee was largely the creation of Mrs. Dorothy Rosenman (wife of Judge Samuel Rosenman, FDR's counsel and speechwriter) in an effort to establish a center position on housing and related issues. Its members included prominent middle-of-the-road builders, mortgage bankers and other financiers, real estate interests, and manufacturers as well as representatives of organized labor and the public. The Rosenmans themselves were close friends of Blandford's and supporters of the policies he was trying to establish.

Blandford's speech was a remarkable declaration of policy. In effect, he laid down basic principles for the Federal role and Federal goals in housing which, after many ups and downs, were ultimately accepted by Congress in the Housing Act of 1949, over intense opposition. They have since survived through five Presidential Administrations and twelve successive Congresses, even though their observance has frequently been less than perfect.

In this speech, Blandford also took a forthright position on the essentiality of public housing as part of an overall peacetime housing program:

> There is nothing inconsistent between the proposition that private enterprise should serve as much of the housing need that it possibly can, and the proposition that public housing should serve the housing need that private enterprise does not serve. If we reject either of these two propositions, we reject either the goal of decent housing for all Americans, or the principle of maintaining our system of private enterprise and utilizing it to the maximum extent. We cannot afford to reject either the principle or the goal. We must abide by the principle and still achieve the goal. A balanced program, with public assistance supplementing private enterprise to meet the whole need, will in the long run benefit private enterprise.

A few of Blandford's sixteen principles deserve repetition:

> *Housing serves human needs.* The family centers around the home. The Nation centers around the family. Decent housing cannot create utopia. But decent housing is vital to the health, safety and welfare of the families of the nation.

All American families should get decent housing. This includes millions of veterans who will need homes. It includes families in rural shacks and urban slums. It includes all minority groups. We have the manpower, resources, industry, and brains to do the whole job.

The slums must go. Their economic and social cost is intolerably high. They must be replaced gradually through a rounded program which includes decent housing within the means of slum dwellers.

Housing should conserve when it can. Investments in present housing have value. Fundamentally sound housing that has commenced to run down should be rehabilitated and repaired before it is too late. Neighborhoods should be maintained, rather than discarded or allowed to decay.

The Federal Government's role in housing should be supplementary. It should do what cannot be done otherwise. It should help private enterprise to serve the largest possible portion of the nation's housing needs. Public agencies must be ready to withdraw from any area when better incomes or lower costs enable individuals, cooperatives, labor groups or business organizations to pick up the responsibility and carry it forward. But the Government's role, while supplementary, involves bedrock responsibility for making sure that decent housing for all the people is gradually achieved.

Shortly after this declaration, there was a significant development in the Senate which had great influence on the direction of the Federal Government's postwar housing proposals. In order to begin preparations for postwar legislation, the Senate had established a special Committee on Postwar Economic Policy and Planning. An agreement was negotiated to establish a subcommittee on Housing and Urban Development and, notwithstanding the Democratic majority in the Senate, to designate Robert Taft as its chairman. The other members of the subcommittee were Senators Wagner, Ellender, Dennis Chavez of New Mexico, George L. Radcliffe of Maryland, La Follette of Wisconsin, and C. Douglass Buck of Delaware. The points of view of the subcommittee members ranged from liberal to middle-of-the-road on housing issues. The subcommittee retained as staff advisers two economists with broad experience on housing matters: Miles Colean and Ernest M. Fisher.

The subcommittee opened hearings on June 1, 1944, with John Blandford as the first witness. His voluminous testimony was primarily an elaboration of the principles he had laid down in his speech before the National Committee on Housing. He also seized the occasion to coin a good phrase on the importance of maintaining the consolidated National Housing Agency after the war: "We cannot make housing hang together instead of hanging all at loose ends unless we continue what we call 'the total approach' to housing."

The subcommittee hearings were interrupted during the summer and fall of 1944, in part because of the distractions of the 1944 Presidential election campaign. During this period, Blandford's office continued its studies of postwar housing. In November, the National Housing Agency published the first authoritative projection of U.S. housing needs for the first decade after the war. This estimated a need for 12.6 million nonfarm dwellings, about one-half to meet estimated population increases, establishment or re-establishment of war veterans' households, and the undoubling of married couples living with others. The other half represented proposed replacement of substandard housing, assuming a 20-year replacement period.

While conservative in terms of the actual national population growth over the succeeding 25 years, the NHA estimates set targets far above any past accomplishments in housing production. The projection of needs for an annual average of 1.25 million new dwellings was one-third higher than the peak production year in 1925 and 79 percent higher than average annual construction during the Twenties. It was also 76 percent higher than the peak prewar year in 1941 and over three and one-half times larger than actual average production in the immediate postwar decade. Of equal significance was the NHA projection of the rent or sales price distribution of the 12.6 million dwellings which would be necessary in order to accommodate the range of incomes within the U.S. population. Based on 1944 prices and civilian income levels, the NHA estimated that 22 percent of the total need for new housing would be at rent levels of less than $20 a month. This clearly was at a level requiring subsidies, as under the low-rent housing program. The NHA further estimated that about one-half of the total postwar need could be accommodated by the established private residential building industry, using FHA insurance aids or savings and loan financing, but that about 30 percent of the total need representing lower-middle-income households would require improved methods of private financing, production techniques, and marketing.

The NHA projections promptly drew fire from the conservative elements in the private building industry. The arguments were that the projections were greatly in excess of any achievable capacity by the industry or by its materials and equipment suppliers, that construction at this scale would lead to overbuilding, and that the results would be to add to the wartime inflation. The underlying motivations for these attacks, while never precisely so stated publicly, were twofold: first, that the scale of the projected housing production in effect supported the need for a continued major role by the Federal Government in housing after the war, and, second, that the NHA projections exposed the inability of the private building and financing industries to meet the housing needs of one-half of the population. However, the NHA study was so carefully documented and substantiated that no acceptable refutation of its conclusions was ever achieved. On the contrary, the NHA projections gained increasing acceptance among outside organizations and within the Congress.

A basic issue which was surfacing in 1944 was increasing concern with the prospects for the national economy and for continued full employment after the war. With public memories still fresh as to the economic consequences of the great depression, this concern was understandable and urgent, especially since large unemployment had been eliminated only with the advent of the war economy and the drafting of over 11 million men into the armed forces. The NHA postwar studies involved extensive research on the role of housing in the national economy and on the economic implications of the NHA housing production projections, if achieved. Based on this research and other studies, I prepared a paper under the heading "Housing and Full Employment" which was widely circulated in Congress and among outside organizations. Among other things, this paper estimated that achievement of the NHA's production goals, along with farm housing construction and major residential repairs, would produce an average annual housing investment of $7 billion. This coincided with an estimate by the Federal Reserve Board of the amount of new residential investment which would be required as part of an overall program to achieve full employment in the early postwar years. The paper cited also that this volume of home building and investment would provide approximately 4.5 million jobs, directly and indirectly over and above stimulating supplementary construction to provide stores and other commercial buildings, new schools, and other facilities needed to service new housing developments.

In the fall of 1944, even while Franklin D. Roosevelt was moving to his reelection for a fourth term over Governor Thomas E. Dewey of New York, the conservative private housing interests were forming a common front in opposition to any public housing and to the continuation of the National Housing Agency after the war. An immediate issue was presented by John Blandford's successful negotiation with the War Production Board to release materials and priorities for the construction of 90,000 dwellings in congested areas, as a first step toward meeting general civilian housing needs as distinguished from the needs of in-migrant war workers. The issue was whether any portion of these 90,000 dwellings should be low-rent public housing under existing but deferred contracts with local housing authorities. The NHA was proposing that 7,000 to 9,000 such units be authorized out of the 17,000 which had been deferred during the war.

In a belligerent joint letter to Blandford on November 4—which began with the rhetorical question: "Do you believe in private enterprise?"—Frank W. Cortwright and Herbert U. Nelson, the executive vice presidents of the National Association of Home Builders and the National Association of Real Estate Boards, demanded that the priorities for the 90,000 units be reserved exclusively for private builders and that no public housing be authorized.

But Blandford held his ground. In his reply to Cortwright and Nelson, he retorted:

> Let me, in turn, ask a question. You know that the segment of private enterprise you represent cannot build for low-income families of the type which would be taken care of in these publicly-financed units. Are you asking me to ignore the needs of such families—including returning veterans, dependents of veterans, and other Americans who happen to be the victims of low incomes—and to ignore the mandate of Congress and the legal commitments to a score of crowded cities and towns?

When the Senate postwar housing subcommittee resumed its hearings in January, 1945, the common line of the organizations making up what had come to be labeled as "the real estate lobby" was conspicuous. In addition to the home builders and the real estate boards, these consisted of the Chamber of Commerce of the United States, the U.S. Savings and Loan League, the National Association of Retail Lumber Dealers, the Mortgage Bankers Association, and the Producers Council. Without exception, the spokesmen for these organizations opposed the continuation of the National Housing Agency consolidation after the war, even though praising the wartime job done by NHA. Their alternative was a return to the loose organizational alignment before the war when the FHA and the Federal Home Loan Bank Board were nominally under the jurisdiction of the Federal Loan Agency and the USHA was under the Federal Works Agency. With only one limited exception, these spokesmen opposed the low-rent public housing program. Here are some excerpts from their remarks on the latter issue:

> *Morton Bodfish of the U.S. Savings and Loan League:* "We consider the public housing program entirely inconsistent with and dangerous to the home ownership and private credit service objectives for which our institutions are established."
>
> *Joseph E. Merrion, president of the National Association of Home Builders:* "We do not concede the need or the right of the Federal Government, either directly or by subsidy to local housing authorities to enter the housing field by building, owning or operating permanent housing projects. We feel that in so doing the Government is invading the field of private enterprise, setting itself up in business in competition with citizens and taxpayers."
>
> *Douglas Whitlock of the Producers Council:* "Building brand new homes at public expense is not the only way to house low-income families. Indeed, it is a last resort, for it is wasteful to build thousands of new homes for the needy if there is, or will be, a sufficient number of sound, decent, acceptable existing developments in which the needy families can live."
>
> *Herbert U. Nelson of the National Association of Real Estate Boards:* "We recommend that no further appropriation be made for public housing and that all of the public housing now in the possession of the Federal Government and the local housing authorities be disposed of after the war."

Nelson's far-out position drew a terse rejoinder from Senator Taft: "If you are going to oppose the public housing program I think you have an obligation to present some alternative."

Nelson responded lamely: "If you go ahead with the public housing program, you necessarily will stop a lot of private enterprise just through plain ordinary fear."

On the opposite side of the coin, the permanent continuation of the National Housing Agency, the extension of the public housing program, the establishment of an urban redevelopment program, and the validity of the NHA postwar housing need projections were all supported by the AFL, the CIO, the National Public Housing Conference, the National Association of Housing Officials, the National Committee on Housing, and the other groups identified generally as public interest organizations. This dual alignment of the real estate interests on the one hand and the liberal forces on the other was to persist throughout the controversies on housing and related issues during the Forties and the Fifties.

With the death of Franklin D. Roosevelt on April 12, 1945, and the succession of Harry S. Truman to the Presidency, there gradually began the inevitable change in style and personalities at the White House and eventually in the top positions throughout the Federal establishment which accompanies the advent of a new President. However, there never was cause to question the general support of President Truman for progressive housing programs. While his Senate assignments had not directly involved him in housing legislation, as chairman of the Temporary National Economic Committee in the immediate prewar period he had sponsored a unanimous committee report which, among many other things, commended programs of slum clearance and low-rent public housing.

In the summer of 1945, there were two Congressional reports of great significance to postwar housing programs. The House of Representatives had its own special committee on Postwar Economic Policy and Planning, under the chairmanship of Representative William M. Colmer of Mississippi. While more conservative in overall composition than its Senate counterpart and lacking a specific concentration on housing, the report of the committee recommending a long-range program of public works and construction gave general support to many of the programs being advocated by the National Housing Agency and its allies. The report recommended further liberalization of FHA insurance for housing construction, including additional incentives for rental housing such as yield insurance on housing investments; extension of Federal financial aid for low-rent public housing, and Federal assistance in the technical development and financing of housing. On the specific issue of public housing, the House report said:

> The committee recognizes that there is an area of housing at the lowest rent levels which private industry cannot afford to serve and which local government is not fully capable of serving. The problem of public housing is therefore one of national as well as of local concern. Any program of Federal cooperation with local governments for postwar construction must accord a permanent place to making up the large deficiency in housing for low-income families.

On August 1, 1945, the Senate Subcommittee on Housing and Urban Redevelopment issued its long-awaited report and recommendations. The report, which was unanimous, represented a major victory for the National Housing Agency and its allies and a setback to the real estate lobby. After praising the NHA for its "excellent performance," the subcommittee recommended that the Agency be made permanent. The report substantially adopted the NHA's projections of postwar housing needs by estimating those needs at 1.2 million dwellings a year for the first ten postwar years. It called for a resumption of the low-rent public housing program at an annual rate of 125,000 dwellings per year for four years. It rejected the real estate lobby's proposal for so-called "rent certificates" to low-income families as a substitute for public housing on the grounds that this approach would be likely "to maintain the profitability of slum areas and blighted areas." It recommended extensions to FHA and FHLB aids to encourage lower-priced private housing and investment in rental housing, a comprehensive program for farm housing, and government research on construction methods and techniques, markets, and needs.

The report made this significant policy statement:

> The subcommittee feels that the importance of a well conceived comprehensive housing policy cannot be exaggerated. There is no problem before the American people with more varied aspects than that of housing, each of them important to the future welfare of the country. From the social point of view, a supply of good housing, sufficient to meet the needs of all families, is essential to a sound and stable democracy. Every family must have a decent home in which to live. . . . From the viewpoint of industry and

employment a large volume of residential construction would make a vital contribution to our postwar economy. . . . Few industries have shown such violent fluctuations from year to year, with resulting unemployment and hardship. Slums have inevitably grown up in all our cities and in our towns and in the open countryside and overcrowding and makeshift alteration have necessarily been utilized to balance our shortcomings. We can no longer accept these conditions as unavoidable . . .

Since the subcommittee did not have authority to introduce legislation, it was necessary to prepare and file a bill through the established channels. This was done by Senators Wagner, Ellender, and Taft who jointly introduced the General Housing Act, embodying the subcommittee's legislative recommendations. Jurisdiction was assumed by the Banking and Currency Committee of which Senator Wagner was chairman.

Then on August 6 and 9, the atomic bomb was dropped on Hiroshima and Nagasaki. On August 14, Japan surrendered unconditionally, thus ending World War II.

So the nation moved abruptly into the postwar era.

CHAPTER 3

Postwar Adjustment and Reaction

The fine goals projected by the Taft subcommttee, by the Senate Banking and Currency Committee, and by the Truman Administration for a comprehensive and orderly attack on national housing problems quickly encountered the realities of the immediate postwar psychology.

The preponderance of the civilian public was fed up with wartime rationing, shortages, and controls. For the most part these had been accepted as inevitable while the war was being fought; after V-J Day, attitudes rapidly shifted. Among most businessmen and other capitalists, the slogan was a quick return to normalcy and reliance on private enterprise. The attitude of the organized builders, mortgage lenders, real estate operators, and materials producers had been foreshadowed by their testimony at the Senate hearings.

The sharpest impact of the postwar psychology on housing proposals developed as the demobilization of the armed forces gained momentum. The troops returned from the war to find that housing was in the shortest supply of all essential commodities. In 1945, because of material shortages and wartime controls, only 326,000 dwellings were produced throughout the country and only about 200,000 in 1944 compared with over 1,000,000 in 1941 and about 890,000 in 1940. In the meantime, the national population was continuing to increase. Furthermore, since Pearl Harbor housing production had been channeled almost entirely into war industry areas and its occupancy was limited to civilian war workers; at the end of the war most of it was occupied.

Many of the newly demobilized veterans had married before the war and had children waiting for them; many others were planning on early marriage. Their mounting demands for quick action on their housing needs were understandable and justified and clearly carried important political implications. Against this background, the long-range housing and development proposals in the Wagner-Ellender-Taft bill appeared increasingly to lack emergency flavor and immediate political appeal.

This political message registered at the White House as well as in Congress. While generally committed-to the proposals of the Wagner-Ellender-Taft bill, President Truman and his political coterie felt mounting pressure to take specific and dramatic action to demonstrate concern and to propose solutions for the acute housing shortage confronting the returning veterans. The President had two alternate courses of action open to him. The first, which would have been the more logical and orderly, was to order special veterans' programs and actions to be undertaken by the National Housing Agency which contained the principal Federal programs in housing and housing finance and which, under the proposals of the Wagner-Ellender-Taft bill, would have become the permanent peacetime housing arm of the Federal establishment. But John Blandford, the able wartime administrator of NHA, was considered an FDR man, not a Truman man. Furthermore, Blandford was felt to be not closely enough aligned with the Democratic Party apparatus by politicos such as National Democratic Chairman Hannegan and was held to lack the color and sex appeal to exert effective political leadership in the veterans' housing crisis.

The second course of action, which Truman chose, was to bring in a new flamboyant face to compose and direct programs exclusively aimed at relieving the shortage of housing for veterans. On January 26, 1946, the President issued an executive order establishing the office of Housing Expediter charged with the task of preparing plans and programs and recommending legislation for the provision of housing for veterans. He named to this post Wilson W. Wyatt, former mayor of Louisville and a successful corporation lawyer.

Wyatt filled the bill as a new and flamboyant face. He was a figure of great charm and vivacity, voluble and frequently eloquent, imaginative and dynamic (although events were to prove that he misjudged the strength and direction of some of the basic political and economic forces which were crystalizing in the immediate postwar era). He quickly aligned himself with the aggressively liberal forces in the Truman Administration, such as Chester Bowles, then the Director of Economic Stabilization, and Paul Porter, then the Administrator of the OPA. He recruited or borrowed staff from them and other wartime agencies to help develop and later administer his program.

After hectic brainstorming sessions, in February, 1946, Wyatt unveiled with great fanfare the Veterans' Emergency Housing Program, which had already gained the endorsement of President Truman. Wyatt's program was primarily aimed at applying wartime production techniques and controls to the solution of the veterans' housing shortage. One of the basic elements of his program was the continuation and strengthening of price controls on building materials and the setting up of allocations and priorities for residential builders in purchasing materials and equipment, subject to a stiff preference for veterans in the sale or rental of the resulting housing. He proposed subsidy payments of $600 million to stimulate the production of building materials and equipment which had been drastically curtailed by wartime controls. Likewise, he called for the postponement of all deferrable and nonessential construction in order to release materials and labor for veterans' housing. He proposed a large expansion in factory fabrication of houses through allocations of surplus war plants and materials and through guaranteeing the market for the product. In addition to price and rental ceilings on new housing, the Wyatt program went beyond wartime controls in housing and asked for price ceilings on the sale of existing houses and of building lots. Wyatt set an overall target for production of 1.2 million houses in 1946 and 1.5 million in 1947.

He also recommended passage of the Wagner-Ellender-Taft bill, an objective which he did not aggressively pursue. In the clamor aroused by his other proposals, this recommendation was largely lost sight of.

Most of the proposals in the Veterans' Emergency Housing Program required new legislation and the battle lines were quickly formed in Congress and especially in the House of Representatives. The political alignment reflected the position of the various interests which would be affected by the program. In general, the Wyatt proposals were supported by the veterans' organizations, their ranks swollen by returning World War II veterans. Organized labor was a champion of the program. Most of the organizations strongly committed to the Wagner-Ellender-Taft bill—such as the Conference of Mayors, the National Public Housing Conference, and the so-called public interest organizations—supported the proposals, albeit with misgivings (which turned out to be well-founded) that this political struggle would dilute the chances for passage of the long-term basic legislation.

In opposition, the National Association of Real Estate Boards mounted the most vociferous lobby. To the real estate industry, the proposal to establish price ceilings on the sale of existing houses and building lots was anathema. The projected $600-million subsidy to stimulate production of building materials and equipment had a mixed reaction within industry: on the one hand it offered short-term financial benefits; on the other, it was part of a package which blocked the resumption of non-residential construction and which was predicated on the continuation of wartime price controls and priorities. There was also a mixed reaction within the home building industry: it offered them a preferred position in securing scarce materials at the same time that it would prevent them from reentering the profitable higher-priced home market.

When debates began on the floor of the House, the alignment pro and con took on a strongly partisan flavor. The right-wing Republican extremists attacked the legislation as "communistic" and a "dictatorship bill." Congressman Wright Patman of Texas, the floor manager for the bill, charged that many of the telegrams he had received opposing the legislation were from phony addresses or had been sent without the knowledge or consent of the alleged signators. Wilson Wyatt attacked the real estate lobby in these words:

> I charge that its motives are to perpetuate the housing shortage in order to gain speculative profits from inflationary real estate prices.
> I charge that its motives are to secure profits at the expense of veterans by breaking price ceilings on existing materials.
> I charge that its motives are to protect vested interests based on limited production of building materials.

The opponents won two victories in the House. The proposal to establish price ceilings on sales of existing houses was defeated 246 to 133, with Republicans voting 161 to 8 against. Then, the proposed subsidy for building materials production was initially defeated 161 to 91, with 46 Southern Democrats joining 115 Republicans in opposition.

In the Senate, a more temperate attitude prevailed with regard to material subsidies. These were approved by a vote of 53 to 20, with the Republicans dividing closely 18 to 16 and with only four Democratic Senators voting against. With this backing from the Senate, House Speaker Sam Rayburn cracked the whip on his Southern colleagues and eventually secured approval of the material subsidies by a vote of 185 to 158; however, the Republican Representatives still voted 133 to 29 against. Thus, on May 22, 1946 the Veterans' Emergency Housing Act became law, minus only the price ceilings on existing housing.

In the meantime, the supporters of the Wagner-Ellender-Taft bill had been striving to maintain its previous political momentum by seeking to establish its essentiality to the success of the Veterans' Emergency Housing Program. In the Senate, the Banking and Currency Committee, which had legislative jurisdiction over both the Wyatt program and the long-term legislation, marshalled these arguments when it unanimously recommended passage of the Wagner-Ellender-Taft bill on April 8, 1946:

> In view of the fact that the committee has just reported favorably upon . . . the veterans' emergency housing bill of 1946, it is necessary to point out precisely and unequivocally how the bill now being reported is equally a part of the veterans' emergency housing program and equally indispensable to its achievement. . . .
>
> The factual basis for the foregoing statement is unmistakably clear. The veterans' emergency housing program calls for 2,700,000 houses to be started during 1946 and 1947. It is intended that these houses be for veterans and their families. Measures such as premium payments and allocations and priorities . . . are essential to getting the materials with which to build these houses. But when these houses are built, and even to provide an effective and sound demand for them when they are built, they must be priced for sale or rent within the financial means of the majority of veterans and their families. . . .
>
> For these reasons, the vitally necessary expediting of production of building materials and of houses . . . cannot be focused directly or adequately upon the needs of veterans and their families unless reinforced simultaneously by the provisions of the bill now being reported, which in a variety of carefully developed ways stimulates

and encourages private enterprise to meet the needs of veterans' families of middle income, and which makes provisions for veterans' families of very low income as well.

These economic realities, as they bear upon veterans' housing, should be carried constantly in mind to avoid any confusion resulting from erroneous allegations that the present bill, since it deals with a long-term program, is not necessary at once during the current emergency shortage for veterans.

These arguments were persuasive to the body of the Senate. In any event, the Wagner-Ellender-Taft bill was passed in the Senate by voice vote in late April, 1946, and sent to the House of Representatives. There were some who concluded cynically that the known opponents of the legislation in the Senate held their fire and avoided a record vote not so much because of the prestige of the bill's bipartisan sponsors but because they were confident the bill would be blocked in the House.

This conclusion turned out to be accurate. After the hectic struggle to secure House acceptance of the Veterans' Emergency Housing bill, the Republican opponents of the Wagner-Ellender-Taft bill on the House Banking and Currency Committee began a covert campaign of frustrating and delaying the necessary committee hearings on the legislation. Their tactics included such little used technical points of order that a quorum of the committee was not present and refusal to grant unanimous consent for the committee to meet while the House was in session. With the session drawing toward its close in a Congressional election year, it also began to appear that the Democratic leadership of the House was not pressing strongly to break the Republican technical filibuster. President Truman sent urgent letters to Speaker Rayburn, Majority Leader John McCormack, and Congressman Brent Spence, the chairman of the Banking Committee, urging that the bill be forced to a vote in the House prior to adjournment. But finally it fell to the aging Spence to announce that it would not be possible to complete committee hearings in time for floor action. The inference was that the House leadership, having forced through one housing bill, preferred to throw the long-term measure into the lap of the next Congress. And so the Wagner-Ellender-Taft bill was allowed to die.

Meanwhile, the Veterans' Emergency Housing Program was in motion. Shortly after the announcement of the Wyatt program, John

Blandford was tapped by President Truman to accompany General George C. Marshall on an ill-fated mission to China and Wyatt was named National Housing Administrator, while continuing to serve as Housing Expediter. Thus, he had jurisdiction over the existing programs and staff of NHA as well as the additional staff he recruited to administer and promote the new programs in the Veterans' Emergency Housing Act. There was intense activity, particularly within his top staff. He reinstituted the wartime six-day work week, and Sunday or evening staff meetings became almost routine.

Notwithstanding his drive, energy, and intelligence, Wilson Wyatt was not an expert administrator. Lines of authority were confused and overlapping jurisdictions developed. He had a proliferation of special assistants (of which this writer was one), appointed for special tasks. While the President had given him directive authority over other Federal agencies on matters related to the emergency program, he soon encountered the classic Federal roadblocks in attempting to exercise these powers. It became clear that he needed an effective deputy. But rather than selecting an experienced administrator, he chose Joseph L. Rauh, brilliant but more flamboyantly liberal and freewheeling than himself. (Wyatt and his deputy soon were characterized privately by some of his staff as the team of "Riot and Wow.")

Nevertheless, despite some administrative confusion, there were substantial accomplishments under the Veterans' Emergency Housing Program in 1946. This was illustrated most directly by the increase in construction starts of new dwellings to 1,023,000 units from 326,000 in 1945, an expansion made possible in good part by the materials priorities and allocations for home building under the program and by the substantial increase in production of building materials and equipment stimulated at least in part by the subsidies offered by the program. It was true that the houses and apartments produced were primarily priced at levels suitable only for middle-income and at best lower-middle-income veterans. There was no production for low-income veterans or other families requiring housing subsidy for the simple reason that there was no financing program to accomplish this result. But the spurt in home-building, combined with the veterans' preference, did begin to have a visible impact on the shortage.

The program nonetheless was swimming against the tide of the postwar political psychology. The concept of maintaining wartime type production controls, even in support of the veterans' housing program, was running counter to powerful economic and political forces pressing for a quick return to so-called normalcy, for decontrol rather than a continuation of controls. These forces were particularly potent in the building materials and equipment field and its related financing sources which were at the core of the nation's industrial power structure, as distinguished from the diffused and fragmented construction industry.

A foretaste of the strength of these pressures occurred in mid-June, 1946, when a Republican drive in Congress to eliminate price controls almost succeeded. At that time, Wilson Wyatt warned: "A breakdown in price controls would mean inevitably that the Veterans' Emergency Housing Program, as now planned, would be unattainable. It would almost certainly eliminate the hope of producing moderate or low-cost homes in the next year or two." However, this near thing was a portent of things to come.

A second front where the program was combatting the realities of the American economic system was in its emphasis and reliance on the development rapidly of large-scale industrialization and factory fabrication of housing production. In theory, this concept had much to support it in logic and in comparable experience in other fields. The construction of homes was (and largely still is) outside the mainstream of American industrial mechanization and technological advance. Since it was therefore largely not possible to absorb rising labor costs through increased productivity as in other major industries, the increase in construction costs historically outran the rise in the general wholesale price level by a wide margin. Furthermore, the so-called home building industry was almost entirely a conglomeration of small builders unable to secure the cost benefits of mass production and mass purchasing. In contrast to this picture, the remarkable achievements during World War II in mass production of planes, ships, tanks and other military hardware appeared to offer a persuasive example of the potential for achieving comparable production benefits through large-scale factory fabrication of complete houses, using advanced industrial techniques.

Appealing as this vision was, there was arrayed against its accomplishment a wide range of entrenched interests and built-in obstacles. These included the AFL building trades unions (although not the CIO industrial unions). They included most home builders who saw in this industrialized approach a threat to their own businesses. The large industries producing building materials, equipment and appliances were generally hostile, particularly with regard to systems involving new materials or built-in equipment. The local distributors of materials and supplies were strongly opposed to a system which might upset their profitable dealings with the typical small home builders. Mortgage lenders were generally indifferent or skeptical. There was no established system for marketing industrialized houses or for financing the erectors up to the point of sale of the completed house. Local building codes were usually a barrier. Against this array, the market guarantees, loans, and priorities for industrialized housing offered by the Wyatt program were not enough to launch a large-scale new industry.

The threats to the Veterans' Emergency Housing Program became academic when the political roof fell in on election day in November, 1946. In a classic postwar reaction and revulsion against wartime restraints, the people gave control of both houses of Congress to the Republican Party for the first time since 1930. In the Senate, the Republicans gained 11 seats to control by 51 to 45. In the House, the Republican gain was 56 seats to control by 246 to 188. Exultingly, the Republicans read the election results as a mandate for the election of a Republican President in 1948.

Harry Truman read the returns, in part at least, as a public repudiation of wartime price controls. On November 9, he ended price and wage controls, including, of course, price controls on building materials. As a gesture, he asked Wilson Wyatt to chart a new course for the Veterans' Emergency Housing Program in the absence of price controls.

Wyatt responded on November 20. He called for continuation of all other aspects of the program, for 100 percent loans for rental housing for veterans, and for 100 percent loans for industrialized housing producers. He also kept the rhetoric of the program:

> We met the emergency production needs of the war by giving all-out government assistance to manufacturers of war materials. Now we need homes and apartments for veterans. The way to get them quickly is to continue to follow the emergency pattern we set up during the war. Then we put the tank manufacturer ahead of less essential competitors. Now we are putting the manufacturer of homes ahead of the manufacturer of less needed products. . . .

It will require your leadership to see that the people of this country are kept aware of the veterans' need for homes, to see that the problem is met by a national unity of purpose and action, to see that every necessary branch of the Federal Government puts its full energies and resources into the emergency housing. We cannot face our veterans with a half-hearted housing program . . .

Some of us who worked with Wyatt in the preparation of his report to the President were convinced that he was writing for the record and submitting a package which he knew would be politically unacceptable to the White House under the changed circumstances. In any event, that was the way it worked out. The President quietly turned down most of Wyatt's proposals. Wyatt promptly resigned and returned to his lucrative law practice in Louisville.

On January 11, 1947, the President signed an executive order terminating most aspects of the program, two weeks less than a year from his order initiating it.

The Veterans' Emergency Housing Program was dead. But the housing needs and problems of the nation were still alive.

CHAPTER 4

The 80th Congress and Housing

With the advent of the Republican-controlled 80th Congress, there immediately was a realignment of political forces related to housing legislation. On the conservative side, there was hopeful anticipation of the election of a Republican President in 1948 and the perpetuation of Republican control of Congress for the indefinite future. At the same time, there were the seeds of a coalition of liberals and middle-of-the-road leaders which eventually would frustrate these ambitions.

The reactionary lobby on housing legislation had clearly defined objectives. From an overall economic standpoint, the lobby of course sought for rapid elimination of the remaining wartime controls on production, construction, and prices. Except for Federal rent control on existing housing, which was to survive for several years, this objective had largely been accomplished in the aftermath to the 1946 Congressional elections and was formalized in the Housing and Rent Act of 1947, enacted on June 30, which officially repealed the Veterans' Emergency Housing Act.

With regard to housing legislation specifically, the lobby sought to liquidate any consolidated Federal interest and activity in the housing field generally. During the war, the National Housing Agency had developed a strong foothold in this direction and the Wagner-Ellender-Taft bill had proposed that NHA be made a permanent consolidation of the major Federal housing programs and functions. The lobby also was strongly opposed to the revival of the Federally subsidized public housing program for low-income families which had been suspended during the war except for financing the development of temporary housing for war industry workers. It followed that the lobby was adamantly against any comprehensive housing legislation like the Wagner-Ellender-Taft bill.

On the positive side, the lobby favored the restoration of so-called independent status for the Federal Housing Administration and the Federal Home Loan Bank Board, both already closely aligned with building and mortgage finance interests through their functions and their staff sympathies. The FHA-insured mortgage system was responsible for providing insured private mortgage credit for the construction and long-term financing of about 20 percent of the new private housing for sale or rent in the immediate postwar years. The Federal Home Loan Bank Board, through its regional banks, was the source of reserve credit for savings and loan associations which were aggressively moving toward becoming the largest force in mortgage financing for individual homes throughout the country. The lobby also favored legislation expanding the resources and liberalizing the financing terms of FHA and FHLB. It was clear likewise that the lobby felt that as independent Federal agencies, there would be assurance of their continuing rapport with their building and financing clients.

The principal figures and personalities in the lobby presented an intriguing cross-section of business attitudes in the early postwar era. Behind the scenes, the master-mind of the lobby was Stuart Fitzpatrick, the astute and sophisticated director of the construction division of the United States Chamber of Commerce. Always avoiding the limelight, Fitzpatrick contributed a measure of coordination and tactical guidance to the activities of his individualistic colleagues.

The most conspicuous member of the reactionary housing lobby at that time was Herbert U. Nelson, executive vice president of the National Association of Real Estate Boards. Fresh from his victory in saving real estate operators from the disaster of Federal price controls on sales of existing housing, Nelson brought a missionary-type fervor to his attacks on the threats—real or imaginary—to private enterprise in real estate from the Federal Government. Another prominent member of the lobby was Morton Bodfish, executive vice president of the United States Savings and Loan League, the trade association for the savings and loan institutions. Bodfish was intellectual, highly educated, vocal, and inclined to be arrogant and bombastic in his attacks on public housing. Frank Cortwright, executive vice president of the National Association of Home Builders, was shrewd, opportunistic, and more effective as a trade association executive than as a lobbyist. "Cotton" Northrop, prematurely white-haired, directed the lobbying activities of the National Association of Retail Lumber Dealers in a sarcastic and frequently vituperative manner. Then there was Douglas Whitlock, director of the National Clay Products Association (brick and clay pipe) and lobbying spokesman for the Producers Council, representing the large manufacturers of building materials and equipment. Florid-faced and portly, Whitlock in appearance was almost a caricature of the popular conception of the professional lobbyist; in manner he could be alternately suave or arrogant.

These were the principal figures in the lobby, and the other trade groups at that time usually followed their lead with regard to housing legislation. It was significant that, with the exception of the United States Chamber of Commerce and the Producers Council, the membership of these organizations while numerous consisted of relatively small-scale business enterprises as compared with the large industrial corporations. As a membership technique, the executives of these trade organizations felt it necessary to keep their members enflamed and frightened in order to assure their continued participation and financial support. At the same time, the local builders, savings and loan officials, and retail lumber dealers who made up the membership of those associations wielded considerable political influence, especially with members of the House of Representatives.

The political forces in the 80th Congress with which the lobby had to deal were mixed. In the House of Representatives, the new Republican leadership—Speaker Joseph Martin from New Bedford, Massachusetts, and Majority Leader Charles Halleck from small-town and rural Indiana—generally saw eye-to-eye with the lobby. Of great significance also was the point of view of the new chairman of the House Banking and Currency Committee, Congressman Jesse Wolcott from suburban Detroit. With close ties to the banking field and to savings and loan associations. Wolcott was strongly opposed to public housing and to major Federal activities in housing except for the FHA and the Home Loan Bank Board. Roly-poly and owlish in appearance, Wolcott was wise and adept in the ways of the House.

The lobby was not firmly assured, however, of clear sailing for its point of view within the Banking and Currency Committee as a whole. Notwithstanding the Republican victory in the 1946 elections, the party division in the House was sufficiently close that the proportionate alignment within the Banking and Currency Committee was 16 on the Republican side and 11 on the Democratic side. Moreover, one of the seats on the Republican side was held by Congressman Merlin Hall of Wisconsin, representing the dwindling La Follette Progressive Party of Wisconsin, who on most substantive issues could be counted on to vote with the Democrats. Thus, the authentic Republican majority on the committee was only 15 to 12, since on housing matters the committee Democrats were cohesive. This margin was too close for complacency.

In the Senate, the political situation was more precarious from the standpoint of the lobby's objectives. Senator Taft, "Mr. Republican," retained his commitment to the principles of the Wagner-Ellender-Taft bill, which was soon to become the Taft-Ellender-Wagner bill. On the Senate Banking and Currency Committee, through seniority the chairmanship fell to Senator Charles W. Tobey of New Hampshire, elderly and garrulous but also liberal and forceful. Also on the Republican side of the committee were Senator Taft and Senator Ralph E. Flanders, a taciturn Vermonter, successful manufacturer, former president of the Federal Reserve Bank of Boston, and a follower of Taft on housing policies. The 1946 election also had the result of bringing two new reactionary Republicans to the committee. One was Senator Joseph McCarthy who had upset Senator Robert La Follette in Wisconsin and who promptly began searching for appealing demagogic issues, alighting first on housing. The second was Senator Harry Cain of Washington who had earned a favorable reputation as the progressive mayor of Tacoma but who was reported to have made commitments to the real estate lobby to assure his election to the Senate.

On balance, a comfortable majority of the Senate committee remained favorable to comprehensive housing legislation. On the Democratic side of the committee, the former chairman, Senator Robert F. Wagner of New York, remained the ranking Democrat. Now bedridden and senile, he retained his Senate seat for political reasons throughout the 80th Congress and, under the Senate rules, could cast his committee votes by proxy. In practice, the senior Democrat on the committee became Senator Burnet Maybank of Charleston, South Carolina, who was a supporter of comprehensive housing legislation. Initiative was soon shown also by the able young Senator John Sparkman from Huntsville, Alabama, recently elected to the seat long held by Senator John Bankhead.

A foretaste of the continuing dispute between Senator Taft and his followers and the lobby was given in a written debate on the Wagner-Ellender-Taft bill between Taft and Herbert U. Nelson which was published in the magazine *Modern Industry* on October 15, 1946, before the Congressional elections. Taft, highly conservative on most issues, expressed his philosophy of the obligations of capitalist society to the poor and the disadvantaged:

> I believe that the Government must see that every family has a minimum standard of decent shelter along with subsistence, medical care, and education. . . . The hand-me-down theory works, but it works to provide indecent housing for those who get it on the last hand-down. This hand-me-down method of taking care of the lowest-income group at low rents is inconsistent with that group getting good housing. . . . The present bill does what can be done to help private construction and sale of homes. . . . But all of these proposals do not eliminate the need for public low-rent housing. . . . The problem must be attacked from every angle. I believe we cannot pour in all the assistance from the top, and that is all private industry can do, or be expected to do. I think we must also attack it from the bottom . . .

The response by Herbert Nelson was replete with the lobby's emotional distortions and non-sequiturs:

> The Bill didn't get through the 79th Congress despite the all-out propaganda pressure put behind it. . . . It is one of the most dangerous pieces of legislation ever proposed. Under the guise of aiding private enterprise, it calls for the largest public housing program in history. It proposes to set up vast Federal controls over building and municipal affairs and to launch the nation on the path to government ownership of homes and other property. . . . But the most significant aspect of the WET bill grows out of this fact: because public housing inevitably competes with private housing, the bill subsidizes further competition by the Federal Government

with private enterprise. . . . This legislative hodge-podge is dangerous, not only for the vast expansion of Federal authority into new fields of private enterprise and the vast inflationary spending it contemplates—but it also meddles to the detriment of Federal aids already in effect to help private enterprise in the building industry. It is a new Federal beachhead in the local community and in the area where private enterprise—if freed of Federal restraints—should and can do the job.

Consistently with his position, Senator Taft introduced early in the first session of the 80th Congress comprehensive housing legislation which incorporated the main principles of the Wagner-Ellender-Taft bill, with some technical modifications. Additional hearings were held and on April 24, 1947, the bill was recommended to the Senate for passage by the Banking and Currency Committee. The committee vote for the bill this time was not unanimous; Senators McCarthy and Cain were prominent in the minority opposing it.

Thus the main issues remained very much alive. A closely related question was the fate of the National Housing Agency as the consolidated housing arm of the Federal Government. The liquidation of NHA was one of the prime objectives of the lobby. In 1946, after the shelving of the Wagner-Ellender-Taft bill in the House, President Truman at Wilson Wyatt's urging sent a proposed Reorganization Plan to Congress which would have made NHA a permanent agency unless rejected by both houses. The plan was in fact turned down by both the House and the Senate, ostensibly because of objections that it would place too much directive power over FHA and the Home Loan Bank Board in the hands of the Administrator but also no doubt in reflection of Wyatt's waning popularity in Congress.

After the retirement of Wyatt, President Truman named Raymond M. Foley, the head of FHA, to succeed Wyatt as National Housing Administrator. Cautious and conservative by nature, Foley had had serious personal misgivings about the 1946 reorganization plan. But he also was a man of conscience and of deep loyalty to Harry Truman. A strategy was devised to gain the objective of a consolidated housing agency by two changes from the rejected 1946 plan: first, to drop the name of the National Housing Agency, with its wartime connotations, and to propose the new name of Housing and Home Finance Agency, and, second, to give the Administrator only coordinating rather than directive powers over the FHA and the

Home Loan Bank Board. On June 27, 1947, the President sent 1 Congress a reorganization plan incorporating these proposals.

These compromises in no way lessened the lobby's fervent oppos tion to a permanent central voice for housing in the Federal Estal lishment. Just previously, the lobby had almost achieved its objectiv via the back door of the Appropriations Committees. Because of th conservative makeup of the Appropriations Committees, especiall in the House, this was a favorite device for crippling programs withou undergoing the risks of attempting substantive legislation to accon plish the same end. In the House, the Appropriations Committe denied all money for staff salaries in the NHA Administrator's offic except for the Administrator himself and a skeleton staff, presumabl to perform temporary liquidating functions. When the measur reached the Senate, the Appropriations Committee under Senatc Homer Ferguson of Michigan voted to follow suit. It was only th last-minute intervention on the floor of the Senate by Senatc Alben Barkley of Kentucky, then the minority leader, strongl seconded by Robert Taft, which upset this manoeuvre to force liquida tion of NHA through the appropriations process.

When the housing reorganization plan reached Congress, th lobby sprang into action. In the House of Representatives, the Truma Administration and the Democratic leadership deliberately avoide a show-down fight since under the Reorganization Act the pla would become effective if approved by only one house. So the pla was rejected in the House by voice vote, with little debate. Th Senate became the real battleground.

The lobby mobilized its full forces to seek the rejection of th plan by the Senate. As a personal note, in my role as Raymon Foley's assistant for Congressional relations, I was seated in th Senate gallery on July 27, 1947, awaiting the start of floor debate o the plan. By coincidence, about a half dozen leaders of the lobb were seated in the row ahead of me. I recall that Whitlock, Cortwright Northrop, Calvin Snyder (of Nelson's organization), and a few others were there. I overheard them exchanging intelligence, sottc voce, about their last-minute interventions with various Senators either directly or through telegrams from the field.

Their efforts were unsuccessful. Senator Taft ridiculed the op- position of the real estate lobby to the plan, including the claim tha it constituted a public housing plot. Senator Flanders was the Republican floor manager in support of the plan. The Republican opposition was led by the right-wing: Senators Bricker, Wherry, and Cain. On this occasion, the Democratic Senators were largely united in support of the plan, aside from a handful of bitter-enders like Senators Byrd and Robertson of Virginia, McCarran of Nevada, and O'Daniel of Texas. The affirmative Democratic forces were led by Senator Barkley of Kentucky, the minority leader and future Vice President, Senator Ellender of Louisiana, and Senator Myers of Pennsylvania.

Senator Taft's strong support of the plan was sufficient to carry 11 other Republican Senators with him, principally from the moderate wing of the party. In combination with strong support from the Democrats, who voted 35 to 6 for the plan, this was sufficient to win approval of the plan, 47 to 38. Thus, the Housing and Home Finance Agency became a permanent arm of the Federal Government, to survive until it was elevated to cabinet status in 1965 as the Department of Housing and Urban Development.

In the meantime, there had been delaying tactics with regard to Senate consideration of the Taft-Ellender-Wagner bill, which had been on the Senate calendar since April 24. There had been strong intervention by the House Republican leadership to the effect that the bill faced certain defeat in the House if it came over from the Senate. In the interests of party unity, they urged that Senate action on the measure be deferred at least until 1948. Robert Taft reluctantly agreed to a compromise under which the bill would remain on the Senate calendar until 1948 and still another investigation of the housing problem would be undertaken by a joint Congressional committee, to give some semblance of action on housing in 1947. The Senate agreed to the House Resolution to this effect on July 26, 1947.

The Democrats in Congress made *pro forma* objections that another investigation was unnecessary and would produce no housing but were powerless to block the action.

The joint committee was to consist of seven members from the Banking and Currency Committee of each house, and divided between four Republicans and three Democrats from each committee. The selection of members was to be made by the political majority and minority in each instance. It turned out that among the 14 members of the joint committee, there was a majority of eight who were generally in support of legislation comparable to the Taft-Ellender-Wagner bill. From the Senate committee, the Republican members were Chairman Tobey and Ralph Flanders, offset by Senators McCarthy and Cain. However, the three Democratic members were solidly for the legislation: Senator Wagner (bedridden but able to vote by proxy under the Senate rules), Senator Glen Taylor of Idaho, and John Sparkman. In the House committee, the four Republicans were solidly in tune with the lobby: Ralph Gamble from Westchester County, New York, the second-ranking Republican on the full Banking and Currency Committee; and Congressmen Frank L. Sundstrom of New Jersey, Rolla C. McMillan of Illinois, and Charles K. Fletcher of California. However, the three Democrats selected were all liberals: Wright Patman, the long-time populist Democrat from Texarkana, Texas; Hale Boggs, the able and intelligent young Representative from New Orleans; and Albert Rains, the able young liberal Democrat from Gadsden, Alabama.

The organization meeting of the Joint Committee did not occur until August 19, 1947, after the adjournment of Congress. This occasion was marked by Senator Joseph McCarthy's first major display of the unscrupulous, Machiavellian tactics for which he was to become notorious.

Senator Tobey appeared at the meeting armed with proxies from several absent Democratic members which, together with the votes of his supporters actually present, would have been sufficient to elect him as chairman of the joint committee. This would have resulted in a much different kind of investigation than actually ensued. But Senator McCarthy, observing that among the members present at the meeting there was a majority of one which was opposed to legislation such as the Wagner-Ellender-Taft bill, quickly moved that the joint committee adopt the rules of the House of Representatives, which prohibit the use of proxies in committee, rather than the rules of the Senate which permit the honoring of proxies. Over the strenuous protests of Senator Tobey and his supporters, this motion was carried by a majority of one. McCarthy then moved the election of Congressman Gamble as chairman and, in turn, McCarthy was elected vice-chairman.

Through this maneuver, the minority which shared the views of the reactionary housing lobby seized control of the organization of the joint committee. Furthermore, recognizing that the majority could upset these arrangements at any subsequent committee meeting at which they were all present, McCarthy prevailed on Congressman Gamble not to call another meeting until March 4, 1948, just 11 days before the joint committee was required to present its final report to Congress. Gamble, a nonaggressive type, was also content to have McCarthy exercise *de facto* control over the operations of the joint committee, including the recruitment of staff who were selected primarily for the conformity of their views with those of the lobby.

In order to present the façade of participation in the investigation by the individual members of the joint committee, the chairman and vice-chairman assigned topics for individual investigation and report. With characteristic McCarthyist cynicism, the basic topic of slum clearance was assigned to Senator Wagner, in full knowledge that the bedridden Senator was in no condition to carry out any kind of investigation.

However, this superficially shrewd move backfired. Senator Wagner's office was being managed by Joseph P. McMurray, his administrative assistant, with occasional supervision from New York City by Robert F. Wagner, Jr., on behalf of his father. I called on McMurray, who had had extensive staff experience in the Senate, and proposed that a detailed questionnaire on housing problems and needs and on the elimination of slums be circulated over Senator Wagner's name to mayors and governors and to a selected list of prominent citizens throughout the country. I predicted that, with the continuing prestige of Senator Wagner's name, such a questionnaire would elicit responses which would confound the propaganda of the anti-housing lobby as well as the minority on the joint committee and support the objectives of the Taft-Ellender-Wagner bill. McMurray was appalled by Joseph McCarthy's ruthless and cynical tactics, was strongly opposed to the objectives of the anti-housing lobby, and had a deep personal commitment to the comprehensive legislation sponsored by his Senator. He promptly accepted my proposal as a counter-move which would serve all three causes.

I prepared the questionnaires with the help of HHFA staff. McMurray dispatched the questionnaires to approximately 750 individuals throughout the country, including the mayors of all cities of 50,000 population or more, the governors of all the States, and representative individuals in business, industry, finance, organized labor, and the professions. The responses to the questionnaires were fully up to our expectations. There was almost unanimous agreement on the widespread existence of slums and other substandard housing. Nine out of ten of those responding asserted that private enterprise could not then or in the foreseeable future provide decent housing, new or old, for the low-income families occupying the slums. An equally high percentage favored the provision of publicly assisted low-rent housing for families not able to afford decent private housing. With regard to slum clearance and redevelopment, 66 out of the 68 mayors responding asserted that public financial assistance would be necessary in order to make the cleared land available for rebuilding at reasonable prices.

I collaborated with Joseph McMurray in preparing a report presenting the results of the questionnaires. Since the report was in response to an official assignment to Senator Wagner, the Joint Committee staff, however reluctantly, was obliged to publish the report in substantial volume as a Joint Committee print and to make it available to Senator Wagner's office for widespread public distribution.

The Joint Committee assignment to Senator Tobey was to prepare a report on the effect of taxation upon housing. Here again, at Senator Tobey's request, I undertook to prepare his report, with staff help from HHFA. Based on a broad interpretation of his assignment, we analyzed 13 pending proposals to reduce the monthly cost of housing through various forms of subsidy, including tax exemption and tax abatement. The principal conclusion of the report, supported by detailed analyses, was that "only the low-rent public housing formula, involving annual Federal subsidies and local tax exemption, would reduce rents sufficiently to meet the requirements of the average family in the lowest income third." Again, the Joint Committee staff was reluctantly required to publish Senator Tobey's report.

The second course of action determined upon by the controlling minority of the Joint Committee was to conduct extensive hearings, beginning and ending in Washington in September and January and including one-day hearings in 32 major cities. The hearings in the field were scheduled by McCarthy's committee staff and selected witnesses were lined up by the staff's advance men. There were compaints from a number of cities that sufficient advance notice of the hearings had not been given to the mayors and especially to the local organizations likely to testify in support of the Taft-Ellender-Wagner bill. There were also complaints that in some cities, the local building and real estate organizations supporting the anti-housing lobby's line were given preferred position and time and that liberal groups wishing to express contrary views were restricted in their opportunity to testify.

However, if it was the intent of Senator McCarthy and the Joint Committee staff to load the record of the field hearings with the views of the local representatives of the anti-housing lobby and to prevent expressions of support for the Taft-Ellender-Wagner bill, this tactic was unsuccessful. A coordinated intelligence program was carried out by the United States Conference of Mayors, the National Housing Conference, the national labor organizations, and others to alert municipal governments and local organizations to the field hearings and about the importance of insisting on an adequate opportunity to present their views. As a result, while some of the hearings were stormy and while the local spokesmen for the anti-housing lobby had more than ample time to state their position, the record of the hearings also contained impressive evidence of grass-roots support for comprehensive housing and redevelopment legislation.

The Joint Committee held its final public hearings in Washington between January 13 and January 28, 1948. On the latter date, the deadline for submission of the committee's report to Congress was little more than six weeks away. Yet there was still no meeting of the full committee and no formal consultation by the committee staff with the majority members on the content of the report.

The moment of truth finally arrived on March 4. The afternoon before, Congressman Hale Boggs telephoned me to report that he had just received a draft of the proposed report together with a notice of a committee meeting the following morning. He told me that from a cursory look at the draft it appeared to be entirely unacceptable and that he was at a loss about how to proceed before the committee meeting to act on the report the following morning. This was clearly the McCarthy strategy.

At Boggs's suggestion I went to his office to pick up his copy of the draft report. I returned to the headquarters of the Housing and Home Finance Agency late that afternoon where we quickly assembled an emergency group to analyze the voluminous staff report and to prepare a memorandum to be available to the Joint Committee meeting the following morning. One group included B. T. Fitzpatrick, the general counsel of HHFA and a leading authority on housing law; Neal J. Hardy, later to become the Federal Housing Commissioner; William L. C. Wheaton, an expert on housing finance and planning and later the Dean of the College of Environmental Design at the University of California at Berkeley; Warren J. Vinton, long-time expert on public housing; several other HHFA staff members, and myself. We worked through most of the night to prepare an answer and rebuttal to the draft report.

The report prepared by the staff of the Joint Committee was shot through with errors of fact, distortions, and omissions. Its main thrust was a bitter attack on the low-rent public housing program, an unsupported claim that private builders could meet all housing needs, and equally unsupported claims that the states and cities could assume the responsibility for housing the poor and for slum clearance and redevelopment without Federal financial aid. More significantly, the report was clearly an expression of the most extremist views of the anti-housing lobby. It was these views which our memorandum undertook to answer and to refute.

Early on the morning of March 4, I telephoned Congressman Wright Patman to tell him of our memorandum and its main conclusions. He agreed to call Congressmen Boggs and Rains and Senator Sparkman to his office for an immediate briefing on our memorandum before the Joint Committee meeting. After B. T. Fitzpatrick and I had made this briefing, which resulted in complete agreement to oppose the draft report in its entirety, we undertook to advise Senators Tobey and Flanders of this agreement and also to alert Senator Taylor.

When the Joint Committee met behind closed doors later that morning, the majority was finally in control. After stormy exchanges with Senator McCarthy and some of his cohorts, the committee majority voted *en bloc* to reject the draft report as inaccurate and inadequate. However, with characteristic resilience, McCarthy proposed and secured tacit agreement that the Joint Committee staff be instructed to revise their report in accordance with the criticisms of the majority, with the revised report to be submitted at a further meeting of the committee prior to the March 15 deadline.

Later that day I called on Senator Flanders at his office and expressed my conviction that the revised report, so long as it was prepared by the Joint Committee staff, would not conceivably be a document to which the Senator would be willing to sign his name. I added that in my opinion the same view would be shared by the other members of the committee majority. Puffing on his pipe, Senator Flanders pondered on my statement and ultimately agreed with it. However, he asked what alternative was open to him. I replied that the same HHFA staff group which had prepared the quick memorandum supporting the majority's rejection of the draft report would be willing to draft, on a strictly confidential basis, a committee report corresponding to his views and to those of the others on the committee majority. I emphasized that the report would be subject to his approval, line by line, and if it received his concurrence, would thereupon become his report.

So it was that our HHFA group undertook the intensive task of preparing what became the final majority report of the Joint Committee on Housing. In his conscientious and thorough manner, Senator Flanders read our product word by word, as did his personal staff. With only a few minor changes, it became the Flanders report. At the final showdown session of the Joint Committee on March 13, 1948, the revised draft presented by Senator McCarthy and the committee staff was rejected by the committee majority as again not presenting accurate findings or acceptable recommendations. Senator Flanders then presented his alternative report which was adopted by the majority, after what was reported to be acrimonious argument. In an effort to preserve a semblance of unity within the Joint Committee and to mask the extent of the defeat of the committee apparatus, Congressman Gamble moved that the Flanders report be unanimously adopted as the final majority report of the committee. This motion was adopted, with Senators McCarthy and Cain reserving the right to oppose the report's recommendations on the extension of the low-rent public housing program.

Two days later, Senator Flanders presented the Joint Committee report on the floor of the Senate for its consideration. He stated, in part:

> First of all, I desire to draw attention to the fact that the studies and investigations of the Joint Committee on Housing, and the conclusions and recommendations embodied in its report, confirm all of the essential findings and recommendations resulting from

earlier investigations of the housing problem. This is especially
true in the case of the intensive study and investigation carried out
by the Senate Subcommittee on Housing and Urban Development
headed by Senator Taft, and which led to the preparation of the
comprehensive housing bill now on the Senate calendar. One result,
therefore, is that the report of the Joint Committee on housing
recommends substantially the long-range proposals embodied in the
Taft-Ellender-Wagner bill.

All of us, I am sure, recognize that housing is one of our most
important domestic problems. I think perhaps we would all agree
that there has been enough investigation and study, and that decisive action must not be longer delayed.

Thus in his terse New England manner, Senator Flanders de-
molished the pretenses and subterfuges of Senator McCarthy and his
supporters and prompters in the real estate lobby. Joe McCarthy was
as vindictive in defeat as he was in his frequent interim successes. His
tactic on this occasion was to ridicule Senator Flanders, to attempt to
fluster him by technical questions, and to insinuate that he was un-
familiar with the content of the report which originally had carried
his name.

Senator Flanders was not adept at the rough and tumble of
Senate floor debate, especially when dealing with an antagonist with
the cynical and slippery virtuosity of Joe McCarthy. Flanders handily
won the vote that day, with the help of his supporters on both sides of
the aisle. But the treatment he received from McCarthy that afternoon evidently rankled over the years. It is significant that by the
mid-Fifties, when McCarthy's demagogic career had passed its crest,
it was Ralph Flanders who first had the political courage to stand
up on the floor of the Senate and make the motion of censure which
led to McCarthy's downfall.

The significant tactical victory of the supporters of comprehensive
housing legislation was still in jeopardy from the standpoint of legislative action by reason of the political timing situation in 1948. The
Republican National Convention was assembling in late June in Philadelphia against a general consensus that the Republican presidential
nominee would sweep the 1948 elections. This meant that Congress
would adjourn or at least recess in advance of the convention. In the
House of Representatives there was total foot-dragging from the
standpoint of legislative initiative on the issue.

As a countermove, the supporters of the legislation moved with relative speed to secure passage of the legislation in the Senate. After brief hearings, the Banking and Currency committee on April 8 reported amendments to the Taft-Ellender-Wagner bill to conform the measure with the recommendations of the Joint Housing Committee. Floor debate began in mid-April.

The opposition centered its fight in support of an amendment by Senator Cain to eliminate the public housing provisions of the bill. The Cain amendment had strong backing from Senator McCarthy and other rightwing Republican Senators. Of future significance, it also was backed by a majority of the Southern Democrats, excluding such stalwarts as Ellender, Hill, Maybank, Sparkman, and Pepper. But Senator Taft by a major effort pressed a majority of the Republican Senators to oppose the Cain amendment. The proposal was defeated, 49 to 35, with 25 Republicans and 24 Democrats opposing Cain and 18 Republicans and 17 Democrats supporting him. After this test vote, the Taft-Ellender-Wagner bill was approved by the Senate on April 22.

The critical issue then became whether committee action and a floor vote on the legislation could be forced in the House of Representatives before the recess for the Republican National Convention. The opposing forces, inside and outside Congress, mobilized for action. The real estate lobby and their allies in the House of Representatives felt that time was on their side and that the safest course was to prevent a vote on the floor before the adjournment.

These tactics drew increasing criticism. Even as conservative a Republican newspaper as the *Kansas City Star* made these editorial comments:

> The Taft-Ellender-Wagner bill has come out of the Senate as the main hope for housing in this session of Congress. This is the bill that makes the real estate boards see red and it seems that their worst "red" is Senator Taft. Anyway he got his bill through the Senate. From here on everything depends on the House of Representatives. . . . The bill is a broad, over-all program for stimulating all types of housing with generous Federal lending policies and other encouragement. . . . The public housing feature is comparatively restricted and modest. There is nothing in it to scare the nation with a trend toward general socialization of housing. But the hysterical real estate lobby has swarmed over Capitol Hill

whenever there was fresh talk about reviving this long dormant bill. The screams of "socialism" have been effective, especially in the House.

The public supporters of the legislation had formed a coalition of 26 national organizations to rally pressure for Congressional action. These included the AFL, the CIO, the U.S. Conference of Mayors, the National Public Housing Conference, the National Farmers Union, two of the veterans' organizations, Negro groups, religious organizations, women's groups, and others. President Truman made a strong appeal over the radio for passage of the bill by the House.

However, the forces for delay and inaction, under the direction of Chairman Jesse Wolcott of the House Banking and Currency Committee, appeared to have the upper hand. These tactics were succinctly described by Lee F. Johnson, executive vice president of the National Public Housing Conference:

> The trick is to stall, to hear other bills, to question witnesses for hours on end, to adjourn the moment the House goes into action each day, to do anything that permits the clock to run out.

On May 20, word was leaked to the press that Speaker Martin and Republican leader Halleck had made a final decision that the Taft-Ellender-Wagner bill would not be allowed to come to a vote on the floor unless the public housing provision was deleted by the committee.

These tactics almost backfired. In an effort to bypass the blockade imposed by the committee and House leadership, the supporters of the legislation began to circulate a petition to discharge the Banking and Currency Committee from jurisdiction over the Senate-passed bill. If signed by an absolute majority of the House membership, this would have brought the bill to a vote on the floor of the house, without amendment. Strong pressure was brought to bear by the national organizations and by local groups, including mayors, to secure signatures to the petition.

As this pressure gained momentum, Chairman Wolcott, as a countermove, felt impelled to call an executive session of his committee in early June to approve a substitute bill which he hurriedly had prepared, lacking any public housing and otherwise representing a watered-down version of the Taft-Ellender-Wagner bill. The assumption was that the Chairman had enough votes on the committee to carry out this maneuver.

The nominal party division in the committee was 16 Republicans and 11 Democrats. However, as previously noted, Congresman Merlin Hull of Wisconsin was committed to vote with the Democrats on this occasion. Another Republican, Representative William G. Stratton, had ambitions to run for Governor of Illinois and was under heavy pressure to support the Senate bill. Finally, Representative Hardie Scott of Philadelphia had been told by his Republican mayor that he would be denied renomination for his House seat if he failed to support the Senate bill.

At the morning executive session it appeared that Chairman Wolcott's strategy would succeed since Hardie Scott reneged on his commitment to suport the Taft-Ellender-Wagner bill. But this word was passed to Mayor Bernard Samuel of Philadelphia who read the riot act over the telephone to his wayward Representative. When the committee reassembled that afternoon, the Democrats moved to substitute the Senate-passed bill for the Wolcott bill. To the consternation of Wolcott and his regular Republican colleagues, Congressman Scott switched his vote and voted for the Democratic motion. With Congressmen Hull and Stratton also joining forces, the motion passed by a vote of 14 to 13 and the committee adopted the Taft-Ellender-Wagner bill without amendment.

This was a humiliating, even if temporary setback for Chairman Wolcott and the House Republican leadership and a psychological victory for the Democrats and the liberal Republicans. The Republican leadership fell back on their second line of defense—the House Rules Committee, packed with rightwing Republicans and reactionary Southern Democrats. By a vote of 6 to 2, the committee refused to grant a rule to permit the bill to be taken up on the floor of the House. The only hope for action rested with the discharge petition but leadership pressure on the House Republicans was sufficient to prevent the necessary majority of signatures.

After extensive maneuvering, the Wolcott bill was finally forced through the House on June 19, the final day of the 1948 session. But, in the Senate, Senator Ellender refused permission to have the House bill considered and stuck to his position notwithstanding demagogic personal attacks by Senator Joe McCarthy. In the early morning hours of the closing session, with cots installed in the corridors for exhausted Senators, Alben Barkley returned to the Senate floor. He was rested after a nap, freshly shaven, and immaculate in a white linen suit. He remarked:

> I understand hope has been abandoned of getting a housing bill, but I have been told tonight that the Republican moguls in Philadelphia have sent word down here that we are not to adjourn until a housing bill is passed—just anything that has got a house in it.
>
> Senators recall having read that one of the great English kings on a historic occasion shouted, "A horse! a horse! my kingdom for a horse!" And so the Senator from Ohio, and the Speaker of the House of Representatives, and the majority leader of the House, and the chairman of the Committee on Banking and Currency of the House are shouting "A house! a house! my candidacy for a house!"

This was an apt description of the minuscule measure which was passed as the final act of the session. It was limited primarily to increasing funds for Government purchase of FHA mortgages and GI loans. In due course, President Truman signed this "so-called housing bill," but with the following comments:

> It was passed by the Congress in the final hours of the session, after the Republican leadership refused to permit the House of Representatives to vote upon the Taft-Ellender-Wagner housing bill. . . . It fails to provide for farm housing or for slum clearance. It fails to provide for housing research, for financial assistance to large-scale home construction, or for encouraging large-scale production of prefabricated housing. It fails completely to aid in meeting our greatest housing need—low-cost rental housing. It makes no provision for publicly-assisted low-rent housing, or in fact, any rental housing. Contrasted with the T-E-W bill, this measure was properly labeled as the "teeny-weeny" housing bill.

Chairman Wolcott retorted:

> He has raised the basic question of socialism versus Americanism. This will be debated at length during the campaign. Mr. Truman will be asked many times to explain why he thinks it desirable to change the American form of Government under which we have become the greatest nation on earth.

Wolcott was correct in predicting that the housing issue would be debated extensively during the 1948 campaign. After the national conventions President Truman called Congress into special session, primarily to act on housing legslation. While no substantive legislation ensued, the special session served to fix the record clearly as to party responsibility for the lack of action on housing.

Throughout his barn-storming election campaign, the "teeny-weeny" housing bill ranked high in Harry Truman's attacks on the "do-nothing, reactionary 80th Congress." And it was one of the prime issues in his upset victory over Governor Thomas E. Dewey.

CHAPTER 5

The Struggle Over the Housing Act of 1949

Harry Truman's amazing upset of Governor Dewey in the 1948 Presidential election created a dramatic shift in the political perspectives for domestic legislation. Since the failure of the Republican 80th Congress to enact comprehensive housing legislation had figured prominently in Truman's barn-storming campaign, the prospects for such legislation were greatly enhanced.

The swing to the Democratic Party was even more marked in the Congressional elections than in the Presidential vote. In the Senate, there was a Democratic gain of nine seats, all of them liberal. This resulted in a party division of 54 Democratic Senators and 42 Republicans and further enhanced the prospects for long-term housing legislation in that body, particularly in view of continued support by a sizable group of Republican Senators. In the House, the political realignment was still more pronounced: there was a net gain of 75 Democratic representatives which more than canceled the Republican gains in 1946 and resulted in at least a nominal Democratic majority of 263 to 171.

Within the Administration and the organizations which had been supporting the basic housing legislation, there was jubilation as well as prompt preparation for immediate renewal of the legislative effort when the new Congress convened in January, 1949.

On the right, there was amazement and consternation at the outcome of the election. This was coupled with acute embarrassment on the part of most of the national opinion-polling organizations which had predicted a sweeping victory for Governor Dewey as well as by *Time* magazine which appeared on the newsstands after the election with a cover portrait presenting the Governor as the next President of the United States.

The real estate lobby doubtless shared this immediate reaction of dismay. However, their ranks quickly reformed behind the dual tactics of, first, presenting public housing as a program which did not house the poor and which was somehow socialistic or communistic, and, second, raising 'the specter of public housing as threatening compulsory racial desegregation. Their prime objective was alienation of the Southern Democrats, especially in the House of Representatives.

The housing legislation transmitted by the Truman Administration, immediately after the convening of the 81st Congress in early January, 1949, was essentially a revival of the Taft-Ellender-Wagner bill which had been blocked from a vote in the House the previous summer. There had been unpublicized bureaucratic infighting within the Administration about the provisions of the bill for Federal grants to subsidize the clearance of slums and blighted areas for redevelopment. This involved social as well as economic overtones. The principle established by the Taft Subcommittee in 1945 and reaffirmed in the subsequent major legislative proposals was that the primary objective and justification for this use of Federal funds was the elimination of predominantly residential slums and the adequate rehousing of the slum occupants. Therefore, a project eligible to receive such grants either must be a predominantly residential slum, in which case the new use of the land could be whatever was considered most appropriate by the community, or, if predominantly nonresidential, the new use would have to be primarily housing. In either case, the availability of satisfactory relocation housing within the means of the families to be displaced by the project would be a fixed requirement.

At a late hour, the then Federal Works Agency, responding to the interests of conservative city planners and central city real estate and construction interests, proposed to the White House that the housing focus of the redevelopment legislation, as well as the fixed relocation housing requirement, be eliminated. The FWA also urged that legislation lodge the administrative responsibility for redevelopment in itself, as more responsive to city planning and public works considerations, rather than in the Housing and Home Finance Agency. Through certain conservatives who had the ear of the President, the FWA proposal received serious consideration. Raymond Foley, the HHFA Administrator, responded that the major objective of the proposed redevelopment legislation

> has been, is now, and should continue to be, the elimination of slums—not just because, as the Federal Works Agency substitute suggests, they "cause deterioration of investments and serious deficiencies in the production of economic wealth," but primarily because they cause deterioration and serious deficiencies in the human beings who are forced to live in them—deterioration and serious deficiences in the real wealth of the nation.

Foley finally won his point with the President.

There also were policy differences between the Administration and legislative leaders, on the one hand, and certain liberal and labor organizations on the other about the content of the legislation. The principal point at issue was whether the Housing Act of 1949 should contain a program of direct Federal loans at low interest rates to finance the development of housing for middle-income and lower-middle-income families, in addition to the public housing program of Federal subsidies for the housing of the lowest-income groups. A number of organizations including labor and religious organizations strongly advocated the inclusion of a middle-income program. But there were fears on the part of the Administration and others that the innovation of direct Federal housing loans, which had not been proposed in the predecessor bills or committee reports, might dilute the political support for the measure and intensify the opposition by private financial interests.

In reporting the Housing Act of 1949 on February 25 of that year, the Senate Banking and Currency Committee recognized these differences and attempted to reconcile them:

> Your committee is not, in this bill, attemping to deal with all of the main areas of the housing problem. . . . This bill does not purport to be . . . legislation authorizing the full and comprehensive housing program that is needed; or providing a complete and final solution to every phase of the complex housing problem. Convincing testimony presented during the hearings indicates that this bill does, however, represent the essential first action toward, and will

provide the sound foundation for such a comprehensive housing program.

When the bill reached the floor of the Senate, it had 22 sponsors, equally divided between Democrats and Republicans. The bill contained five principal provisions. First, as had been proposed in the predecessor measures and reports, it contained a declaration of national housing objectives and policies, the key phrase being that "the general welfare and security of the Nation require the realization as soon as feasible of the goal of a decent home and suitable living environment for every American family." (Subsequent chapters of this book examine the social, economic, and political forces which prevented the achievement of this goal during the two ensuing decades.) Second, the bill established the Federal urban redevelopment and slum clearance program, focused on the elimination and redevelopment of predominantly residential slums and blighted areas. It authorized Federal loans of $1 billion, becoming available over a five-year period, to finance local redevelopment agencies in the acquisition of slum properties and the related costs of preparing the sites for redevelopment. It also authorized a five-year program of $500 million in capital grants to absorb two-thirds of the difference between the gross cost of acquiring and preparing slum sites and the fair value of the land for new building.

Third, the bill reactivated the low-rent public housing program for low-income families, which had been in suspension since before Pearl Harbor. It made available annual subsidies to local housing authorities sufficient to finance 810,000 dwellings over a six-year period.

Fourth, the legislation authorized Federal grants for research in housing and related matters. Referring to the many previous studies which had emphasized the absence of effective research in housing, the committee said:

> These reports have pointed out the relative technological backwardness of the housing industry, compared to other major industries, and have described some of the conditioning social, economic, and political factors that have caused this lag. The housing business is far too important a segment of our economy, and the benefits that could be derived from modernizing it are too large in terms of the improvement in the housing conditions of American

families as well as in stability of employment and investment, to permit us to accept this situation any longer.

Finally, the bill established an extensive program of financial assistance and subsidies to improve housing conditions on farms. The committee report pointed out that a much higher proportion of farm than urban dwellings were in bad physical condition and that the majority of farm houses lacked the amenities considered essential in urban housing.

When the Senate began to debate the Housing Act of 1949 on April 13, the tactical direction of the forces supporting the legislation was in the hands of Senator Sparkman of Alabama who had gained major stature in less than three years in the Senate. He delegated the management of the redevelopment title of the legislation to Senator Paul H. Douglas, the remarkable 57-year-old economist and Marine combat veteran who had been elected in Illinois the preceding fall.

The opposition was managed by Senator John W. Bricker of Ohio, far to the right of his colleague Senator Taft, and Senator Harry Cain of Washington, the prisoner of the real estate lobby. The main thrust of the opposition was an outright attack against the public housing program, with a spillover of crippling amendments to the redevelopment and farm housing proposals. But the most cynical maneuver was a proposed amendment by Senator Bricker, who was anything but a civil rights advocate, to prohibit racial segregation or discrimination in public housing projects. This was a transparent attempt to force liberal members of the Senate to vote for a provision which would antagonize southern supporters of the program. (The subsequent Congressional investigation of lobbying organizations confirmed that this strategem originated with the real estate lobby which in fact was violently opposed to housing desegregation.)

The issue was succinctly put by Senator Edward J. Thye, the progressive Republican from Minnesota:

What is the necessity for the amendment? If there is no mention of class, creed, religion or color in the bill then why is the amendment necessary? . . . My only fear in connection with the proposal to write specific language into the bill . . . is primarily that if the amendment shall prevail, and because of the amendment the entire housing legislation is defeated, we would be endangering the chance of the people or the families who have no place to rent or live in now to obtain suitable living quarters.

And Senator Taft told his colleague from Ohio:

> . . . there is no reason that I know of for such a requirement as is proposed. It seems to me the system has worked with entire justice, and there is no charge made of discrimination of any kind.

The Bricker amendment was defeated by a vote of 46 to 32, although this was the closest margin of any of the opposition amendments. Northern Democratic liberals, such as Hubert Humphrey and Paul Douglas, explained that they had the difficult choice of voting for nondiscrimination and assuring defeat of the legislation, or voting against desegregation and saving the bill. Ultimately, they voted against the Bricker amendment and were joined by most of their Democratic colleagues together with a few Republicans such as Senators Taft, Tobey, Flanders, and Morse.

From a substantive standpoint, the key vote in the Senate was on a motion by Senator Bricker to strike the public housing and farm housing titles of the bill. This was defeated 58 to 19. On this vote even Joe McCarthy deserted, and Bricker was able to muster only 13 Republican and 6 Democratic votes. The entire bill was then passed, 57 to 13, on April 21.

The struggle now moved to the House of Representatives where hearings on a comparable bill had started on April 9 and continued through May 7. In contrast to the Senate, the power and influence of the real estate lobby and its allies, all of which were united in strong opposition to the Housing Act of 1949, were extensive in the House. Notwithstanding the massive Democratic majority, there was serious doubt over the passage of the bill and especially its public housing provisions. The lobby intensified its propaganda and pressures against the measure. In addition to the National Association of Real Estate Boards, the National Association of Home Builders, and their friends in the building materials field, a particularly potent force in the House was in the United States Savings and Loan League. Under the direction of Morton Bodfish, its executive vice president, the League had shrewdly urged its member savings and loan associations to follow a policy of electing their Congressmen to their boards of directors and also providing a source of campaign financing. As a result, a majority of the members of the House served as directors of savings and loan associations in their home towns.

Arrayed against the real estate lobby were the forces of a formidable group of organizations: the AFL, the CIO, the United States Conference of Mayors, the American Municipal Association, all the principal veterans' organizations, national religious organizations of all faiths, the National Association for the Advancement of Colored People and allied groups, and a number of the principal national women's organizations. The main coordinating group was the National Public Housing Conference. The Truman Administration was also active in exerting pressure in behalf of the legislation; as Assistant to the Housing Administrator I was a principal agent in this campaign and in seeking support from local groups and national organizations. I worked closely with Lee F. Johnson, executive vice president of the National Public Housing Conference, and with B. T. Fitzpatrick, general counsel of the Housing and Home Finance Agency, who was the principal drafter of the bill and was in overall charge of legislative strategy.

On May 16, 1949, the House Banking and Currency Committee by a vote of 14 to 7 reported out the Housing Act of 1949 in substantially the same form in which it had passed the Senate. The report observed at the outset:

> Your committee heard testimony by a great number of witnesses and was impressed not only by the overwhelming support of its provisions from spokesmen of a wide variety of citizens groups but also by the increasing acceptance of its major objectives even by industry leaders who disagreed with detailed provisions.

This "increasing acceptance" did not extend to the real estate lobby and its spokesmen within the House of Representatives. In fact, the most violent attack on the bill was appended to the committee report itself in the form of the minority views of Representative Frederick C. Smith, a right-wing extremist from Marion, Ohio:

> Political ownership of human shelter is the mark of the beast. Nothing can be more communistic. Those who live in houses owned by the political authority are in the nature of things so completely beholden to it as to make them amenable to its dictation in the

selection of persons to perform the duties of government. . . . The title of H.R. 4009 should be—"A bill to further enslave the people of the United States."

The real estate lobby and their allies shifted their pressure to the House Rules Committee, dominated by conservatives of both parties, in an effort to block the issuance of a rule to bring the bill to the floor of the House for action. The lobby intensified its propaganda and distortions concerning the provisions and impact of the legislation. There was an initial success when the Rules Committee voted 7 to 5 to table the bill, the same tactic which had blocked floor action on the comparable legislation in June, 1948.

The Truman Administration and the Democratic leadership of the House were resolved to break these blocking tactics, bring the bill to the House floor, and secure its passage. With regard to the Rules Committee, the leadership had seized the opportunity presented by the large Democratic majority and, upon the opening of the 81st Congress, had forced through a change in the House rules permitting the chairman of a legislative committee to call up for floor action a committee bill if the Rules Committee had not authorized its consideration within 21 days. Speaker Sam Rayburn, after the Rules Committee vote to table the bill, made it clear that he was prepared to resort to the 21-day rule. This led several of the committee conservatives to see the handwriting on the wall; three of them accordingly switched their vote and, on reconsideration, the bill was cleared for floor action by a vote of 8 to 4.

There continued to be serious concern about the impact of the real estate lobby's intensive propaganda campaign on marginal members of the House, especially Representatives from small-town and rural constituencies and from the South. In a search for a technique to dramatize the blatant distortions and inaccuracies of the lobby's propaganda, it was decided at the White House to expose them in detail in a letter from President Truman to Speaker Rayburn. With a few of my associates in the Housing and Home Finance Agency, I was asked to collaborate with Charles Murphy, then White House counsel, and David Bell, then a White House assistant, to prepare and document such a letter.

The letter was dispatched and released on June 17, five days before the House debate on the legislation was scheduled to begin. The Truman letter pulled no punches. I will cite a few excerpts:

> I have been shocked in recent days at the extraordinary propaganda campaign that has been unleashed against this bill by the real estate lobby. I do not recall ever having witnessed a more deliberate campaign of misrepresentation and distortion against legislation of such crucial importance to the public welfare. The propaganda of the real estate lobby consistently misstates the explicit provisions of the bill, consistently misrepresents what will be the actual effect of the bill, and consistently distorts the facts of the housing situation in the country.

The letter then proceeded to examine the principal charges made by the lobby and to present the actual facts. In summary:

> 1. The real estate lobby claims that H.R. 4009 will cost the Federal Government 20 billion dollars. . . . This is an exaggeration of approximately 100 percent. The actual cost of the bill will be about 10 billion dollars, spread over a period of some 30 years.
> 2. The real estate lobby claims that each low-rent public housing unit will cost more than $15,000. The facts are that the amount of money provided . . . will permit an average cost, at the most, of $8,465. . . .
> 3. The real estate lobby claims that "there is no longer any pretense that public housing is for the poor." The facts are that H.R. 4009 requires local public housing authorities to give preference for admission to public housing projects to low income families having the most urgent housing needs. . . . In the first half of 1948, the average income of the families admitted to the present low-rent projects was $1,480.

The Truman letter went on to refute the other principal distortions of the lobby: that the Housing Act of 1949 would not clear slums, that public housing programs could be imposed on unwilling communities by the Federal Government, that the private housing industry was prepared to meet the needs of low-income families, that the provision of adequate housing for low-income families "will encourage indolence and shiftlessness and destroy thrift and initiative." The President was particularly vehement in responding to the charge that the legislation was "socialistic":

> Insofar as this argument is intended seriously, it is false. H.R. 4009

will strengthen, not weaken, private enterprise. . . . I am sure, however, that this argument by members of the real estate lobby is not meant seriously. They know better. And so do the many individuals and organizations who have studied the facts of the matter and concluded that the bill is desirable. The 24 Republican and 33 Democratic members of the Senate who voted for a comparable bill did not believe the charge of socialism. The many distinguished newspapers throughout the country who support the bill do not believe it is socialistic. The American Legion, the Veterans of Foreign Wars, the American Veterans of World War II, the American Veterans Committee, the Disabled American Veterans, the Jewish War Veterans, the Catholic War Veterans—all of them have seen through the charge of socialism and support the bill. So do the American Municipal Association and the United States Conference of Mayors. The American Federation of Labor and the Congress of Industrial Organizations support the bill. So do the National Conference of Catholic Charities and the Congregational Christian Churches. So do the League of Women Voters, the National Council of Negro Women, the National Council of Catholic Women and the National Council of Jewish Women. So do the National Grange and the National Farmers Union. And so do the many other outstanding organizations and individuals who have testified that this legislation is necessary to the public interest.

Yet the real estate lobby, shortsighted and utterly selfish, continues to cry "socialism" in a last effort to smother the real facts and real issues which this bill is designed to meet.

These attempts to mislead and frighten the people and their representatives in the Congress—these false claims designed to prejudice some groups of people against others—these malicious and willful appeals to ignorance and selfishness—are examples of selfish propaganda at its worst.

The President's letter clearly did not change any votes among the committed opponents of the legislation. However, it did presumably have a favorable impact on some undecided votes, especially among the Democratic members, and provided valuable ammunition for the organizations lobbying in support of the bill. On the other hand, in sharp contrast to the position of the Republicans in the Senate, the House Republican leadership—Minority Leader Joseph Martin and Minority Whip Charles Halleck, strongly prompted by Representative Jesse Wolcott of the Banking and Currency Committee—made it a party issue for the Republican members to vote against the bill and especially against its public housing provisions.

When debate began on the floor of the House on June 22, the

now familiar arguments, pro and con, were presented by both sides. The opposition, notwithstanding the exposures in the Truman letter, filled the record with the distortions of the real estate lobby. A few examples:

> *Representative John C. Kunkel* (a leading Republican member of the Banking and Currency Committee): ". . . this so-called housing bill is a hoax in many ways. It will not provide housing for those who cannot afford to pay."
>
> *Representative Jesse Wolcott of Michigan* (ranking Republican on the committee): "No one argues that there is anything in this bill for any locality outside of 10 metropolitan areas. If any of you who live in cities with populations or from 20,000 up to 500,000 think there is anything in this bill for your people, read it over and become disillusioned. You are not going to get any of the benefits."
>
> *Representative Charles W. Vursell of Illinois:* "I oppose it because it is, in fact, using the power of the Federal Government to destroy the great building industry of private enterprise. I am opposed to this bill because it will take money, through excise taxes and otherwise, from the really poor . . . who will not be permitted as occupants in these low-rent buildings. . . . I am opposed to this legislation because it will rob the men and women of their cherished ambition to work and save to build and own their own homes."
>
> *Representative George A. Dondero of Michigan:* "If this colossal program is adopted, the first fatal step toward national socialism will have been taken and the first real imitation of the Russian ideology of government will have gained a foothold on the shores of freedom."

The supporters of the legislation marshalled the arguments which had been presented in the committee reports and summarized in the President's letter:

> *Representative John W. McCormack of Massachusetts,* the Majority Leader: ". . . it is rather strange, and in a sense amusing, to listen to members denouncing this bill as constituting socialism and protesting against it as a bill to give governmental assistance in the field of public housing. . . . Yet those very people, in fact not only now but in the past, have been the strongest advocates of government aid and assistance. . . . I appreciate opposition on other grounds, if members are opposed to slum programs . . .

but as to opposition on the grounds that it is socialism there is no justification."

Representative Frank M. Karsten of Missouri: "If we pass this legislation we will have a program that can reduce slums and provide low income housing. If we do not pass this bill, the slums must stand and grow and millions of men, women, and children of low income in this country will be doomed to wasteful, unnecessary, and disgraceful conditions of life. No more false and unjust attack has been leveled at public housing than the cry of those who oppose any housing relief for low income families on the grounds that public housing has not been serving low income needs. This is simply not so."

Representative William A. Barrett of Pennsylvania: "As private enterprise has made no mentionable contribution toward offering decent, low-cost housing, we are left with no alternative but to authorize Federal financial assistance to communities to start on a slum clearance program. . . . And finally in spite of the lies so assiduously spread by the opposition, all of this will be accomplished under the direction of local housing authorities and local government."

The floor debate ground on for four days. A number of crippling amendments affecting both the public housing program and the new urban redevelopment program were voted down. But the key issue was raised by Representative Edward H. Rees, a conservative Republican from Kansas, who moved to strike the public housing provisions from the bill. In a so-called teller vote, in which names are not recorded, the Rees motion prevailed by a vote of 168 to 165.

When the House assembled for final action on the bill, Representative Spence, chairman of the Banking and Currency Committee, demanded a record roll-call vote on the Rees amendment. In a tense atmosphere, the roll-call vote seasawed narrowly. Finally, the Rees amendment was defeated by a vote of 209 to 204. A switch of only three votes would have eliminated public housing from the legislation.

With the key issue disposed of, the House approved the entire bill on June 29 by a roll-call vote of 227 to 186. After a conference with the Senate, the legislation was sent to the White House and was signed by President Truman on July 15, 1949. Thus, the four-year struggle for enactment of a comprehensive national housing policy finally ended in victory. The goal established of a decent home in a suitable living environment for every American family was to survive all the political vicissitudes of the next two decades, even though its accomplishment was to be beset with serious frustrations.

At the same time, the narrow margin by which the public housing program survived in the legislation was a forecast of the political troubles in store for liberal housing legislation. It was also a classic illustration of the informal coalition of conservative Republicans and conservative or reactionary Southern Democrats which was a threat to all progressive legislation. In the ten Southern states, all nominally Democratic, the vote was almost two to one against public housing. Only in Alabama and Georgia did a majority of the State delegation vote in favor of public housing. The House Republicans voted 140 to 22 against public housing. Even though the other Democrats voted overwhelmingly (157 to 5) for public housing, it was the votes of the 22 maverick Republicans, 14 of whom were from Northeastern or Middle Atlantic districts, which preserved the program.

This alignment was to haunt the housing program in the coming years.

CHAPTER 6

First Steps to Meet the Housing Crisis in the Cities

After the enactment of the Housing Act of 1949, there was a mood of great expectations among the individuals, local governments, and organizations which had struggled for four years for the passage of the legislation. Notwithstanding the narrow margin of the victory in the House, the outcome had special political significance as the first demonstration of the potential of an urban crisis.

The forces which had overcome the political opposition of the real estate lobby and the large bloc of rural-oriented Representatives in the House constituted in truth an urban coalition, even though the term was not in popular usage at the time. It embraced virtually without exceptions the mayors of all sizable cities as well as many smaller towns organized under the various State leagues or municipalities. It included organized labor. It included the various national veterans' organizations, which exerted substantial political influence at a point of time only four years after the end of World War II. As recited by President Truman in his letter to Speaker Rayburn, it covered many of the principal national public interest, religious, and women's organizations. Furthermore, even though the voting record in the House was largely negative among the Southern Representatives and spotty among the Midwestern delegations, there was extensive regional grass-roots support for the legislation. This reflected largely the interests of mayors and the more than 600 local housing authorities which already were in existence.

The real problem was to begin to produce results against these great expectations. The revival of the public housing program was supported by the existence of active local housing authorities and the plans of many of them to expand their programs. But it soon developed that there were obstacles and roadblocks, partly because of staff shortages and other deficiencies both in the local authorities and in the Federal Public Housing Administration. More basic were the difficulties immediately encountered by many local authorities in finding sites for new public housing projects which were acceptable to the neighborhoods involved and hence to the city councils which had to approve the sites. Since a rising percentage of the occupants of and applicants for public housing was Negro, this site selection problem was already a reflection of the racial issue which was to plague the program in the years ahead.

Furthermore, the real estate lobby, after its narrow defeat in the House of Representatives, had openly launched a national campaign to block the public housing program at the local level. Its technique centered on creating or exploiting local controversies on the selection of sites for new public housing projects, controversies which at least covertly generally focused on the race issue. Through its local affiliates, the lobby sought to generate direct neighborhood political pressure on city councils against the approval of public housing sites or, where permitted or required by State law, to stimulate petitions forcing the city-wide referenda on the public housing program. In this way, the lobby was successful in blocking, at least temporarily, the expansion or initiation of public housing programs in a number of localities. These tactics were primarily effective in smaller cities where projects were proposed in white middle-class or lower-middle-class neighborhoods. In the South, with well-established patterns of neighborhood racial segregation and with local authorities committed to the maintenance of those patterns, the tactics were generally inapplicable. Here, the lobby's approach was necessarily limited to the ideological issue of "socialism."

Through this combination of circumstances and roadblocks, the progress of the public housing program was far less than the schedule of 135,000 dwellings per year authorized by the Housing Act of 1949. At the end of 1951, almost two and one-half years after the enactment of the legislation, only 84,600 public housing dwellings had been placed in construction.

For the new program of Federal loans and grants for slum clearance and urban development, the problems of accomplishment were of a different nature. While sharing in the general conservative attack on the 1949 Act, this program did not have the controversial stigma which was unjustifiably attached to the public housing program. The language of the statute made it clear that most of the redevelopment construction on the slum or blighted sites cleared with Federal financial assistance was intended to be under private rather than public auspices. There was considerable potential real estate interest in redevelopment, which tempered the otherwise automatic opposition of the real estate lobby to Federal subsidy programs affecting private property. The concept of slum clearance and redevelopment had the enthusiastic support, if not full understanding, of most mayors who saw it as an opportunity to rid cities of the social problems and fiscal deficits emanating from slums and blighted areas and to revive the central cores against the competition of the suburbs. The program also had the general support of all the organizations which had backed the Housing Act of 1949.

The principal obstacle against quick accomplishment under the slum clearance and urban redevelopment program was simply that it was an entirely new program. At the time of enactment of the 1949 Act, 27 states had adopted urban redevelopment laws. But, with the single exception of Metropolitan Life's Stuyvesant Town project in New York City, and the unique Golden Triangle project in Pittsburgh, there had been no actual activity. This reflected the fact that none of the state statutes provided any means of financing the almost inevitable writedown between the costs of assembling slum sites, demolishing the dilapidated or obsolete structures, and installing new utilities and site improvements, and the feasible value of the cleared land for new development. Furthermore, the constitutionality of most of the State laws was untested. Redevelopment required the backstop of the use of public powers of condemnation and thus needed judicial affirmation of the principle that the public purpose was the clearance of slums or blighted areas, regardless of whether the cleared land was ultimately disposed of for private development. In anticipation of the passage of the 1949 Act, a few of the large cities—Philadelphia, Detroit, Chicago, St. Louis, San Francisco, and Los Angeles—had begun to plan their initial redevelopment projects. In New York City, the astute and forceful Robert Moses had seen to it that the new program would be under his control. But elsewhere it was largely a matter of aspirations and expectations.

In September, 1949, I was appointed to be in charge of the new redevelopment program for the Housing and Home Finance Agency. Starting with an initial staff of one assistant, two secretaries, and a messenger, I had the job of recruiting and organizing a competent staff and establishing policies which would be consistent with the objectives and requirements of the law and still workable from the standpoint of the communities. In addition to this time-consuming process, it was essential to establish a simple procedure permitting interested communities to take initial steps without waiting for the completion of the staffing and policy-setting process. By the end of 1950, 222 communities had received preliminary grant commitments for almost $200 million and planning or other work had started on 124 slum clearance and redevelopment projects. By the end of 1951, these totals had increased to $283 million and 201 projects.

It was also important to avoid the crystallization of the conservative, doctrinaire business opposition which was hemming in the public housing program and to seek a broad base of support. To this end, I initiated a series of conferences with the local power structure in communities with an identified interest in redevelopment, including business leaders as well as city hall, labor, and local public interest groups. For the same purpose, I established a national advisory committee of 21 members.

Another basic obstacle to achieving the fine goals of the Housing Act of 1949 was the fact that the nation still did not have a complete comprehensive housing program. As the Senate Banking and Currency Committee had emphasized in its report on the 1949 Act, there remained a gap in the Federally-aided housing programs represented by lower-middle-income households whose economic position was above the low-income levels eligible for public housing but not high enough to afford typical new private homes or apartments at prevailing market prices and mortgage charges. This segment of the population comprised a substantial part of the blue-collar labor force as well as the lower-paid white-collar workers, in short the nonpoor two-fifths of the population which could afford radios, televisions, washing machines, and automobiles but which could not afford new houses at prevailing prices.

The Senate Committee had lived up to its promise to attempt to close this gap by proposing a massive program of direct Federal loans to housing cooperatives and other non-profit housing corporations at approximately the Federal bond interest rate and for fifty-year terms. However, this proposal sparked strong opposition, not only from the real estate lobby as such but also from mortgage lenders. Somehow, the concept of direct Federal housing loans was considered a dangerous precedent. Somehow, it was contended that this program to reach an unserved housing market would be inflationary, even though the booming private housing market in higher priced homes was not considered inflationary. Doubtless, the fact that private housing construction exceeded 1.4 million dwellings in 1949 and was to exceed 1.9 million in 1950 lessened some of the political support for the proposal.

Early in 1950, a compromise was attempted, after consultation with the Federal Reserve Board. In lieu of direct Federal lending, it was proposed that the program be financed by Federally-guaranteed debentures which would be offered in the private bond market; the total size of the program would be reduced by about one-half from $6 billion to $3.6 billion. The issue came to a vote in the Senate on March 15, 1950. As usual, Senator Bricker of Ohio offered a motion to strike the new program from the pending legislation; this time he prevailed by a vote of 43 to 38. In contrast to the wide margin by which Bricker's comparable motion to strike the public housing program had been defeated a year before, htis vote significantly revealed the heightened political pressures stimulated by a program which might impinge on the housing finance field traditionally reserved to the mortgage lending institutions. The Republican Senators voted 31 to 6 for the Bricker motion, with such Republican Senators as Taft, Tobey, Vandenberg, and Morse not voting. The Democratic Senators voted 32 to 12 against the Bricker motion but, in the Deep South, the vote was 10 to 6 in favor. It was to be eleven years before a middle-income housing proposal bypassing the regular mortgage market would again come up for a Congressional vote.

A new and unexpected threat to the expansion of housing and related programs then occurred. On June 23, 1950, the armies of North Korea invaded South Korea. On July 18, President Truman directed the Housing and Home Finance Administrator to curtail housing credit in order to conserve building materials for the Korean emergency and to limit the start of construction of public housing to not more than 30,000 dwellings from that date until the end of the year. On July 19, the President requested legislation authorizing him to establish wartime production and credit controls. While never reaching the intensity of World War II restraints, these controls were an inhibiting influence on housing production. Coming only five years after the end of World War II, they also had an immediate political impact.

This impact was promptly reflected in the 1950 Congressional elections. The Republicans made a net gain of five Senate seats, reducing the Democratic majority to only two votes. In the House, the net Republican gain was 28 seats, reducing the Democratic majority to 35.

This election added new Republican faces to the Senate which long would be prominent on the conservative scene. These included Richard M. Nixon of California who had successfully concluded his red-baiting campaign against Helen Gahagan Douglas, Everett M. Dirksen of Illinois, and Wallace F. Bennett of Utah, a former president of the National Association of Manufacturers.

The Korean war also made it possible for the real estate lobby to cloak its opposition to public housing in the robes of patriotism. The argument was that public housing construction was an unessential diversion of materials and manpower from the war effort (this, notwithstanding that private housing construction continued at a rate of over 1.4 million dwellings in 1951). President Truman went part way toward this argument by proposing that construction of public housing be limited to 75,000 dwellings in the fiscal year beginning July 1, 1951, as against the annual rate of 135,000 units contemplated by the 1949 Act. The House Appropriations Committee went further and recommended a limitation to 50,000 dwellings. But the representatives of the lobby stole a march. At seven o'clock on the evening of Friday, May 4, when most of the Northeastern members of the House had already left for the weekend at home, Representative Ed Gossett, a right-wing Democrat from Texas, maneuvered a vote on his motion to cut the public housing program to the token amount of 5,000 dwellings. This carried by a vote of 181 to 113, with 139 not voting. The Republicans supported their Texas Democratic colleague, 123 to 14. The Democrats from the Deep South went with Gossett,

53 to 22. Those other Democrats who were present voted against the Gossett motion 76 to 5.

The real estate lobby had overplayed its hand. In the Senate, the Appropriations Committee again recommended a ceiling of 50,000 units. When Senator Dirksen, newly elected from Illinois, moved to substitute the House figure of 5,000 units, he was soundly trounced by a vote of 47 to 25 and barely carried a majority of the enlarged Republican bloc in the Senate. During the debate, Senator Taft tersely put the issue when he said: "This is not a matter of economy. It is merely an effort to stop the public housing program."

After extended controversy between the House and the Senate, the Senate finally prevailed. The showdown vote in the House, which supported the Senate figure by 206 to 169, evidenced a substantial counterreaction to the May 4 debacle. Even the Deep South Democrats produced a bare majority of 41 to 38 for the 50,000 unit ceiling. While the Republican Representatives voted two and one-half to one against the Senate figure, there were 47 Republican votes in support of public housing. Significantly, 35 of these votes were from Republican districts east of Indiana. In the Middle West and West, the Republicans were almost solidly against public housing.

However, the fact that this outcome was considered a great victory—only two years after the 1949 Act had established an annual rate of 135,000 dwellings—was striking evidence of the political problems besetting the accomplishment of the goals of that law.

With the intensification of the Korean war and the deepening of domestic controversy concerning that conflict, the political climate for progressive programs was bleak. This reaction was augmented by the centering of public discontent with the war on the person of President Truman, leading to his decision to renounce Democratic nomination for reelection.

In housing, the low-rent public program continued to be the whipping boy of the real estate lobby, which was exploiting the economic and social tensions of the war situation as well as the mounting anti-communist hysteria that gave an added fillip to charges of "socialism" in housing. In 1952, the annual housing appropriations battle illustrated the political impact of these tensions. President Truman had again requested approval of 75,000 public housing units for the fiscal year beginning July 1, 1952, notwithstanding the Korean war.

This time, the House Appropriations Committee, under the astute but conservative leadership of Representative Albert Thomas of Houston, cut the President's request by two-thirds to 25,000. Again, a right-wing Texas Democrat, Representative O. C. Fisher, moved to cut the program to 5,000 units. This was initially approved by a vote of 192 to 168, with the Republican-Southern Democrat coalition once more prevailing.

As in 1951, the Senate rescued the public housing program and approved a construction level of 45,000 dwellings. However, in a significant reflection of the worsening political climate, the vote was only 37 to 31, a margin of 6 as compared with 22 a year earlier. The affirmative Republican votes dropped to 8 from 15 in 1951. The ultimate compromise, hard-fought in the House, was 35,000 units. Furthermore, Representative Thomas had successfully sustained a provision that the 35,000 annual level applied not only to the coming fiscal year but to all succeeding years unless modified by Congress in the future. This in effect was an amendment of the Housing Act of 1949 and thus constituted legislation in an appropriation bill, which theoretically was contrary to the rules of the House of Representatives. Nonetheless, the limitation became the law of the land.

Meanwhile, the 1952 Presidential campaign was proceeding at full steam, amid increasing indications that General Dwight D. Eisenhower's war-hero halo combined with the increasing public revulsion with the Korean war would produce a victory over Adlai E. Stevenson. On housing, the platforms of the two parties offered an interesting contrast. The Republican platform was succinct, to say the least —a single sentence which said: "Slum Clearance: With local cooperation we shall aid slum clearance." The Democratic platform stated:

> We pledge ourselves to the fulfillment of the programs of private housing, public low-rent housing, slum clearance, urban redevelopment, farm housing and housing research as authorized by the Housing Act of 1949. We deplore the efforts of special interests groups, which themselves have prospered through government guarantees of housing mortgages, to destroy those programs adopted to assist families of low income. . . . We pledge ourselves to enact additional legislation to promote housing required for defense workers, middle income families, aged persons, and migratory farm laborers.

In the campaign, General Eisenhower avoided the housing issue, except for generalities, while Adlai Stevenson pressed for the forthright position outlined in the Democratic platform.

On the secondary campaign between the two Vice Presidential candidates, Lee F. Johnson, executive vice president of the National Housing Conference, made the following ironic observation: "For Vice President we have two United States Senators with 100 percent housing records. Senator Richard M. Nixon on low-rent public housing has been 100 percent wrong. Senator John Sparkman has been 100 percent right."

The Eisenhower landslide in November, 1952, ended twenty years of control of the White House by the Democratic Party. In contrast to 1948, when the housing issue loomed large in the Presidential campaign, the Eisenhower victory was achieved without any specific commitment, pro or con, on housing.

The outcome in the Congressional elections was considerably less than a landslide. The Republicans gained two seats in the Senate but in effect lost one when Senator Wayne Morse of Oregon declared himself an independent. So the party division in the Senate was 48 Republicans, 47 Democrats, and 1 independent. (In the House, the Republicans gained only 22 seats and controlled by the narrow margin of 221 to 210, still sufficient to organize the committee and the leadership apparatus.) Furthermore, the Republican-conservative Southern Democrat coalition promised a working majority.

The Eisenhower Administration inherited a low-rent public housing program which, despite its buffeting, had started or completed 156,000 dwellings since the enactment of the Housing Act of 1949 and which had firm contracts for 53,000 additional dwellings. This was about half the rate contemplated by the Act. It inherited a slum clearance and urban redevelopment program which was active in 253 communities, which had 259 projects in execution and $329 million in capital grants committed. It inherited a private residential building trend which produced 1,446,000 dwellings in 1952, off 24 percent from the peak in 1950.

The Eisenhower Administration also inherited unsolved housing problems and mounting pressures in the cities.

CHAPTER 7

Gradualism and Stalemate, 1953-57: The Eisenhower Regime Seeks a Republican-Business Consensus on Housing

During the first flush of the Eisenhower Administration, housing did not rank high on the agenda. There were more vital matters to attend to, such as the installation of John Foster Dulles as Secretary of State, "Engine Charlie" Wilson—"What's good for General Motors is good for the nation"—as Secretary of Defense, and George Humphrey as Secretary of the Treasury.

With Sherman Adams functioning as White House Chief of Staff, it was a very comfortable coalition of high corporation finance and Republican politicians.

The task of recruiting the new top echelon for the Housing and Home Finance Agency was assigned by the White House and the Republican National Committee to Douglas Whitlock, the florid-faced director of the National Clay Products Institute and a prominent figure in the real estate lobby. This assignment presumably was in recognition of valuable campaign support by Whitlock and his allies. It was not until March, 1953, that the White House sent up the nomination of former Representative Albert M. Cole to replace Raymond M. Foley as Housing and Home Finance Administrator. Even under the circumstances, this seemed a remarkable appointment. Cole, a Kansas Republican, had served four terms in the House during which time he had advanced in seniority on the Banking and Currency Committee. He had been a consistent opponent of the public housing program and of the comprehensive legislation eventually embodied in the Housing Act of 1949. In fact, in June, 1949, Representative Cole had appeared before the House Rules Committee to oppose the granting of a rule for floor debate, claiming that the legislation was socialistic and discriminatory against the poor. He had been defeated for reelection in 1952 because he had opposed a flood-control project considered important by his rural constituents. It was understandable that Cole was questioned closely by Senator Sparkman and others during the Senate Committee hearing on his nomination about his readiness to administer fairly and sympathetically programs which he had strongly opposed while in Congress.

Subsequently, the Whitlock machine produced Guy O. T. Hollyday of Baltimore as Commissioner of the Federal Housing Administration. Hollyday was closely identified with the mortgage banking field. To head the public housing program, the White House selected Charles E. Slusser, the former Republican mayor of Akron, Ohio, a realtor by profession and a member of the National Association of Real Estate Boards which was the core of the lobby. Albert Cole asked me to remain for the time being as Director of the slum clearance and urban redevelopment program; I agreed in order to help maintain the momentum of this still new program during the transitional period. Finally, in late June, 1953, Cole advised me that he had gotten the word about my successor, namely James Follin. This appointment also had the mark of the Whitlock group since Follin had been staff director of the Producers' Council which represented the interests of the building material and equipment manufacturers in the real estate lobby. Follin, an Eisenhower Democrat, had also as Deputy Administrator spearheaded the effort by the Federal Works Agency to secure control of the redevelopment program in 1949 and to eliminate its housing emphasis.

The real estate lobby clearly had fared well in the selection of the men who would direct the Federal housing programs under the Eisenhower Administration. However, in all fairness, it should be recorded that at no time did these men attempt to sabotage the programs they were administering even though there were strong differences of opinion in the field about the correctness and vigor of some of their policies. In fact, the pressure of events was to transform some of them from antagonists to protagonists. This was especially true of Albert Cole with respect to public housing.

In Congress, the chairmanship of the principal committees concerned with housing passed to conservatives and outright opponents. With the retirement of the venerable Senator Charles W. Tobey, a strong supporter of liberal housing programs, the chairmanship of the Senate Banking and Currency Committee was assumed by Senator Homer Capehart of Indiana. A successful manufacturer, the portly, cigar-smoking Senator Capehart had voted for the Bricker motion to strike the public housing program from the Housing Act of 1949 and likewise for the successful Bricker amendment to strike the middle-income housing proposal from the Housing Act of 1950. The comparable views of Capehart's counterpart in the House of Representatives, Representative Jesse Wolcott, were well-established and immutable. Furthermore, the chairmanship of the key House Appropriations Subcommittee on Independent Offices passed to Representative John Philips of California, an irreconcilable opponent of the philosophy and programs of the Housing Act of 1949.

The first test of the political climate in the House of Representatives on housing matters occurred on the appropriations bill for the fiscal year beginning July 1, 1953. In his lame-duck budget message, President Truman had recommended again a ceiling of 75,000 public housing units. The revised Eisenhower budget reduced this request to 35,000 units, the same level as authorized the preceding year. But the Philips Appropriations Subcommittee recommended that the new public housing units be discontinued on July 1. Ironically, the motion to restore the Eisenhower Administration's request for 35,000 units was made by a Democratic member of the subcommittee, Representative Sidney Yates of Illinois. The motion was defeated 245 to 157, with Majority Leader Charles Halleck and Majority Whip Leslie Arends both voting against restoring their Administration's request. The House Republicans as a whole voted 176 to 33 against public housing. And the coalition with the conservative Southern Democrats was working well: the Representatives from the Deep South voted 52 to 22 against the Yates motion.

In what had become the typical pattern, the Senate restored some order by approving the Administration's request for 35,000 units. After the usual bitter battles in the conference between the Senate and House, the final outcome was an authorization to start construction on not more than 20,000 public housing units in the coming fiscal year. But this was accompanied by a prohibition against entering into any new contracts with local housing authorities for the planning of additional projects unless thereafter authorized by Congress. The real estate lobby had scored heavily in its first round with the Eisenhower Administration.

There were, however, some cooler heads in Republican circles who recognized the political importance of establishing some kind of rational consensus on a gut issue such as housing and urban development. The first step was the announcement by Administrator Cole of plans for a study of the Government's long-range housing objectives through a series of field conferences. Then, on September 12, 1953, President Eisenhower by executive order established an Advisory Committee on Government Housing Policies and Programs.

The 23-man advisory committee, headed by Albert Cole, grew largely from a recommendation to the White House by Aksel Nielsen, a prominent Denver mortgage banker and golfing and fishing companion of President Eisenhower. Its membership consisted principally of figures from the financial, construction, and real estate fields. Included were a few extreme die-hard opponents of public housing— George L. Bliss, a savings and loan executive from New York City, Alexander Summer, a realtor from New Jersey, and Rodney Lockwood, a builder from Detroit. But there also were more sophisticated and realistic members such as Miles Colean, an economist, Ehney A. Camp, a life insurance executive from Alabama, R. G. Hughes, a Texas builder, Robert M. Morgan, a Boston savings bank official, and James W. Rouse, a Baltimore mortgage banker. Another member was Ernest J. Bohn, the able director of the Cleveland Housing Authority and a veteran of the public housing movement. Bohn, who had impeccable Republican credentials, was persuasive in convincing a majority of the committee of the essentiality of public housing, in the tradition of Senator Taft. These voices prevailed and the result was a moderate and reasonably progressive report, which was issued on December 14, 1953.

In response to the Advisory Committee's recommendations, President Eisenhower sent a special message on housing to Congress on January 25, 1954, incorporating most of the proposals suggested by the committee. These included 140,000 additional public housing units over a four-year period at an annual rate of 35,000 units. They also included the proposals for special FHA financing for new or rehabilitated housing in urban renewal areas and for displaced families.

Once again there was a breakdown in Republican communication and party discipline on the issue of public housing. When the House Banking and Currency Committee reported out the Housing Act of 1954 encompassing many of the President's requests, Chairman Wolcott and his cohorts saw to it that there was no provision for an extension of the public housing program.

The political issue was put by Representative Isidore Dollinger of New York, a Democratic member of the Committee:

> The housing bill before us offers no new, helpful, or substantial solutions for our grave housing problems; we can safely assume that no new private housing available to those in the low or middle income groups would be built as a result of this legislation; we find no proposal to provide public housing for low income families for which no new shelter is possible under any other plan or method yet found. . . . Are we to abandon the millions now living in places unfit for human habitation, those being displaced by slum clearance and public improvements, those forced to live in dangerous firetraps?

Once again, it remained for a Democratic Representative, this time Richard Bolling of Kansas City, Missouri, to put the motion to restore President Eisenhower's public housing request. Once again, the motion was defeated by a roll-call vote of 211 to 176. Majority Leader Halleck finally voted to support the President's program but the Republican Representatives as a whole, including Majority Whip Arends, voted 150 to 48 against it.

In the Senate, the progress of the 1954 legislation was complicated by the explosion of the so-called "Section 608" scandal. In layman's language, this involved the disclosure that in a number of FHA-insured rental housing projects, the proceeds of the insured mortgages not only covered all of the developers' costs plus normal profits but also additional "windfalls." These were the combined result of loose statutory language and loose appraisal practices by FHA, both of which were generally intended to stimulate the production of rental housing in the post-World War II period.

Senator Capehart seized on this situation to exploit its political potential through special investigatory hearings. (An immediate victim of the hearings was FHA Commissioner Hollyday, whose resignation was brutally demanded by the White House for alleged failure o correct these abuses prior to their exposure.) Senator Capehart made extensive headlines from his investigation but also soon found that he was handling a two-edged sword. Many of the builder-recipients of the "windfalls" were prominent in the residential construction field and thus represented the Senator's normal constituency in the broad sense of the term. The National Association of Home Builders, the National Association of Real Estate Boards, and the Mortgage Bankers Association were anything but appreciative of the exposure of various of their members and the unfavorable picture of the ethics of the private residential development industry generally which grew out of the Capehart hearings. Furthermore, the record was replete with instances of intervention with HHFA and FHA by members of Congress, including Capehart himself, on behalf of builders seeking Section 608 commitments. Also, the record was clear that Congress itself, under pressure from builders, had on several occasions disregarded recommendations by former Housing and Home Finance Administrator Raymond Foley that the Section 608 program be phased out. In addition, notwithstanding the ethical implications, there was nothing outright illegal about the windfalls.

The one constructive outcome of the investigation was the establishment of a new legal requirement for all FHA multi-family housing programs that builders certify their actual costs upon completion and that savings from the estimates on which the mortgages were based be applied to reducing the mortgages rather than going into the builders' pockets. An indirect negative effect of the investigation was the demoralization of the FHA bureaucracy, leading to an overcautious attitude which was to slow down progress under FHA multi-family housing programs for many years to come.

With this distraction disposed of, the Senate proceeded to pass the Housing Act of 1954, including the President's requested four-year public housing program. In the conferences with the House, however, the President's program went by the boards, the only surviving remnant being an authorization of up to 35,000 units in the fiscal year beginning July 1, 1954, limited to communities with active slum clearance and urban redevelopment programs.

There was a concerted effort by the Eisenhower Administration to portray the Housing Act of 1954 as the most far-reaching legislation ever enacted in this field, not excluding the Housing Act of 1949. The law did, in fact, contain a number of important provisions and innovations, especially in the fields of what was now termed urban renewal and in urban planning. The broadening of the slum clearance and urban redevelopment statute to give specific recognition to conservation and rehabilitation of existing residential structures in urban renewal areas was constructive in principle. The establishment of special FHA programs to insure private mortgages on development or rehabilitation in urban renewal areas and on lower-priced private relocation housing recognized the need for more liberal financing terms in these areas. The authorization for Federal purchase of these mortgages or other special purpose loans provided a realistic safeguard against the cautious lending practices of private mortgage institutions in these new fields. The establishment of the new requirement for a "workable program for community improvement" as a prerequisite for participation in the urban renewal, public housing, and new FHA programs would give impetus to local planning, the creation of more adequate housing and related codes, and more effective local relocation programs. The initiation of a new program of urban planning assistance grants would prove to have long-range significance in stimulating local planning in smaller cities and ultimately on a regional basis.

However, on an objective reading, the gaps remaining in the national housing program were more significant than the additions to it made by the 1954 Act. The meager provision for public housing was absurdly out of balance with the actual housing needs of the poor. There was still no financing program for new housing in the no-man's land between public housing and the going private housing market. Among other things, these two deficiencies made it generally impossible to develop new housing in redevelopment areas which would be financially suitable for the families to be displaced (a fact which would be overlooked or forgotten by many later critics of urban renewal). The new emphasis on conservation and rehabilitation was constructive in principle; what was lacking was a functioning financing mechanism which would work for existing owners or tenants. This would lead to many future delays and frustrations.

This disparity between the requirements for an effective national housing program and the tools at hand as well as actual accomplishment began to stimulate a revival of proposals by the coalition which had ultimately secured the enactment of the Housing Act of 1949. The recapture of control of both houses of Congress by the Democratic Party in the 1954 mid-term elections provided generally a more sympathetic backdrop for such proposals. This meant that two sagacious and progressive legislative leaders—Senator John Sparkman and Representative Albert Rains—resumed the chairmanship of the Housing Subcommittees of the Banking and Currency Committees of the Senate and House.

Perhaps the best informed and most searching analysis of this disparity and projection of future requirements for a balanced comprehensive program was prepared in 1954 by William L. C. Wheaton, then a Professor at the University of Pennsylvania and a long-time student of the housing economy. Dr. Wheaton's analysis and projection became the basis for an emerging consensus among such organizations as the National Housing Conference and its allied public interest organizations, and the AFL and the CIO. The Wheaton projections were predicated on meeting the housing requirements resulting from new household formation, including internal migration, on providing sufficient vacancies to permit reasonable freedom of housing choice for consumers, and on replacing 10 million substandard dwellings over the succeeding twenty years. His conclusion was that to reach this objective would require an average annual rate of housing production of about 2 million units between 1955 and 1960, increasing to an annual rate of 2.4 million after 1965. His further conclusion was that less than three-fifths of this production could be financed and marketed under existing modes of financing and FHA aids, that about one-third would need added financial help to reach middle and lower-middle income families otherwise unable to afford new homes, and that about one-tenth should be public housing for low income families. He also found that this rate of production would be economically feasible and would require no increase in the proportion of total national income, assuming continued growth in the national economy at rates comparable to the trend since the end of World War II.

Wheaton's findings were substantially adopted by the National Housing Conference in 1955 and were subsequently incorporated in a bill introduced by Senator Herbert H. Lehman of New York. The NHC proposals called for public housing authorizations at a rate of 200,000 units a year, and a middle-income housing program involving $3 billion a year in 3 percent loans, generally along the lines rejected by the Senate in 1950. The NHC also urged the creation of a Federal Department of Housing and Urban Affairs, becoming the first national organization to formally make this proposal.

While experience over the next fifteen years confirmed the general accuracy of his projections if the goals of the Housing Act of 1949 were to be met, these proposals were too rich for the political blood of the 84th Congress. However, there were some straws in the wind as to a potential revival of a more progressive majority in Congress. In June, 1955, Senator Sparkman secured committee support for a return to the 135,000 units per year public housing level set by the 1949 Act and beat down on the floor of the Senate a Capehart motion to substitute the Administration's request for only 35,000 units. The margin was 44 to 38. The old order seemed reconfirmed in the House when on July 29, 1955, Representative Wolcott moved successfully to strike public housing entirely and received a majority of 217 to 188. But four days later the House accepted a compromise figure of 45,000 public housing units agreed to in conference with the Senate. This was the largest amount of public housing accepted by the House since 1951. On this vote, for once a majority of the Deep South Democrats either deserted their Republican allies or absented themselves from the floor.

There was significance also in the impact of the realities of the housing problem for low-income families on Administrator Albert Cole. Addressing the annual convention of the National Housing Conference on June 8, 1955, Cole said:

> This Administration is convinced, and I am convinced—and it is no secret that I had to be convinced—that additional public housing is absolutely essential for carrying forward the President's comprehensive housing and urban renewal program. Public housing is not just something we would like to have—it is something we have to have.

Commissioner Charles Slusser, like Cole no long-time friend of public housing, defended the program against new charges by the National Association of Real Estate Boards which he established were based on false statistics.

Lee Johnson of the National Housing Conference made this comment at that time:

> When the National Association of Real Estate Boards resorted to

faked statistics, their case blew up. It is significant that NAREB
stood alone this year in violent, irresponsible opposition. Their old
colleagues were content to say they were against public housing
and let it drop.

Similar comments were made in the July, 1955, issue of *House
and Home,* the Time, Inc. publication for the private housing industry and related fields. The article began: "One of the most startling
trends of the spring of 1955 has probably been one of the least noted:
the private housing industry's decades-old fight against public housing
shows some subtle signs of weakening." Among other reasons for
the change, the magazine stated: "Working quietly in the grass roots,
public housers have made important converts among eastern Republican Congressmen and Senators." An unnamed Texas mortgage
banker was quoted as having said: "The boys are just worn out—
tired of the fight. The public housers outlasted us."

There were other signs of a breakaway by significant power centers from the parochial semi-hysteria of the real estate lobby. Of
great significance was the emergence of associations of the power
structure in major cities and metropolitan areas dedicated to the
revitalization and redevelopment of the urban centers. The forerun-
ner of this trend was the Allegheny Conference in Pittsburgh. The
Conference had been established primarily on the initiative of the
Mellon interests to rescue Pittsburgh from total decay, loss of industry, loss of population, and loss of trade. United States Steel, Jones
and Laughlin Steel, the banks, and the large department stores joined
forces with the Mellons in this effort. The Conference worked in
closest concert with Mayor David Lawrence, the astute and powerful
Democratic leader of Western Pennsylvania and a strong influence in
organized labor. While the members of the Conference were predominantly Republican in political affiliation, there was a tacit but
potent political alliance between the Conference and Mayor Lawrence on local issues of importance to the remarkable Pittsburgh
program.

Comparable organizations with generally similar sophistication began to appear in other cities like Philadelphia, Chicago, Cleveland,
Detroit, St. Louis, San Francisco, Washington, Buffalo, and New
Haven. While the primary focus of these organizations from the
standpoint of Federal programs was on urban renewal as an essential

tool for the revival of urban centers, the necessity of public housing as a companion to these efforts was accepted by them as a fact of life.

A comparable event was the emergence of a new breed of large developers with the imagination and know-how to recognize the investment potential in developing new housing and commercial facilities in urban renewal areas where sizable cleared land was finally becoming available. In 1954, William Zeckendorf, the flamboyant and brilliant head of Webb & Knapp who was then at the pinnacle of his adventurous real estate career, swept into Washington and, with the blessing of the White House, unveiled his plans for redeveloping a large segment of Southwest Washington which was all in an urban renewal area. In 1955, as a private consultant, I was instrumental in persuading Roger Stevens, a successful real estate financier, and James H. Scheuer, a wealthy young real estate man in New York City, to become the redevelopers of another sizable section of Southwest Washington. Scheuer went on to similar urban renewal undertakings in St. Louis, Sacramento, Brookline, Mass., and San Juan, Puerto Rico. Herbert Greenwald of Chicago and Detroit was a similar type. Gradually, as the urban renewal program evolved, a number of the large construction and real estate development firms became involved.

To men of this stripe, the essentiality of accompanying public housing was taken as a matter of fact. They considered the new stale charges of "socialism" and "competition with private enterprise" from the real estate lobby as so much nonsense; in fact, a number of them had successfully and profitably built public housing projects for local housing authorities. Their prime concern governmentally was to receive what they considered to be realistic treatment from the FHA and from the local renewal agencies. Eventually, their sophistication began to rub off on the more conventional private developers.

There was also evidence of a more mature attitude on the broad housing issue by mortgage bankers and building materials and equipment manufacturers. After the passage of the Housing Act of 1954, I collaborated with James W. Rouse, an intelligent and successful mortgage banker from Baltimore, in preparing a long-range renewal and housing program for the District of Columbia Government (our report, entitled "No Slums in Ten Years," proved to be somewhat optimistic). While not sharing the anti-public housing hysteria of the real estate lobby, Rouse started out as a skeptic on the role of public housing in such a program. However, when confronted by the evidence that the program could not be accomplished without a substantial amount of additional public housing, he accepted the facts. Rouse, who had been chairman of the urban renewal subcommittee of the President's Advisory Committee, joined with other mortgage bankers, building materials officials, a few more-enlightened builders, a few representatives of organized labor, and the top echelon of Time-Life-Fortune, to establish ACTION (the American Committee to Improve our Neighborhoods). While it became overly preoccupied with residential rehabilitation as the basic solution to the housing problem, ACTION did serve as a catalyst for more realistic thinking by local business men through local meetings and publications. It also provided a healthy antidote for the stale propaganda of local real estate boards.

The gradually changing climate was reflected in the relative ease with which the Housing Act of 1956 passed through Congress. This measure broadened the urban renewal program and the related FHA financing programs, made the first specific authorization for housing for the elderly (including public housing), and authorized new contracts for up to 35,000 units of public housing in each of the two following years. While this annual rate was less than the 45,000-unit level authorized the year before, the combined total of 70,000 units was the largest action by Congress since the passage of the 1949 Act. Furthermore, it was contended by some critics—friendly as well as unfriendly—that 35,000 units a year was the maximum which could be realistically anticipated, given the increasing problem of securing local approval of sites and the weight of Federal bureaucratic controls. The recent production rate lent some substance to these claims.

Meanwhile, the 1956 Presidential election campaign was in process. As in 1952, the Democratic platform called for greatly expanded efforts in housing and community development. The Republican platform had this to say:

> We have supported measures that have made more housing available than ever before in history, reduced urban slums in local-federal partnership, stimulated record home ownership, and authorized additional low-rent public housing.

If the first clause of this statement was meant to say that housing production had reached record levels during President Eisenhower's first term, it was inaccurate; actually, total housing production in the four years 1953-56, inclusive, was 7 percent less than in the preceding four years. Also, the rate of construction in 1956 was declining 18 percent from 1955. This initiated a six-year stagnation in housing production, reflecting the fact that the peak of the post-war housing demand in the upper-income brackets had been satisfied and that no large programs for lower-middle-income and low-income households had been undertaken.

As a measure of Republican priorities, the platform stated: "To meet the immense demands of our expanding economy, we have initiated the largest highway, air and maritime programs in history, each soundly financed."

The second Eisenhower landslide made it clear that Ike was the people's choice. However, in the curious political dichotomy of the American voting public, notwithstanding the landslide, the Democrats maintained their narrow control of the Senate, 49 to 47, and increased their control of the House by one vote net, 233 to 200.

So for the next four years, the country again would have a politically divided government.

CHAPTER 8

Gradualism and Stalemate, 1957-61: The Eisenhower Regime Moves to the Right

With the advent of President Eisenhower's second term, a swing to the right quickly became evident in domestic economic and social policies and programs. While the conspiratorial demagoguery and character assassination of the era of Senator Joe McCarthy had finally been liquidated, this was not followed by an era of progressivism in so far as the Eisenhower Administration was concerned. The basic theme was to be fiscal soundness, curtailment or restraint of Federal domestic programs and expenditures, and putative transfer of Federal domestic responsibilities to the States. This attitude reflected the philosophy of the dominant coterie influencing the White House: George Humphrey as Secretary of the Treasury, Percival Brundage as Director of the Bureau of the Budget, Raymond Saulnier as Chairman of the Council of Economic Advisers, and William McChesney Martin as Chairman of the Federal Reserve Board.

The trend to the right soon was reflected in the Administration's attitude toward housing and community development. Whereas the 1956 housing legislation had authorized new contracts for 35,000 public housing units per year for two years, restrictive administrative policies limited the actual contracts executed in 1957 to 5,391 units and in 1958 to 24,293 units. The increasing demand for urban renewal funds from communities around the country made this program a new target for retrenchment by the Administration. Early in 1957, with all urban renewal funds committed or reserved, the Administration arbitrarily declared a moratorium on acceptance of applications for new projects in order to avoid accumulating a back-log which might become a pressure point for substantial additional appropriations by Congress. The official request was for only $175 million, less than a third of the going annual rate of demand from communities. (This was doubled by Congress to $350 million in the Housing Act of 1957, as one facet of a growing trend in the Democratic-controlled Congress to exceed the President's parsimonious requests.)

The White House coterie's long-term objective for curtailing urban renewal was made clear in President Eisenhower's budget message to Congress in January, 1958. In this, he requested legislation reducing the Federal participation in urban renewal costs to 50 percent from the 67 percent established by the law. In view of the financial stringencies confronting almost all municipalities, this would have cut the effective demand for Federal urban renewal funds, notwithstanding the urgent need. Failing to get the necessary legislation, the Administration attempted to secure substantially the same result by imposing by regulation an arbitrary rationing formula designed to restrict the urban renewal program. Writing in a National Housing Conference publication in 1959, I commented: "the growing strength of redevelopment has led the advocates of small government and small programs to attempt to cut redevelopment down before it attains a stature demanding and getting Federal support equivalent, let's say, to about one-tenth of the annual subsidy for agriculture."

The restrictive policies of the Administration also had a major adverse impact on the private housing industry, notwithstanding the verbal commitment of the Administration to the primacy of private enterprise in all fields of economic endeavor. (One major exception to this principle under the Eisenhower Administration was, of course, the $26-billion interstate highway program which was lobbied through the Administration and the Congress with ease by the automobile and petroleum industries and allied groups.) In 1957, construction starts of private housing dropped to 1,175,000 units, the lowest level since the immediate postwar year of 1946, 11 percent below 1956, 28 percent below 1955, and 38 percent below the peak year of 1950.

The fragmented private housing industry, while ranking high within the American economy in total volume, obviously did not pack the political clout within the White House coterie which was assumed as a matter of course by the big concentrated industries like autos, petroleum, metals, and chemicals. The recession in private housing construction was not caused by a decline in total housing demand and need, especially for lower-priced units, but rather by the lack of any Federal financing program for the lower middle-income market and by the relatively weak position of the sources for private residential financing—dependent almost entirely upon consumer savings—in competition with the large corporations in the capital markets. In these circumstances, the line of the White House coterie was to exercise fiscal controls strictly on a *laissez-faire* doctrine—let the market decide in which direction money should flow, without regard for the social consequences. This doctrine obviously favored the large corporations which could readily absorb higher interest costs and pass them along to the consumer and threw the brunt of the credit crunch to the small builder and individual seeking a mortgage to buy a home.

This philosphy was illustrated in an exchange between William McChesney Martin and Senator Joseph S. Clark, the liberal former mayor of Philadelphia, during hearings before the Senate Banking and Currency Committee in March, 1957:

> *Senator Clark:* ". . . there was an administration recommendation for a fairly severe cutback in urban renewal and slum clearance. We also know that in the last few years the President has been unwilling to recommend a continuation of the public housing program at the rate advocated by the late Senator Taft. I wonder whether from where you sit on the Federal Reserve Board you feel that these two contractions in our effort to supply adequate housing for lower and middle income groups are necessary to the strength of a sound economy?"
>
> *Mr. Martin:* ". . . I think at the present time anything we can do to postpone commitments which can be postponed, until the supply of savings increases, is desirable."
>
> *Senator Clark:* "And your policy is nonselective postponement without regard to social need?"
>
> *Mr. Martin:* "Our policy is directed toward the overall pool of credit."

In keeping with this philosophy, President Eisenhower early in 1957 sent a special message to Congress advocating various measures to hold Federal costs and activities to a minimum. In the field of private housing where tight money was already restricting production, rather than proposing steps to increase the flow of private credit to residential construction, he recommended legislation reducing the resources of the Federal National Mortgage Association to purchase privately-originated FHA mortgages in the most critical segments of the new housing market, such as housing in urban renewal areas and cooperative housing. Here again, Congress rejected the President's recommendations. Instead, in the Housing Act of 1957, it increased FNMA's special purpose mortage purchasing authority by $450 million and increased its general authority by $650 million.

By the winter of 1958, the policies enforced by the White House coterie had produced a general recession in the national economy, not limited to housing. Since the White House refused to push for any substantive measures to counter the economic decline, Senator John Sparkman, as chairman of the Senate Housing Subcommittee, took matters into his own hands in so far as the housing economy was concerned. He introduced the Emergency Housing Act of 1958 to increase the FNMA special assistance fund by $500 million and to establish a new FNMA special assistance revolving fund of $1 billion for the purchase of FHA and Veterans Administration mortgages not exceeding $13,500 on new single-family homes. Under the political pressure generated by the growing public disaffection with the Administration's economic policies, the Sparkman measure passed the Senate without a dissenting vote and was approved in the House by an overwhelming voice vote.

Confronted by this decisive political consensus in Congress, which reached into both parties, President Eisenhower reluctantly approved the Sparkman bill on April 1, 1958. However, he felt compelled to lecture the Congress on the unsoundness of direct Federal action to reverse the recession in housing:

> . . . the legislation ignores the responsibility and ability of private enterprise to function without imposing a direct burden on the Federal purse. It has been the fixed policy of this Administration, and should be the consistent purpose of the Federal government, to seek in every way to encourage private capital and private investors to finance in competitive markets the myriad activities in our economy, including housing construction. This legislation contans provisions that are wholly inconsistent with that policy and with

the philosophy of the free enterprise system that has made this nation strong.

As a footnote, the Emergency Housing Act of 1958 was primarily responsible for checking the decline in private housing construction and for achieving a 12 percent gain for 1958 as a whole over 1957.

The Senate Banking and Currency Committee, under Senator Sparkman's leadership, went on to propose an omnibus housing bill, going well beyond the retrogressive recommendations of the Administration. The bill as passed by the Senate would have strengthened local control of public housing projects as a relief from restrictive Federal regulations, would have liberalized the types of projects which could be developed, and would have authorized an additional 35,000 dwellings. The bill also would have funded the urban renewal program for six years at a rate of $350 million a year.

In the House of Representatives, the Senate-passed bill was supported by the Banking and Currency Committee but was blocked in the Rules Committee under the leadership of Chairman Howard Smith, the right-wing Virginia Democrat who saw eye-to-eye with the Eisenhower Administration on fiscal and budgetary matters. This impasse forced the Democratic leadership to attempt to suspend the rules in order to bring the measure to a vote on the floor of the House. Under the House rules, this motion required a two-thirds majority; it failed by only six votes, with 251 members voting to suspend the rules and 134 opposing. This remarkable vote was a clear reflection of the political disaffection being generated by the 1958 recession. The Democrats from the Deep South voted 55 to 21 to overturn their colleagues on the Rules Committee. A total of 67 Republicans deserted their leadership and voted for the motion. The Democratic members from the Border and Northern states voted for the motion by a margin of 129 to 6.

The vote was also an accurate signal of what was to happen in the off-year Congressional elections in November, 1958. In the Senate, the Democrats gained 15 seats, to control by 64 to 34. In the House of Representatives, the Democratic gain was 49 seats, to control by 282 to 152. In both houses, the Democratic majority was the largest since the peak of Franklin D. Roosevelt's popularity in the mid-Thirties. Quite naturally, the scent of victory in the 1960 Presidential election was in the air. This quickened the political maneuverings by the potential Democratic Presidential candidates—John F. Kennedy, Lyndon B. Johnson, Hubert H. Humphrey, and Adlai E. Stevenson. It also gave further impetus to forward planning by groups in and out of Congress who were committed to progressive legislation in fields such as housing and community development.

In fact, there already had been considerable activity in charting courses for future legislation on housing and related fields based on existing and projected needs during the coming decades and anticipating changes in the political climate which would make it impossible to mount programs to begin meeting those needs. For example, in January, 1957, the Senate Housing Subcommittee issued a staff report on "Income and Housing." This report reinforced what should have been an obvious finding: that serious housing shortages persisted, notwithstanding the lessened pressure from the immediate postwar housing demands created by returning military veterans, and that low-income families, Negro and Puerto Rican households, and elderly persons were especially hard hit by the shortages. The report concluded that the current production of housing was not materially reducing the shortages, that the prevailing prices of dwelling units were generally too high for the families in greatest need, and that Federal programs such as urban renewal and interstate highway· development which were displacing families were intensifying local housing needs. Based on surveys, the report stated that the great majority of city mayors felt that expanded housing programs were needed and that the Federal government should provide more effective assistance in meeting the needs.

Outside the Congress and the Federal establishment, the principal focal point for forging new concepts and proposals for housing and community development and arriving at a progressive consensus was the National Housing Conference. The Conference, although chronically underfinanced, brought together the points of view, expertise, and insights of leading local administrators of housing and urban renewal programs, the AFL-CIO establishment, mayors and other public officials, the nucleus of progressive and sophisticated private entrepreneurs in the urban field, and the involved academic community. It also had the confidence of the liberal leaders in Congress.

In 1957, under the informal aegis of the National Housing Conference, a small group was assembled by Ira S. Robbins, then the chairman of its board of directors, to consider the state of the nation in so far as housing and community development was concerned and to survey potential courses of action. Robbins was then a commissioner of the New York City Housing Authority, had been the director of the New York City Citizens' Housing and Planning Council, and was close to Senator Herbert H. Lehman and Governor Averell Harriman of New York. Others in the group included Coleman Woodbury, who had been active in formulating the postwar housing program as Assistànt Administrator of the National Housing Agency and then a professor of city planning at Harvard and Yale; William L. C. Wheaton, then the director of the Institute for Urban Studies at the University of Pennsylvania; Lee F. Johnson, the executive vice president of the Conference; Dr. Frank Horne, an expert on Negro problems and relations; Charles Abrams, lawyer and author and international expert on housing and urban affairs; Elizabeth Wood, for many years the director of the Chicago Housing Authority and an expert on public housing; Albert Mayer, a distinguished architect and urban expert; James H. Scheuer, the redeveloper, and others. I was asked to prepare a position paper and recommendations for the group, based on intensive discussions and independent research.

The outcome was a working paper entitled "Blueprint for Full Community Development, 1957-1975." While never formally published, in retrospect this paper identified the main issues which were to dominate legislative efforts and local programs in housing and community development over the ensuing decade and more. Its recommendations formed the basis for the future legislative programs of the National Housing Conference and allied organizations. Many of them have since been incorporated in Federal legislation, even though the scale of accomplishment still leaves much to be desired.

The paper emphasized and clarified the impact on American society of the massive population growth already under way, the full implications of which were still not generally recognized. It pointed to Census forecasts of a U.S. population growth of over 78 million persons, or more than 50 percent, between 1950 and 1975, almost all of which would be concentrated in metropolitan or other urbanized areas. As to the condition of American cities to receive this population growth, the paper had this to say:

> Even though the sharpest proportions of the acute post-war housing shortage have been relieved, millions of American families are

still relegated to slums or substandard housing. Families of minority race are largely confined to deteriorating central city neighborhoods. Schools are overcrowded. Traffic congestion is rampant. There are large backlogs of need for modern water and sewer facilities. The mushrooming growth in the suburbs has been largely unplanned and chaotic, threatening serious problems of future blight and already imposing heavy burdens on suburban populations for the installation of adequate community facilities and services. Municipal finances are strained and are currently further aggravated by tight money and skyrocketing interest rates. Construction costs are rising and the marketing of housing production is being concentrated increasingly within the top income fifth of the U.S. population.

This still reads like a summary of urban conditions in the United States in 1973.

The principal recommendations made by the group and set forth in the paper were the following:

- Establishment of a new Federal Department to consolidate the main Federal functions in housing and community development and to provide Cabinet-level stature and coordination for these functions. Recognition that "the safeguarding of the national interest in full community development is in large measure a Federal responsibiilty which cannot be relinquished to the state and local governments without imperiling the national welfare."

- Expansion in total national housing production to 2 million dwellings per year to meet population growth and replace substandard housing and other demolitions.

- Assurance of adequate financing through a permanent Federal backup when private credit is insufficient or its terms excessive. Exploration of a broadened financial base for housing through investing a portion of Social Security reserves in Federally-guaranteed bond-type security which would be attractive to pension funds and to the general bond market.

- In order to develop new housing within the means of the neglected lower-middle-income market, the establishment by the Federal Government of a financing program at terms comparable to the average cost of money to the Federal Government and local governments.

- Expansion in the low-rent public housing program to an annual rate of 200,000 dwelling units per year. Recasting of the public housing program to encourage the development of smaller projects and single properties, to permit the purchase of suitable existing dwellings for use as public housing, repeal of the requirement for eviction of tenants whose incomes rise above fixed limits, the design of projects on a basis permitting their eventual sale to tenants either individually or on a cooperative basis, and the provision of social services for families admitted to public housing as an essential part of the public cost of operating the housing.

• Rapid expansion of the redevelopment and urban renewal program through annual Federal grant authorizations at a minimum annual rate of $500 million for ten years, with machinery for annual review of the adequacy of this authorization in relation to community requirements. Authorization for advance acquisition of land and relocation. Activation of the open land and predominantly open land provisions of the Federal redevelopment statute in suburban or metropolitan locations to provide housing to meet relocation needs and to accommodate the increasing urban population.

• Establishment of new programs of Federal loans and grants to assist local governments to overcome their backlog in schools, public utilities, parks, and transportation and to keep pace with future growth requirements.

• Establishment of an intensive program of Federally-financed research covering all technological, economic, social and financial problems in housing and community development. Provision of Federal grants for training planning technicians, engineers, public administrators, and other professional personnel needed for greatly expanded housing and community development programs.

Meanwhile, the White House coterie persevered in its restrictive proposals on housing and community development, notwithstanding the Democratic sweep in the Congressional elections. President Eisenhower's budget message in January, 1959, in effect repeated his 1958 proposals for gradual curtailment in Federal participation in urban renewal and for an inadequate level of funding in relation to community requests; again, he requested no additional authorization for public housing.

The Senate, with its greatly enlarged Democratic majority, proceeded to prepare its own legislation, under the leadership of Senator Sparkman. The bill which passed the Senate in early February by a final vote of 60 to 28 went far beyond the President's requests and reversed a number of his proposals. The bill would have authorized 75,000 aditional units of public housing and proposed expanded urban renewal authorizations at an annual rate of $350 million for six years, with an escalator authority of $150 million per year if local demands required and with no change in the Federal share of urban renewal costs. It also initiated a new program of direct Federal loans at low interest rates to finance nonprofit housing projects for elderly households. The key votes were on a series of motions by Senator Capehart: to substitute the Administration bill, defeated 58 to 32; to eliminate the public housing provision, defeated 50 to 37; and to substitute the Administration's urban renewal proposals, defeated 58 to 34.

In the House of Representatives, Congressman Albert Rains, as Chairman of the Housing Subcommittee, fashioned a bill of generally comparable dimensions and secured the majority support of the House. However, when the final bill as compromised between the two Houses was sent to the President in late June, the White House coterie closed in. President Eisenhower said in his veto message on July 7:

> Congress has presented me with a bill so excessive in the spending it proposes and so defective in other respects that it would do far more damage than good . . . the bill is extravagant and much of the spending it authorizes is unnecessary . . -. the spending authorizations taken together with other seriously objectionable provisions would be inflationary and therefore an obstacle to constructive progress toward better housing for Americans . . . the bill would tend to substitute Federal spending for private investment . . .

The veto message prompted strong reactions among Democratic leaders in Congress. Congressman Rains departed from his accustomed temperate language, as follows:

> The truth is that fake charges of inflation have been raised by those whose real opposition to the bill stems from their refusal to accept any measure which would improve the housing condition of lower income families or to raise a finger to help clear slums and rebuild our cities. This callous decree, cloaked in pious sounding phrases, would sacrifice the hopes of many families for better housing. . . . The entire veto message is a jumble of meaningless claims. I would think better of it if it came out and honestly said that this action was based on blind partisanship. The President's action is an attempt to block any further efforts to rid our cities of blight, or to build homes for the elderly at rents which they can afford.

Nevertheless, the Democrats lacked by a few votes the two-thirds majority necessary to override the President's veto in the Senate. The two houses thereupon assembled and passed a compromise bill which was sent to the White House on August 31. Again, the President vetoed. His message this time singled out the proposed 37,000 units of public housing, the authorization of $650 million for urban renewal, a new program of direct loans to colleges for classrooms and related facilities—"this is Federal aid to education in a highly objectionable form"—and the new program of loans for elderly housing as prime reasons for his veto. He also observed:

> This is not the kind of housing legislation that is needed at this time. It does not help the housing industry for the Federal Government to adopt methods that in these times would increase inflationaɪy pressures in our economy and thereby discourage the thrift on which home financing is heavily dependent. Nor does it make sense to purport to assist any group of citizens, least of all elderly persons living on fixed retirement incomes, by legislation that tends further to increase the cost of living.

Again, the Senate lacked by five votes the two-thirds majority needed to override the veto, the vote being 58 to 36. With Congressional adjournment drawing near, the Democratic leadership persisted in a third attempt to secure the enactment of meaningful housing and community development legislation. Finally, in the closing days of the session, a third version of the Housing Act of 1959 was sent to the White House. This time, President Eisenhower capitulated and approved the legislation on September 23 even through it was very similar in most respects to the bill he had vetoed on September 4. It contained 37,000 units of low-rent public housing. It contained $650 million of urban renewal grants (of which $300 million was deferred until July 1, 1960), authorized early land acquisition in urban renewal areas, permitted special writeoffs for public housing sites in urban renewal areas, and established special grants to finance community-wide studies of urban renewal needs. The Act also contained direct loan authority of $50 million for elderly housing and of $25 million for college classrooms, both of which the President had so recently castigated.

The struggles over the 1959 Housing Act had emphasized and clarified the political pressures and alignments which would figure largely in the 1960 Presidential campaign. Predominantly, the mayors, the AFL-CIO, the Negro organizations, and liberal organizations like the National Housing Conference and its allies lined up behind expansive economic policies, including housing and community development, which ran counter to the increasingly conservative trend of the Eisenhower regime. There was also increasing disaffection from the Eisenhower policies of economic restraint by businessmen, especially in the construction and housing fields, who disagreed in principle or who had been hurt by tight money.

The White House coterie, however, kept the Eisenhower regime on its conservative course, which was reflected in tight money and a national economic growth rate of only 2.3 percent per annum. In private housing construction, there was a 17 percent decline in 1960 from 1959. There was an increase in overall unemployment.

The rising expectations of a Democratic victory in 1960 and a consequent shift to expansionist national policies also stmulated forward planning in this direction in a number of interesting quarters. For example, in February, 1960, the Metropolitan Housing and Planning Council of Chicago and Action, Inc. of New York sponsored a two-day Conference on Housing the Economically and Socially Disadvantaged Groups in the Population. The conference, which was held in Chicago, was funded by the Field Foundation and by Sears, Roebuck and Co. It was chaired by Philip M. Klutznick, one of the most imaginative real estate developers in the country and a former head of the Federal Public Housing Administration; its chief consultant was Warren J. Vinton, the long-time Federal public housing expert who had finally been ousted by the Eisenhower Administration in 1957.

The make-up of the 30 participants in the conference was significant from the standpoint of the prevailing attitudes among the more progressive segments of the national business community. They included, among others, Edward F. Blettner, vice president of the First National Bank of Chicago; Albert M. Cole, who had resigned as Housing and Home Finance Administrator in January, 1959, in considerable disillusionment with Administration housing policies and was executive vice president of the Reynolds Aluminum Service Corporation; Neal Hardy, prominent in the National Association of Home Builders and a future Commissioner of FHA; E. E. Hargrave, executive vice president of Jewel Tea Co.: Ferd Kramer, a nationally known mortgage banker; Bruce Savage, an Indianapolis realtor who was shortly to become the last Public Housing Commissioner under the Eisenhower Administration; and Theodore Yntema, vice president of the Ford Motor Co. Also included in the group were two prominent architects as well as representatives from social work, organized labor, and racial relations. There was some overlap with the special National Housing Conference group which had assembled three years before, as referred to earlier in this chapter.

The conclusions and recommendations of this conference, while not all unanimous, were far removed from the conservative standpatism of the Eisenhower regime. In many respects, they paralleled the recommendations of the special National Housing Conference group in 1957. In particular, the report scotched the arguments of the Eisenhower Administration that financial responsibilities in housing and community development should increasingly be transferred from the Federal Government to state and local governments:

> Opinion expressed in the Conference clearly pinpointed the Federal government as that level having the best and most flexible resources for raising necessary revenues, and which can most appropriately assume those obligations affecting the national standard of living; while the local governments, which are already strained to the breaking point by the increased burdens of population dispersal, physical growth, and the needs for services, can properly undertake the responsibilities of planning, programming, administration, and regulating the existing supply.

The Conference report also noted that 13 million of the nation's 55 million dwellings were substandard, with an additional 2 million "slum-locked and environmentally blighted." It found that an increase in total housing production to a sustained rate of 2.2 to 2.4 million dwellings per year was needed to remedy this deficiency and to meet population growth and that at least 500,000 new units a year should be targeted toward families in the $6,000-and-under income bracket. To achieve the latter objective, the report recommended a massive increase in Federal subsidies, including interest rates at low as 1 percent for homes for lower-middle-income families.

In 1959, I was elected the president of the National Housing Conference and therefore became the principal legislative spokesman for that organization. Reflecting the growing consensus that housing and community development would be a major issue in American society during the decade of the Sixties, in May, 1960, I made these comments to the Senate Housing Subcommittee:

> In our opinion, the expansion of the housing economy to meet the needs of the Sixties will inevitably be one of the major domestic issues during the coming decade. Likewise, we are convinced that a national problem of this scope and complexity can be satisfactorily met only through the effective leadership of the Federal government, acting through financial aids, stimulation, and technical assistance. While the execution of such a program must remain with the local communities and largely with private enterprise, we are convinced that the leadership and supporting role of the Federal Government is indispensable. Correspondingly, we feel that the crucial importance of housing and overall community development to the healthy future growth of our urban population and metropolitan centers should be more adequately represented within the Federal establishment itself. Consequently, we strongly favor the enactment of legislation extending Cabinet status to this important sphere of Federal activity. We believe that the present status of Federal housing, renewal and related programs has suffered from lack of representation at the Cabinet table and that the growing importance of these matters to the great majority of the American people makes it imperative to afford them Federal recognition and status on a parity with other major program activities of the Federal government.

In Congress, an attempt was made to pass further substantive housing legislation. The Senate passed a major bill on June 14, 1960, by the large majority of 64 to 16, including a 19-to-11 majority of the Republican Senators voting. A sizable companion bill was favorably reported by the House Banking and Currency Committee on June 20 only to become sidetracked in the adjournment rush for the national political conventions.

However, housing was a major issue in the 1960 Presidential campaign. Amid the traditional verbiage of the party platforms, there was a clear line drawn between the Democratic and Republican party philosophies on this issue. The Democratic platform had this to say:

> A new Democratic administration will expand Federal programs to aid urban communities to clear their slums, dispose of their

sewage, educate their children, transport suburban commuters to and from their jobs, and combat juvenile delinquency. We will give the city dweller a voice at the Cabinet table by bringing together within a single Department programs concerned with urban and metropolitan problems. . . . Today our rate of home building is less than ten years ago. A healthy expanding economy will enable us to build 2 million homes a year, in wholesome neighborhoods, for people of all incomes. At this rate, within a single decade we can clear away our slums and assure every American family a decent place to live. . . . Most of the increased construction will be priced to meet the housing needs of middle and low income families who now live in substandard housing and are priced out of the market for decent homes. . . . The home building industry should be aided by special mortgage assistance, with low interest rates, long-term mortgage periods and reduced down payments. Where necessary, direct Government loans should be provided. Even with this new and flexible approach, there will still be need for a substantial low-rent public housing program authorizing as many units as local communities require and are prepared to build.

The Republican platform conformed to the line of the second Eisenhower Administration:

Vigorous state and local governments are a vital part of our Federal union. The Federal Government should leave to state and local governments those programs and problems which they can best handle and tax sources adequate to finance them. . . . No vast new bureaucracy is needed to achieve this objective. . . . Despite noteworthy accomplishments, stubborn and deep-seated problems stand in the way of achieving the national objective of a decent home in a suitable living environment for every American. Recognizing that the Federal government must help provide the economic climate and incentives which make this objective obtainable, the Republican Party will vigorously support the following steps, all designed to supplement and not supplant private initiative: continued effort to clear slums, and promote rebuilding, rehabilitation and conservation of our cities; stimulate new programs to develop specialized types of housing, such as those for the elderly and for nursing homes . . . adequate authority for the Federal housing agencies to assist the flow of mortgage credit into private housing, with emphasis on homes for middle and lower-income families.

The Republican platform was conspicuously silent on needs for low-rent public housing or other housing for the poor.

During the campaign, Richard Nixon paid little attention to the housing issue. John Kennedy, however, assembled a major meeting on housing in Pittsburgh early in October. The outpouring of mayors, builders, developers, labor officials, and representatives of liberal organizations for that meeting indicated that a broad consensus in the field was looking to a Kennedy victory to break through the political stalemate which had frustrated them during the later Eisenhower years.

Kennedy's narrow victory that November, despite extensive anti-Catholic prejudice, opened the era of the New Frontier—in housing, as in most other basic fields.

CHAPTER 9

Housing in the New Frontier, 1961-63: Promise and Distraction

A new and invigorating spirit pervaded the Washington scene with the advent of the Kennedy Administration, notwithstanding the narrowness of the political victory over Richard Nixon. In contrast to the cautious and often niggardly position of the Eisenhower regime, this spirit was quickly manifested in the Kennedy attitude toward housing and community development.

In his first address to Congress on the state of the Union on January 30, 1961, President Kennedy ranked housing with education and health care for the aged among the principal "unfinished and neglected tasks" of the nation. Concerning housing, he said:

> Our cities are being engulfed in squalor. Twelve long years after Congress declared our goal to be a decent home and a suitable environment for every American family, we still have 25 million Americans living in substandard homes.

Because of the emphasis given to housing in his campaign, there was intense interest in President Kennedy's choice of Administrator for the Housing and Home Finance Agency. This interest was heightened by the expectation that the Kennedy Administration would seek and probably secure the elevation of the Housing Agency to Cabinet-level status. In view of the political importance of the big-city vote and the active role played by many Democratic mayors in his campaign, there was widespread speculation that the President would choose a prominent mayor such as Richard Lee of New Haven.

There was also speculation that he would turn to the liberal private enterprise wing in the development field, which had given him important support. Instead, he opted to nominate a Negro—the first to be proposed as head of a major Federal agency.

There clearly was a political motivation attached to the nomination of Robert C. Weaver in view of the growing importance of the Negro vote, especially in Northern cities, and the rising tide for civil rights. However, in addition to the color of his skin, Weaver had extensve qualifications for the top housing post. Holding a Ph.D. from Harvard, he had served in the New Deal as racial relations adviser on housing, had been professor of economics at New York University, had been Deputy Commissioner of Housing for New York State and later the state Rent Control Administrator, and was currently vice-chairman of the Housing and Redevelopment Board of New York City.

Weaver's nomination came as a surprise to most and drew a mixed reaction, with underlying racial overtones. In Congress, the progressive Southern legislative leaders on housing—Senator Sparkman and Congressman Rains—displayed a correct but cool attitude which spilled over to the professionals in housing and redevelopment in the South. The private-enterprise groups in the field were disappointed that someone from their ranks had not been chosen, and the mayors were generally disgruntled that the appointment had not come from their group. The nomination was, of course, applauded by the Negro organizations and drew general support from organized labor and from liberal groups.

After his nomination was confirmed by the Senate, Weaver promptly neutralized a good part of the incipient negativism toward himself by assembling a vigorous and youngish top staff. As Deputy Administrator, he selected Jack Conway, an energetic and forceful labor official who had been assistant to Walter Reuther of the United Automobile Workers since 1946. To head the public housing program, Weaver appointed Marie McGuire, the charming, beauteous, and highly successful director of the San Antonio Housing Authority. William Slayton, who had strong connections with local urban renewal agencies, with the municipal organizations, and with the new breed of private redevelopers, was named as head of the urban renewal program. As FHA Commissioner, Weaver selected Neal Hardy, who had been an assistant administrator of HHFA during the Truman Administration and was very much *persona grata* with builders and mortgage bankers by reason of seven years of experience in a top office with the National Association of Home Builders.

When the Kennedy Administration assumed office, the nation was in the course of an economic recession induced by the tight money and stringent fiscal policies of the Eisenhower Administration. (Richard Nixon was later to complain that these policies had cost him the election in 1960.) As usual, the private housing industry was the principal sufferer from the recession. Starts of new private housing in 1960 declined 18 percent from 1959 and almost reached the low level of the previous Eisenhower recession in 1957. By the end of 1960, one out of every six construction workers was unemployed, a rise of 25 percent within a year and the highest unemployment rate of any major American industry. Meanwhile, urban renewal activity was at a low ebb due to limited funds and public housing construction was only beginning to recover from the most regressive policies of the Eisenhower regime, with only 26,500 dwelling units placed under construction nationally in 1960.

President Kennedy moved rapidly to attempt to counter the recession in housing construction by reducing the interest rate on FHA-insured mortgages and GI loans and by inducing the Federal Reserve Board to take steps to expand the flow of funds for private housing mortgages. He also ordered a step-up in the rate of Federal approvals of urban renewal and public housing projects.

Of greater long-term significance, he proposed a major legislative program which faced up to the realities of the crisis in housing and community development and which would provide at least partial positive solutions. The President was living up to his campaign commitments on these issues and his promises to the cities. This was a sharp contrast with the official policy of the Eisenhower regime, especially during the second term, to ignore or minimize these issues.

In a special message to Congress on March 9, 1961, President Kennedy emphasized the prospective growth in the national population to 235 million by 1975 and to 300 million by the year 2000 and the fact that 14 million American families were living in substandard or deteriorating housing. He said:

Our policy for housing and community development must be directed toward the accomplishment of three basic national objectives:

First, to renew our cities and assure sound growth of our rapidly expanding metropolitan area.

Second, to provide decent housing for all of our people.

Third, to encourage a prosperous and efficient construction industry as an essential component of general economic prosperity and growth . . .

The Kennedy message also recognized the changed character of the national housing market and the need for concentrating on homes for lower-income households. Referring to the recession in residential construction, he said:

Formerly, this kind of depression in the homebuilding and related industries could be more easily met. But the housing market today is basically different than that of only a few years ago. There is no longer an enormous backlog of economic demand which can be released simply by providing ample credit. Credit devices must now be used selectively to encourage private industries to build and finance more housing in the lower price ranges to meet the unfilled demands of moderate income families. It is these families who offer the largest and the most immediate potential housing market, along with those of still lower incomes who must rely on low-rent public housing.

Specifically, President Kennedy urged new legislation to permit loans for rental or cooperative housing for lower-middle-income families at the average Federal borrowing rate, which was then 3⅛ percent; this was the first effort since 1950 to reach this neglected market. He called for an increase of 100,000 dwellings in the low-rent public housing program, the largest increment since 1949, and for an increase of $2.5 billion in urban renewal funds over a four-year period, one-fourth greater than the total authorization over the preceding twelve years. He also advocated a new program of Federal grants and loans to finance land reserves in metropolitan areas for future development and for open space.

The progressive flavor and comprehensive nature of the Kennedy proposals drew an enthusiastic response from the urban groups and liberal organizations which had been eagerly awaiting the unveiling of the "New Frontier" in housing and community development. My remarks before the House Housing Subcommittee on April 27, 1961 were typical of this reaction as compared with the lean years of the Eisenhower era:

> It is heartening and exhilarating to find informed and incisive recognition of the crisis in housing and community development by the present Administration, and to have presented a set of substantive and constructive proposals to solve this crisis, or at least to make a far-reaching start on its ultimate solution . . . In general, we are enthusiastically in favor of this legislation which we consider to be the most important measure in the field of housing and community development to come before the Congress since the historic Housing Act of 1949.

Even at the peak of the Kennedy political honeymoon, the President's housing proposals did not have easy sailing in Congress. In the House of Representatives, this largely reflected the closeness of the 1960 election and the fact that the Democrats lost 22 seats, notwithstanding the Kennedy victory. Furthermore, these lost seats had been held by Northern liberals elected in the Democratic Congressional landslide in 1958. Also, the Republican organization in the House, headed by Representative Charles Halleck of Indiana, remained loyal to the regressive policies of the Eisenhower second term. When the House Banking and Currency Committee reported favorably on most of the Kennedy proposals on June 1, 1961, all but two of the Republican Committee members signed a minority report which stated in part:

> The overriding issue in this housing bill, in our opinion, is the issue of fiscal responsibility. The bill contains excessive budget spending authorizations. The bill contains unsound and unnecessary provisions. It does not hold tightly to prudent fiscal standards. It will not "preserve our fiscal integrity and world confidence in the dollar." The Congress cannot expect to pass huge budget spending measures of this type without inviting a resumption of the outflow of gold from our country.

(The internal quotes were from a special message to Congress by President Kennedy.)

The critical vote in the House occurred on June 22, when Representative Gordon C. McDonough of California, acting with the full support of the Republican leadership, moved to recommit the bill with instructions to delete most of its new provisions and to cripple the others. The motion was defeated by a margin of 18 votes, 215 to 197. Only seven Republicans deserted their leadership on this vote; of these, four were from New York City, including John V. Lindsay, the future mayor of the city. However, in this instance, largely through the efforts and influence of Representative Albert Rains, the Republican-Southern Democrat coalition did not function effectively; the Deep South Democrats voted 44 to 31 against the motion to recommit.

Even in the Senate, where the Democratic majority was 65 to 35, the political margin for the legislation was narrow. In fact, a peculiar coalition of liberal Border State Democrats, led by Senator Albert Gore of Tennessee, and conservative Republicans came within two votes of striking from the bill the new program for low-interest housing loans for lower-middle-income families. Evidently, the motivation of Senator Gore and the Democrats who followed him was the mistaken premise that the new program would be competitive with conventional home building and mortgage banking operations and even with low-rent public housing. For the legislation as a whole, the key vote in the Senate as in the House was on a motion to recommit offered by Republican Senator Prescott Bush of Connecticut. This motion was defeated by a margin of only five votes, 47 to 52. Only two Republicans—Senators Jacob K. Javits of New York and Clifford Case of New Jersey—voted against the motion to recommit. The Senators from the Deep South split 8 to 7 in favor of the motion.

While the margin of victory for the legislation in Congress was small, the Housing Act of 1961 preserved most of the Kennedy requests and represented the most significant new law in this field since 1949. The lower-middle-income and low-rent public housing programs both survived intact. The added authorization for urban renewal was cut to $2 billion, but this still represented a doubling of funds for this program. The President's proposal for grants and loans for land reserves was lost, but grants for public open space projects were approved. Initial financing for mass transportation projects was established. In short, the legislation was an important initial response to the needs of cities and the expanding urban population.

Events of the next two years, however, were to demonstrate that there were major obstacles in the path of achieving major advances under the programs of the 1961 Act. The reasons were complex.

For one thing, the impact of the 1960 recession carried over into 1961 and it was not until 1962 that there was major evidence of a resumption in economic growth. This trend was reflected in private residential construction; new starts of dwelling units increased only 4 percent in 1961 over the depressed 1960 level of 1,230,000, notwithstanding the intensive efforts by the Kennedy Administration to expand the flow of mortgage credit. By 1963, the total had increased to almost 1,600,000, but little of the growth was in the areas of greatest housing need.

The new program of low-interest housing loans for lower-middle-income families was extremely slow in developing momentum. In part this reflected the growing pains of a new Federal undertaking and the difficulties of adjusting the old-line FHA field bureaucracy to new concepts. But it also reflected the establishment of unduly restrictive administrative policies which had the effect of making the program financially unattractive to typical residential builders. The responsibility was divided between an overcautious attitude by the new top housing officials and unrealistic claims by legislative leaders who had exaggerated the savings in rents which could be achieved solely through a reduction of about two-fifths in mortgage interest cost. In any case, only 4,200 dwelling units were placed in construction nationally in 1962 and 8,700 in 1963. While the latter figure was hailed by the Housing and Home Finance Agency as a major accomplishment, objectively it was a most meager performance in a potential lower-middle-income housing market of several millions of households.

In low-rent public housing, progress was even slower despite a much improved top administration. During the three years ending 1963, only 72,000 low-rent units were placed in construction nationally, a yearly average of 24,000, or less than in the final year of the Eisenhower Administration. This reflected in large part the intensification of the problem, mainly generated by racial issues, of securing local community approvals of sites for new public housing family projects. Only the urban renewal program, among the major elements of the 1961 Act, was performing on schedule in utilization of funds.

The political difficulties encountered in Congress by the Kennedy Administration on housing and related matters were illustrated by its inability to secure Congressional approval of the establishment of the Housing and Home Finance Agency as a Cabinet-level Department. On April 18, 1961, President Kennedy submitted proposed legislation creating a Department of Urban Affairs and Housing, mainly by transfer of functions of HHFA. Hearings were held and the proposal drew strong support from the adherents of a stronger status for housing programs within the Federal establishment. However, Congress dragged its heels. After extended delays, the House Committee on Government Operations recommended passage of the legislation. But on January 24, 1962, the House Rules Committee denied a rule to bring the legislation to a vote on the floor of the House. The Administration thereupon submitted a reorganization plan to accomplish the same result under a procedure which would have given the plan the force of law if not disapproved by one house of Congress within 30 days. On February 21, 1962, the House of Representatives did just that, and by a vote of 264 to 150.

While never publicly stated by Congressional leaders, there were racial undertones to the refusal of Congress to accept the concept of Departmental status for the housing agency. There was a widely held opinion in informed Congressional quarters that President Kennedy had made a serious tactical error in announcing in advance that if the Department were established, he would nominate Robert C. Weaver to become its first Secretary. While this announcement was welcomed by Negro organizations and civil rights groups, its reception among Southern Democrats was generally unfavorable, which was held to be a decisive factor in the negative attitude by Congress as a whole. In the lobbies of the House of Representatives, the view was privately expressed by many that a Department of Housing and Urban Development would never be approved by the House as long as the heir apparent as Secretary was Robert C. Weaver. This point of view was reinforced, however illogically, by the expectation that, under the increasing pressures from civil rights organizations, President Kennedy eventually would issue an executive order prohibiting racial discrimination in Federally-assisted housing and urban development programs.

An ironic postlude to this undercover display of racial bias occurred after Abraham Ribicoff resigned as Secretary of Health, Education and Welfare to run successfully for the Senate from Connecticut. There was serious consideration at the White House of the possibility of achieving two political gains by nominating Robert Weaver as

Secretary of HEW—who would thereby become the first Negro Cabinet-member—and selecting a successor to Weaver at HHFA who would be more acceptable to Congress, thus paving the way for acceptance of a Department of Housing prior to the 1964 Presidential elections. Weaver himself insisted he was not seeking the HEW post and preferred to continue as Housing Administrator. The eventual White House decision was against this strategem. Some cynical White House observers concluded that the final opinion was that the maximum political mileage among Negro organizations had been derived from the President's appointment of Weaver as Housing Administrator and endorsement of him as the first Secretary of Housing and that as HEW Secretary he might carry with him Congressional hostilities endangering the President's proposals for health and education legislation.

Notwithstanding its political problems in Congress, the Kennedy Administration fared well in the off-year Congressional elections in November, 1962. Against expectations that the Democrats would suffer a loss of seats typical for the party in power in an off-year election, the Democrats gained two seats in the Senate, to control by 67 to 33, and had a net loss of only two seats in the House of Representatives, to control by a majority of 258 to 177. From the standpoint of the organizations and individuals pressing for more effective performance by the Federal Government in advancing toward established goals for housing and urban development, the problem was to translate this apparently favorable political situation in Congress into action.

There was growing frustration within these ranks in 1963. The priorities of the Kennedy Administration appeared to be focusing increasingly on military research and development, space exploration, and employment stimulation and training, with less emphasis on the issues of housing and urban development which had figured so largely in the President's special message to Congress in March, 1961. As an illustration, in the fiscal year ended June 30, 1963, actual Federal expenditures for public housing, urban renewal, and community facilities amounted to only $400 million, and Federal activities in support of the private residential mortgage market actually resulted in a net surplus of $536 million. By contrast, expenditures for military research and development were $6,376 million, for manned space flight $1,533 million, and for farm income stabilization

$5,517 million. In his message to Congress in early 1963, President Kennedy renewed his request for establishment of a Department of Urban Affairs and Housing and asked for Federal financial assistance for mass transportation systems and for a modest increase in funds for housing for the elderly. Otherwise he made no substantive proposals on housing and community development. By and large, Administrator Weaver and the other top officials in the Housing and Home Finance Agency retained the personal respect and support of the organizations which had supported and pressed for these programs, but this relationship was being strained by meager performance.

These frustrations rose abruptly to the surface in a resolution adopted at the convention of the National Housing Conference in late February, 1963. The participants in the preparation of the resolution were representatives of municipal organizations, the AFL-CIO, religious organizations, professionals and local organizations—in short, substantially the same groups which had enthusiastically applauded President Kennedy's special message on housing only two years before. The resolution stated, in part:

> New programs must be initiated in several fields, and a number of existing programs must have new or expanded authorizations if they are not to grind to a halt before the end of 1963. Yet the Administration has failed to make any comprehensive analysis of needs or of the adequacy of present programs. This year it has not proposed new programs or authorizations to expand housing production and urban rebuilding. . . . The National Housing Conference is dismayed by these deficiencies of the Administration's proposed housing program and is equally dismayed at the passive acquiescence of our community and civic leadership in the inadequate program which we now have. . . . The National Housing Conference asserts that the Administration's attitude and its proposals are not good enough to meet our needs and aspirations. It urges the Congress to bestir itself and assume leadership in activating and expanding the programs that are now languishing or waiting to be initiated.

As a follow-through on this blunt position, I delivered the keynote speech at a National Housing Conference meeting at which the other speakers were Robert Weaver and the other top officials of HHFA, who naturally spoke in defense of the progress being made under their administration. My views were different. I said, in part:

The fact is that our national housing production has been frozen for years at a level less than 60 percent of the annual requirements lying only a few years ahead. The fact is, notwithstanding a long established and successful public housing program and the beginning of an FHA program for lower middle income families, we have no mass national housing program for families in the lower half of the income scale. The fact is, notwithstanding the successful progress in urban renewal, only the surface has been scratched in the renewal of blighted urban areas, no broad solution has been developed for directing the massive urban sprawl within a sound planning framework, traffic congestion is rampant, and there are grave shortages of classrooms, parks, playgrounds, and recreation facilities. . . .

The hard reality is that we have not done enough, that we will be proceeding in the future from a base already containing serious shortages, and that our national requirements only a few years ahead will vastly exceed present rates of national production and present allocations of Federal, local, and private financial resources. . . .

Many of us are deeply concerned by the glaring disparity between the obvious national requirements and the nation's awareness of those requirements. The complex of community development problems intimately affects the lives of the predominant portion of the American people. The political potential in seeking effective solutions would appear to be almost unlimited. But this political potential is not adequately influencing Congress. This implies a lag by many communities in recognizing and communicating the importance of their own problems . . .

A concerted search was begun for a technique and an approach which could break through the wall of indifference or unawareness that was impeding effective action on housing and community development, could dramatize the issues from the community level to the national level, and could mobilize public attention and political support. A decision was reached by the Conference of Mayors and other municipal organizations, by the National Housing Conference, by the AFL-CIO, and by related professional and public interest groups to urge the President to convene a major White House Conference on housing and community development before the end of 1963. This was a technique which had been used successfully in the past to polarize support for other social issues such as the problems of the elderly, public health, and education.

At first, Robert C. Weaver, whose support would be an essential first step for White House acceptance of the proposal, was lukewarm. But he came to perceive the potential value of such a conference to him and the HHFA programs in helping to overcome the frustrations which he and his top staff were experiencing. Weaver gave his backing to the proposal, made favorable soundings at the White House, and assigned staff to work with representatives of the sponsoring organizations. The latter groups formally urged the President to convene the conference. Representations were made regarding the political importance of such a backdrop in terms of the 1964 Presidential election and especially in relation to the mounting right-wing support for the draft-Goldwater campaign.

A working committee was formed to draft a format and a statement of the issues for the conference. Informal contacts were made with legislative leaders in Congress. A preliminary program was prepared involving the formation of local and regional committees, the scheduling of local and regional public hearings and conventions beginning in early September, and the convening of the White House Conference itself in early December. An extensive panel of experts was proposed to prepare reports and papers for submission to the conference. Inquiries were made about the availability of public meeting rooms for the local hearings, of appropriate major hotel facilities in Washington, and of sources of Federal funding for the expenses of the conference.

All this proceeded with the knowledge and tacit approval of the White House. Suddenly, the signals were changed. The occasion was the first massive civil rights march on Washington in early August. While the march was peaceful, the huge outpouring of participants and the militant tone of many of the speeches raised the specter of providing ready-made settings for a whole sequence of local demonstrations through the local hearings proposed for the autumn in preparation for the White House conference in December. While never publicly stated, it was clear that to the President's advisers, this prospect presented political risks outweighing the potential political advantages. So the word went out from the White House that plans for the conference on housing were to be put indefinitely on the shelf.

Then, on November 22, the shots rang out in Dallas, and the Kennedy era came to a premature end.

CHAPTER 10

The Great Society and the Shadow of Vietnam, 1963-66

After the assassination, the shift in style at the White House between the brief Kennedy era and the incoming era of Lyndon B. Johnson was gradual for a few weeks but soon complete. There was considerable contrast between the two administrations. On the one hand, there was the Groton-Harvard aura of John F. Kennedy, stamped with the style of the Eastern establishment but accompanied by a verve strongly appealing to the intellectual coteries and to the youth of the country as well as to the Catholic blocs and labor groups in the urban areas. On the other hand, there was the twangy Texas style of Lyndon B. Johnson, the former small-town Texas school teacher, deliberately homespun, but at least equally sophisticated in the ways of politics and big business and appealing to the predominant Protestant ethic of the rural Midwest and the South.

The program objectives of the two Presidents, however, were remarkably similar. In fact, President Johnson soon displayed greater self-confidence in his proposals and dealings with Congress than had President Kennedy in the months preceeding his murder. This doubtless reflected in large degree Lyndon Johnson's long career as Democratic leader of the Senate and his successful record as manager and manipulator in the cloakrooms and on the floor. President Johnson also showed his self-confidence by keeping largely intact the top Federal echelon which he had inherited, aside from the immediate White House staff and aside from the potential political threat represented by Attorney General Robert F. Kennedy.

President Johnson's attitude toward housing programs had consistently been favorable. In 1937, when he was a freshman member of the House of Representatives, he applied sufficient pressure on Nathan Straus, the first administrator of the United States Housing Authority, to secure approval of the first public housing project in the country under the United States Housing Act of 1937 for Austin, Texas, in his Congressional district. While he had not served on any of the Congressional committees having jurisdiction over housing and community development legislation, he had played an effective leadership role in supporting the Democratic proposals for housing legislation during the Eisenhower years.

President Kennedy had withheld any recommendations for major additional housing and community development legislation in 1963, in contrast to his major proposals shortly after his inauguration in 1961. President Johnson early in 1964 urged a resumption of major legislation. In a special message to Congress on January 27, he prefaced his recommendations as follows:

> Our nation stands today at the threshold of the greatest period of growth in its history.
>
> By 1970, we shall have to build at least 2 million new homes a year to keep up with the growth of our population.
>
> We will need many new classrooms, uncounted miles of new streets and utility lines, and an unprecedented volume of water and sewerage facilities. We will need stores, and churches and libraries, distribution systems for goods, transportation systems for people, and communications systems for ideas.
>
> Above all, we will need more land, new housing, and orderly community development. For most of this population growth will be concentrated in the fringe areas around existing metropolitan communities.

The major program proposals in his message included authorization for an additional 200,000 public housing dwellings over the following four years plus 40,000 leased units, an additional $1.4 billion in urban renewal funds for a two-year period, and a new program of grants and loans for the development of public facilities in new communities, as well as loan insurance for the private developers of such communities.

The President also renewed the request for legislation establishing a Department of Housing and Community Development, consolidating the existing functions of the Housing and Home Finance Agency at the cabinet level. He did not, however, repeat President Kennedy's tactic of announcing that he would nominate Administrator Robert C. Weaver as the first Secretary if the Department legislation was enacted.

As a further illustration of President Johnson's political self-confidence and aggressiveness, on March 16, 1964, he sent a message to Congress on the poverty problem and proposed the enactment of the Economic Opportunity Act of 1964, including the establishment and financing of the Job Corps, of various manpower training and educational programs for the poor, and urban and rural community action programs.

The President's housing proposals were not, however, to have entirely smooth sailing. In part, this reflected the fact that 1964 was a Presidential election year, marked by Lyndon Johnson's ambition to win the Presidency in his own right and by the increasing coalescence of right-wing political forces behind the candidacy of Senator Barry Goldwater. The result was a tendency both at the White House and among the Democratic leaders in Congress to avoid rocking the boat by pushing too hard on housing legislation. This cautious course was also influenced by the controversy attached to the Administration's civil rights and anti-poverty proposals; the passage of both these measures was considered to be essential for Democratic success in the national elections.

Another factor contributing to the uncertainty was the increasing attacks on the urban renewal and redevelopment program—from the left as well as from the right. Among the conservative factions, urban renewal had largely supplanted the low-rent public housing programs as the primary target for political opposition in the field of housing and community development. This doubtless reflected, on the one hand, the limited volume of public housing which was being accepted by American communities and, on the other hand, the rapidly increasing local demand for urban renewal. By the end of 1964, there were 800 communities participating in urban renewal throughout the country, resulting in a sharp escalation in requirements for Federal urban renewal funds—a development which was distasteful to the advocates of restricted Federal functions.

Among the liberal intelligentsia, the most influential assault on the concept of urban renewal and related programs was a book—

The Death and Life of Great American Cities—by Jane Jacobs, an accomplished writer on architectural and planning subjects. Mrs. Jacobs made a cogent criticism of the massive, institutional, and unattractive projects which typified the public housing program in many of the largest cities. But the main burden of her book was a romantic and emotional defense of the social and human values of life in congested urban neighborhoods, no matter how blighted, and an attack on planners and related urban renewal and housing activities attempting to recast and hence disturb those neighborhoods.

A somewhat related attitude had developed among a number of the leaders of Negro organizations and their liberal white allies, who coined the phrase "Negro removal" as the hallmark of the urban renewal program. This reflected the fact that in most major cities, North and South, a majority of the residents of slums and blighted areas selected locally for redevelopment were Negro. The phrase was frequently accompanied by the charge that most of the Negro families displaced by urban renewal were left to shift for themselves in so far as relocation housing was concerned and ended up in other slums. While this charge was never substantiated factually, by repetition it gained widespread acceptance. The statistics of HHFA (which were later verified by an independent survey in 132 cities by the U.S. Bureau of the Census) showed that 93 percent of all families displaced by urban renewal were relocated in standard housing within their financial means and that the 7 percent who relocated in substandard housing did so of their own volition after declining assistance. There were other inconsistencies in these arguments since by implication they seemed to say either that the Negro ghettoes should be untouched by urban renewal or that they should be redeveloped exclusively for present residents, thereby maintaining rather than dispersing the ghetto. Nevertheless, the increasing prevalence of such attitudes presented a political problem for the future of urban renewal.

Potentially the most dangerous attack on the program grew out of a research study financed by the Joint Center for Urban Studies of MIT and Harvard University, through Ford Foundation grants. The researcher and author of the resulting book—*The Federal Bulldozer* —was Martin Anderson, then a young assistant professor of finance at the Columbia University Graduate School of Business. His book purported to be a critical and factual analysis of the urban renewal program from its inception in 1949, leading inevitably to the conclusion that the program had been and would continue to be a failure and should be repealed forthwith. Although not a lawyer, Anderson brashly questioned the constitutionality of the urban renewal statute, notwithstanding the unanimous opinion to the contrary by the United States Supreme Court in 1953 and comparable opinions on the validity of State redevelopment statutes by the overwhelming majority of State high courts. Anderson's final conclusion was that "only free enterprise" could handle the job of rebuilding cities, presumably with no Federal aid. The multitude of factual errors, misleading use of statistics, and distortions in *The Federal Bulldozer* were carefully exposed and refuted by the National Association of Housing and Redevelopment Officials. Nevertheless, the book was published under the prestigious imprint of the MIT Press and was immediately embraced by the right-wing opponents of urban renewal and related Federal housing programs.

One of the far-right organizations which followed the Anderson line was "Life Line," a radio program subsidized by H. L. Hunt, the Texas oil magnate. The technique used by this program was to distribute to radio stations, predominantly in smaller cities and towns, a taped commentary expressing the right-wing point of view of "Life Line" on pending issues. The financial bait to the local stations was that the use of the tape was accompanied by paid commercials financed by other subsidiaries of the Hunt enterprises. One of these commentaries was an attack on urban renewal à la Anderson and replete with language such as "immoral pork barrel project," "free Federal handouts," "incompetence," "irresponsibility," and so on. As president of the National Housing Conference and with informal help from HHFA, I wrote every radio station which had broadcast this "Life Line" commentary to request time for a reply on the basis of the "Fairness Doctrine" of the Federal Communications Commission which stated, in part:

> Regardless of label or form, if one viewpoint of a controversial issue of public importance is presented, the licensee is obligated to make a reasonable effort to present the opposing viewpoint or viewpoints.

The National Housing Conference offered the stations a 15-minute tape prepared at its expense but without commercial fee. A total of

130 stations accepted and broadcast the Conference tape, some reluctantly but most without complaint. In my tape, I said, in part:

> The fact that during the past year 125 cities in 28 states began their first urban renewal project is, I believe, a clear indication that people in these cities have looked at the advances made by urban renewal in other cities and decided to follow suit. . . . All of us who support urban renewal welcome controversy. Controversy and free speech and open discussion often are necessary before a community can reach agreement and consent. But we deplore the myths and false stereotypes about the urban renewal program. We want the facts to be known.

The Federal Bulldozer was enthusiastically received by the United States Chamber of Commerce. (It should be noted that the United States Chamber of Commerce is not an association of local chambers of commerce but rather a Washington-based national institution financed largely by big corporations and by the magazine *Nation's Business* and consistently conservative in its position on economic issues.) The Chamber sponsored a series of regional conferences attacking urban renewal primarily on the grounds advanced by the *Bulldozer* and with Martin Anderson participating as a paid lecturer. However, a survey of local chambers of commerce in cities with active urban renewal programs, made by the American Municipal Association, disclosed that a large majority opposed the position taken by the U.S. Chamber.

These tactics evoked the following comments by Representative Albert Rains, chairman of the Housing Subcommittee of the House of Representatives. Writing in the 1964 *Yearbook* of the National Housing Conference, Congressman Rains said in part:

> I am particularly disturbed at the unremitting hatchet work being done on the urban renewal program. In my judgement, this is a vital part of our efforts to restore our cities. . . . The program's detractors say that the Federal Government should not concern itself with the problems of our urban population but should turn the whole program back to local government. It is obvious that local government cannot bear the financial burden of urban renewal and it is paradoxical that this should be proposed for a program which is doing more than any other to shore up municipal revenues and is actually helping local government meet the demands

for services and public investment to the maximum extent possible. The attemps to kill the urban renewal program, make the cities pay back Federal aid, reduce the Federal share of the cost, or introduce procedural amendments which would hamstring the program, would actually weaken local governments and make it necessary for them to look to Washington for a growing proportion of their financial needs.

In some mysterious way, the U.S. Chamber of Commerce has taken upon itself to lead the attack on urban renewal in spite of the fact that a great number of local chambers of commerce heartily endorse it. The support of local businessmen and local chambers of commerce was clearly evident in the special urban renewal hearings which my Subcommittee on Housing held in the fall of 1963 and in the legislative hearings in the spring of this year. In spite of this, the attack on urban renewal has become a rallying cry for all those who oppose Federal aid of any kind . . .

Notwithstanding the attacks on urban renewal and the threats to kill the program, the ultimate legislative outcome was to preserve the status quo with some forward progress, even though on a compromise basis. Both the Senate and House housing subcommittees had completed their legislative hearings on the Administration's proposals and other bills by late February. However, because of the political uncertainties, final committee action was deferred in both houses until late July, after the political lines for the 1964 Presidential campaign had been drawn by the Republican and Democratic national conventions. The basic compromise in both houses was to limit the Housing Act of 1964 primarily to a one-year extension and funding of the basic programs, with a commitment for consideration of more extensive legislation in 1965 after the Presidential elections, and to defer action on new proposals such as Federal insurance of loans for new community development.

In the Senate Banking and Currency Committee, Chairman A. Willis Robertson of Virginia, long the junior representative of the Byrd machine in the Senate, strongly opposed the extension of the urban renewal and public housing program. And the four right-wing Republicans on the committee—Senators Wallace F. Bennett of Utah, John G. Tower of Texas, Milward L. Simpson of Wyoming, and Peter H. Dominick of Colorado—waxed into flowery rhetoric in opposing the compromise bill:

We believe strongly that taxpayers' dollars are wasted; are used to little or no advantage other than political, and are used to cover up administrative inefficiencies. . . . We reiterate that in 1965 we will offer to the Congress amendments designed to make major changes in this vast program of grants and loans which has placed our cities in the paradoxical position of being beggars and profiteers; has enticed hundreds of thousands of our people to try to finance homes beyond their means; has created unfair dreams in the minds of the destitute; has sprawled over the country to the point of near domination of urban and some rural life; has lost nearly all semblance of an honest effort by the Federal Government to be helpful to those needing Federal help to obtain safe and sanitary housing.

But the large majority of both the committee and the Senate as a whole supported Senator Sparkman and the other Democratic leaders. So the putative revolt fizzled out and the bill passed the Senate by voice vote.

In the House committee, mainly because of skillful negotiation by Albert Rains with Representative William B. Widnall of New Jersey, the ranking Republican, the compromise bill was unanimously approved by the Housing Subcommittee and was approved by the full Banking and Currency Committee 18 to 1, with 4 abstentions. The principal quid pro quo for Representative Widnall was the inclusion in the bill of his proposal for direct low-interest Federal loans for rehabilitation in urban renewal areas. The bill passed on the floor of the House by a vote of 308 to 66, with the Republicans voting 118 to 41 in favor.

The principal provisions of the bill as finally passed by Congress was an increase of $725 million in urban renewal capital grants, further authorizations for 37,500 additional public housing units, and amendments to various FHA programs.

As a backdrop to the political alignments of the 1964 Presidential campaign, the differences between the Republican and Democratic party platforms on matters relating to housing and community development were significant. The Republican platform was, of course, an extremely conservative document, conforming to the views of Senator Goldwater. (The chairman of the platform committee was Representative Melvin R. Laird of Wisconsin, later to become Secretary of Defense in the Nixon Administration.) The platform contained precisely two references to housing and community development: first, "under housing and urban renewal programs . . . it has created new slums by forcing the poor from their homes to make room for luxury apartments, while neglecting the vital need for adequate relocation assistance" and, second, a pledge for "emphasis upon channeling more private capital into sound urban development projects and private housing."

The Democratic platform had this to say on the same questions:

> Now is the time to redouble our efforts, with full cooperation among local, state and federal governments for these objectives:
>
> The goal of our housing program must be a decent home for every American family.
>
> We will continue to assist broad community and regional development, urban renewal, mass transit, open space and other programs for our metropolitan areas . . .
>
> Because our cities and suburbs are so important to the welfare of all our people, we believe a department devoted to urban affairs should be added to the President's cabinet.

Lyndon Johnson's sweeping landslide victory over Barry Goldwater in the 1964 election cleared the way for "the Great Society" and for his remarkable record in achieving major domestic legislative programs over the next four years. The landslide produced a Democratic margin of 294 to 140 in the House of Representatives, the largest Democratic majority since the peak of New Deal popularity in the Thirties. Along with a 68-to-32 margin in the Senate, this presented a political power base which President Johnson was a past master at exploiting, notwithstanding continuing problems with the Southern conservatives in Congress. The dimensions of the Democratic triumph also led to premature predictions of the long-term emasculation of the Republican party as a national political force. At the same time, in the background were the sinister implications of the Gulf of Tonkin resolution as to the massive escalation of United States participation in the Vietnamese war which was to limit accomplishments under the President's major domestic programs and was to frustrate his political career.

Housing and community development ranked high on President Johnson's legislative agenda for 1965. On March 2, 1965, he presented his program in this area in an eloquent special message to Congress in which he said:

Within the borders of our urban centers can be found the most impressive achievements of man's skill and the highest expressions of man's spirit, as well as the worst examples of degradation and cruelty and misery to be found in modern America.

The modern city can be the most ruthless enemy of the good life, or it can be its servant. The choice is up to this generation of Americans. In our time, two giant and dangerous forces are converging on our cities: the forces of growth and decay.

Let us be clear about the core of this problem. The problem is people and the quality of the lives they lead. We want to build not just housing units, but neighborhoods; not just to construct schools, but to educate children; not just to raise income, but to create beauty and end the poisoning of our environment.

The substance of the President's message was a renewed request for the establishment of a Department of Housing and Urban Development and a wide range of substantive program proposals. In addition to a four-year funding of urban renewal for a total of $2.9 billion and a four-year public housing authorization at the rate of 60,000 dwellings per year, the President recommended a comprehensive package of new urban development programs, including: matching grants for sewer and water facilities on a basis consistent with area-wide plans for future growth; financial assistance for advance acquisition of land for new public buildings and other facilities; Federal insurance of loans for acquisition and development of land for privately-sponsored new communities and planned subdivisions; financial assistance to State land development agencies for land acquisition and development; matching grants for building multipurpose neighborhood facilities for health, recreation, and community activity; and an expansion of the open-space grant program to include small parks and playgrounds in cities, landscaping, tree planting, and improvement of existing city parks.

Within this comprehensive package, what turned out to be the most controversial recommendation was the President's proposal for the establishment of a rent-supplement housing program. Under this plan, Federal rent subsidies would be paid to the private developers and owners of rental or cooperative housing to cover the difference between 25 percent of a tenant's income and the amount necessary to support his dwelling, including mortgage debt service, real estate taxes, operating expenses, and profit. The mortgages would be insured by FHA, would pay a so-called market rate of interest, and would be made by private lending institutions. The motives of the Administration in advancing this proposal were mixed. On the one hand, the proposed housing was intended to accommodate families with a range of income from low to moderate to middle-income, with the rental subsidy to the individual family being geared to its income. This would break away from the pattern of economic segregation which characterized the existing Federal-aid housing programs for low- and moderate-income families. Furthermore, the proposal would have waived for this program the usual Federal requirement that any Federally-aided housing in effect be sanctioned by the local governing body of the locality. The intent here was to help penetrate the wall of exclusion erected by many suburban communities against the introduction of housing for low- and moderate-income families. These both were principles which were supported by the progressive forces in the housing field.

On the other hand, the financing mechanism in the rent-supplement proposal in essence represented Bureau of the Budget gimickry intended to phase out eventually the existing programs for low-interest direct Federal loans for housing for moderate-income families and for the elderly. This gambit stemmed from the intrinsically absurd Federal Budgetary policy of treating an expenditure for the purchase of a guaranteed, repayable housing mortgage, which eventually would be recouped in its entirety and with interest, in precisely the same way as an expenditure to meet a Federal payroll or to pay interest on a Federal bond. Since the mortgages financing rent-supplement projects would be made by private lending institutions, the capital cost of the housing would not enter into Federal budget expenditures and the annual charge to the Federal budget would be limited to the amount of the rent supplement subsidy. Of course, over the long run the cost to the Federal Government of borrowing is almost always less than the interest cost of private mortgages even when insured by FHA.

During this same period, there developed a curious lapse in liaison between the President and the big-city mayors. Notwithstanding the political importance of the urban vote, the President persistently declined repeated requests for direct meetings with the U.S. Conference of Mayors or the National League of Cities. While he reportedly conferred individually on occasion with mayors like Richard Daley of Chicago and Robert F. Wagner, Jr. of New York, he declined formal sessions with the municipal organizations, perhaps because he wished to avoid public identification with the big cities. Finally, this impasse was partially broken when the President designated Vice President Hubert H. Humphrey to be his personal liaison in dealing with the problems and complaints of city governments.

In the committee hearings and in the Congressional debate on the President's program, the rent-supplement proposal proved to be the lightning rod for controversy. This had the indirect effect of smoothing the way for the rest of the legislation, including urban renewal and public housing and also including most of President Johnson's other new proposals. The alignment of political forces, pro and con, on rent supplements was interesting. Since the projects would be sponsored, financed, owned, and operated largely by private building and lending institutions, the proposal gained support from the National Association of Home Builders, the Mortgage Bankers Association of America, and the American Bankers Association. On the other hand, the proposal drew opposition from some of the old-line local public housing authorities who saw it as competitive to their predominant position in developing and managing housing for low-income families and as a program which would draw away scarce financial resources which might better go into additional low-rent public housing. Also, a number of them sincerely believed that private developers lacked the experience and motivation to do a satisfactory job in the management of housing for low-income families.

The strongest political opposition to rent supplements stemmed from the provision which would authorize projects to be undertaken without specific authorization by the local governing body of the community. While never specifically so stated on the public record, this was considered to be a device to bring about the development of housing for low- and moderate-income families in the suburbs and, more precisely for Negro families. It was therefore anathema to most suburban communities. This generated strong political pressures on Congressmen from suburban districts who, in the North, were predominantly Republicans. While normally these Republican Representatives would have gone along with legislation supported by the home building and mortgage financing interests, in this case most of them responded to the opposition from home.

The liberal lobby on housing, headed by the National Housing Conference, the AFL-CIO, and cooperating organizations, supported the rent-supplement proposal. However, the lobby strongly opposed the phase-out of the low-interest direct-loan programs for housing for moderate-income families and for elderly households. Instead, it proposed that the interest rate on these loans, which had risen to 4 percent, be reduced to 3 percent and that substantial additional funds be provided. The legislative committees accepted these recommendations, increased the funds available for Federal purchase of 3-percent mortgages on housing for moderate-income families by more than $1.6 billion over a four-year period, and authorized an increase of $150 million in direct 3-percent loans for housing for the elderly. In response to pressures from the cities, the committees also seized on President Johnson's recommendation for a one-year appropriation of $100 million for 50-percent grants for water and sewer facilities and expanded it to a four-year program at the rate of $200 million a year.

When the time came for final legislative action, the rent-supplement program was the center of opposition, for the reasons previously cited. In the House Banking and Currency Committee, the revised bill was approved by the Housing Subcommittee 10 to 1 and was reported out by the full committee by a vote of 26 to 7. However, the seven Republicans in opposition issued a strong minority report attacking the rent supplement program as "foreign to American concepts" and claiming that it "kills the incentive of the American family" and "is the way of the socialistic state." It was significant that the report made no mention of the real underlying reason for opposition to the program.

It was clear that the key vote on the floor of the House would be on a motion to recommit the bill to the committee with instructions to strike out the provisions establishing the rent-supplement program. The White House mobilized its lobbying forces, still under the direction of Lawrence O'Brien on crucial issues even though he was now the Postmaster General. President Johnson himself was reported to have made personal intercessions with individual members of Congress. The liberal lobby was brought into play, especially the

AFL-CIO with its extensive lobbying force on Capitol Hill. I participated in some of the planning sessions in which the doubtful or uncommitted members of the House were identified, arrangements were made to exert maximum pressure on them either directly or from their districts, or failing results from that route to attempt to arrange "live pairs" in which the opposing Representatives agreed not to vote in return for abstention by a favoring Representative, or to encourage absenteeism on "official business." As was traditionally the case in House votes on critical housing issues, the vote on recommital was extremely close, but the motion was defeated 208 to 202. The Republicans Representatives voted overwhelmingly— 128 to 5—for recommital. The Democrats provided the narrow margin against the motion by a vote of 203 to 74. Even on the vote for final passage of the bill, when opponents frequently shift their vote in order to work both sides of a controversial issue, only 26 Republican Representatives voted for the bill while 109 were in opposition. The Democrats divided 219 for to 60 against on the final vote, with the opposition being entirely from the South.

In the Senate, the key vote likewise was on a motion to strike the rent-supplement provisions, which was defeated by a vote of 47 to 40. Only 5 Republican Senators voted against the motion to strike rent supplements; the Democrats divided 42 against the motion and 17 for. The Senate vote for final passage was 54 to 30. The Democrats voted 47 in favor to 11 against, with all the opposing votes except for Senator Frank J. Lausche of Ohio being from the Deep South. Only 7 Republican Senators voted for the bill, with 19 opposed.

The passage of the Housing and Urban Development Act of 1965, which was signed by President Johnson on August 10 of that year with considerable fanfare, was a major addition to the Federal programs for housing and community development. The only important setback was an amendment setting the income limits for families eligible to receive rent supplements on a level comparable to the income ceilings for low-rent public housing in the same locality, thereby eliminating any benefits for moderate-income families just above the public housing level. This amendment was pressed by long-time liberals like Senator Paul Douglas of Illinois and Senator William Proxmire of Wisconsin on the grounds that the rent-supplement funds should be concentrated on families at the poverty level.

Others who were equally on the progressive side of the housing effort felt that this was a short-sighted position in view of the increasing disenchantment of lower-middle-income white families, and especially blue-collar workers, with the concentration of Federal aid programs on the poor, and in view of the social and political desirability of achieving greater economic integration within Federally-aided housing programs.

During the same period that the housing bill was being considered, the Johnson Administration was also pressing for approval of the legislation establishing the Department of Housing and Urban Development, which was under the jurisdiction of the Government Operations Committees of the Senate and House. On this issue all of the liberal organizations together with the AFL-CIO and the municipal and county associations were united in support. On the private enterprise side there was division. The National Association of Home Builders supported the legislation, with the proviso that the identity of the FHA be preserved and that one of the Assistant Secretaries in the proposed department be designated as FHA Commissioner. The National Association of Mutual Savings Banks was in support. The United States Savings and Loan League and the National League of Insured Savings Associations, potent lobbying forces especially in the House of Representatives, had been neutralized by the fact that the legislation did not propose consolidating the Federal Home Loan Bank Board in the new department, on the grounds that the Board was a supervisory and quasi-judicial regulatory agency rather than a development agency. The Board, which functioned as the principal source of secondary credit for savings and loan associations, had been separated from HHFA by legislation in 1955.

The opposition to the legislation from private sources reflected varying forms of parochial interests. The National Association of Real Estate Boards, the United States Chamber of Commerce, the Mortgage Bankers Association, the National Lumber and Material Dealers Association, and the Life Insurance Association of America, in opposing the departmental bill, urged that FHA be made an independent agency and freed of any social responsibilities. Since these same organizations had taken the identical position in opposing the establishment of HHFA in 1947, their stand reflected no growth in political sophistication in the intervening eighteen years. The National Association of Manufacturers opposed the bill on the grounds that it would run counter to the transfer of responsibility for urban problems to the states and to local initiative. The American Farm Bureau Federation opposed the legislation out of fear that the proposed department would be too responsive to the needs of the cities.

A majority of the Congressional Republicans were in opposition to establishing the new department primarily on their traditional grounds of opposing big government. Nevertheless, with a large majority of Democrats supporting the Administration, the bill was favorably reported by the House Committee on May 11, 1965, and by the Senate Committee on August 2. The House Democrats voted 209 to 67 in favor, while the Republicans were opposed by the overwhelming margin of 117 to 8. In the Senate the Democrats voted 47 to 14 to support the measure and the Republicans were aligned 19 to 10 against.

After the passage of the departmental bill there ensued a bizarre personal drama over who would be the first Secretary of Housing and Urban Development. This was illustrative of Lyndon Johnson's frequently secretive methods of operation in matters involving Presidential power. Throughout the period of consideration of the bill, the President had carefully avoided giving any indication that he would nominate Robert C. Weaver as Secretary or, for that matter, any hint as to any other selection. Even the usually prolific Washington rumor mill was largely silent. There had been some speculation that the President might nominate former Congressman Albert Rains of Alabama, who had retired from Congress because of his conflicts with Governor George C. Wallace and his machine but who had an outstanding record over the years as sponsor of progressive housing legislation. It was held by some that this would be a smart counter-move against Wallace's increasingly raucous demagoguery. However, in view of the critical civil rights developments in Alabama it appeared unlikely that the President would nominate an Alabamian to a Cabinet-level post.

Especially after the successful battle on the Housing and Urban Development Act of 1965 during which Weaver was the principal Administration spokesman, there was increasing general expectation that Weaver would get the Presidential nod. On September 9, when the President was to sign the bill in the White House Rose Garden before a sizable audience, I happened to drive with Weaver to the White House in his official limousine. Without his expressly saying so, I felt that Weaver was confident he would be named. Before he began his remarks, the President beckoned Weaver to his side. But he completed his remarks with no mention of Weaver or anyone else as prospective Secretary.

The Washington rumor mill then began to work overtime. But as weeks went by, the White House preserved an enigmatic silence. There was a well-substantiated report that the President had immediately offered the post to Mayor Daley of Chicago but that Daley felt he should continue as mayor. The terms of the law specified that the new Department and the powers of its Secretary became effective within sixty days of the President's signature or by November 9. But when no nomination had been made by that date, some legal legerdemain was found to defer the deadline indefinitely. As the weeks dragged into months, there were many who felt that Weaver should resign in a dignified response to the President's apparent lack of confidence in him. However, Weaver was doggedly determined to sweat the situation out. Then, unpredictably in early January, 1966, President Johnson confounded all expectations by calling a special press conference to announce that he was nominating Robert C. Weaver. The President explained somewhat lamely that he had combed the country for the best man for the job, had considered about 300 possible candidates, but had finally decided that Bob Weaver was the best man after all.

This belated action cleared the way finally for organization of the Department of Housing and Urban Development. The Act provided for an Under Secretary and four Assistant Secretaries. The organizational structure of the new Department as perfected in late February divided the operating responsibilities of the four Assistant Secretaries as follows: an Assistant Secretary for mortgage credit and FHA Commissioner, an Assistant Secretary for Renewal and Housing Assistance (with responsibility for urban renewal, public housing, and direct loans for housing for the elderly), an Assistant Secretary for metropolitan development, and an Assistant Secretary for demonstration projects and intergovernmental relations. Only one man in the top echelon of HHFA—Philip M. Brownstein of FHA—survived the transition to departmental status. Milton Semer, who had been the number-two man in the HHFA hierarchy as Deputy Administrator and General Counsel, was passed over for the Under Secretary's post and resigned. William L. Slayton, the able head of urban renewal, had fallen out of favor with Weaver, who suspected him, rightly or wrongly, of lobbying for his own interests with the mayors during the uncertain months between the approval of the departmental bill and Weaver's ultimate nomination. Slayton resigned to become executive vice president of Urban America. Marie McGuire, the head of the Public Housing Administration, had also incurred Weaver's disfavor, purportedly because he considered her a poor administrator but presumably because he suspected she had been less than enthusiastic about the rent-supplement proposal and had privately shared the misgivings of some of the local housing authorities.

The composition of the top administrative structure in the new Department also reflected the heightened urban crisis in the United States and the outbreaks of violence in the Negro ghettoes. The bloody conflict in the Watts district of Los Angeles had occurred and so had the outbreaks in Harlem in New York City. There was increasing racial tension in most of the principal cities throughout the country. As one response to this worrisome scene, President Johnson in the fall of 1965 had quietly assembled a "task force" to develop recommendations for more effective use of Federal programs in relieving housing, social, and economic tensions in the ghettoes. The task force, operating without public hearings or publicity, prepared an unpublished report which laid the groundwork for the President's subsequent proposal for a "Demonstration Cities" program (later designated the "Model Cities" program). The head of the task force was Robert C. Wood, chairman of the political science department at the Massachusetts Institute of Technology. In January, 1966, the President nominated Professor Wood to be Undersecretary of the Department.

To round out the top echelon of the Department (which quickly became known as HUD), the President nominated Charles Harr, a professor at Harvard Law School, to be Assistant Secretary for metropolitan development. Harr, who had also been on the task force, was a specialist on land use and zoning law and a student of foreign housing programs. He also selected Ralph Taylor as Assistant Secretary for demonstration projects and intergovernmental relations. Taylor had extensive experience as former director of the New Haven redevelopment program and in private redevelopment activities. Through one of the quirks of White House politics, the word had been passed to Secretary Weaver that the Assistant Secretary for renewal and housing assistance must be a mayor, presumably to improve the President's relationships with the municipal organizations. As it turned out, none of the well-known mayors was willing to accept the appointment, so the post went by default to Don Hummel, the former mayor of Tucson, with little or no experience in or knowledge of either urban renewal or public housing.

The principal proposal of the Presidential task force became the Johnson Administration's main thrust for urban legislation in 1966 and likewise became a main focus for political controversy. On January 26, in a special message to Congress, the President said, in part:

> We know that cities can stimulate the best in man, and aggravate the worst. We know the convenience of city life, and its paralysis. What we may only dimly perceive is the gravity of the choice before us. Shall we make our cities liveable for ourselves and our posterity? Or shall we by timidity and neglect damn them to fester and decay?
>
> If we permit our cities to grow without rational design; if we stand passively by, while the center of each becomes a hive of deprivation, crime and hopelessness; if we devour the countryside as though it were limitless, while our ruins—millions of tenement apartments and dilapidated houses go unredeemed—if we become two people, the suburban affluent and the urban poor, each filled with mistrust and fear for the other—if this is our desire and policy as a people, then we shall effectively cripple each generation to come. We shall as well condemn our generation to a bitter paradox: an educated, wealthy, progressive people, who would not give their thoughts, their resources, or their wills to provide for their common well-being.
>
> I do not believe such a fate is either necessary or inevitable. But I believe this will come to pass unless we commit ourselves now to the planning, the building, the teaching, and the caring that alone can forestall it. That is why I am recommending today a massive demonstration cities program. I recommend that both the public and private sectors of our economy join to build in our cities and towns an environment for man equal to the dignity of his aspirations.
>
> I recommend an effort larger in scope, more comprehensive, more concentrated than any that has gone before.

The President went on to define the sweeping objectives of the program as follows:

> I propose a demonstration cities program that will offer qualifying cities of all sizes the promise of a new life for their people.
> I propose that we make massive additions to the supply of low and moderate cost housing.
> I propose that we combine physical reconstruction and rehabilitation with effective social programs throughout the rebuilding process.
> I propose that we focus all the techniques and talents within our society on the crisis of the American city.

The financial mechanism of the demonstration cities proposal was the offer of a supplementary Federal grant to cities, based on 80 percent of the local participation in all Federal-aid programs having an impact on the blighted area selected for upgrading—housing, urban renewal, health, education, public works, manpower training, and so on. This supplementary grant would be available to the city government for any purpose related to the improvement of physical or social conditions in the selected area and thus, in essence, was a first step toward offering cities block grants for the relief of urban problems.

This objective was naturally appealing to the hard-pressed city governments. But there were strings attached to the proposal. For one thing, in reflection of President Johnson's still unadmitted financial dilemma in relation to the mushrooming war in Vietnam, the extent of the Federal resources which the President proposed to commit were much more limited than was implied by the rather grandiose language of his message to Congress. While his appeal was to all cities of all sizes, it soon became clear that his proposed funding of the program—about $400 million a year in supplementary grants—could make a significant impact only in a much smaller number of localities. In fact, by the time that Robert C. Weaver was testifying in behalf of the proposal before the House Banking and Currency Committee on February 28, 1966, the predicted number of cities to participate in the program had been reduced to 60 to 70. Also, the proposed legislation provided no additional funds for urban renewal, which clearly would be the largest physical program underlying the demonstration-cities projects and which was already grossly underfinanced. This problem led the U.S. Conference of Mayors, the National Housing Conference, and other organizations to press for a special appropriation of urban renewal funds for use in the demonstration cities areas.

The financial limitations of the program prompted Mayor John Lindsay of New York City (which could readily have used the entire $400 million per year itself) to testify, as follows:

> For this demonstration to make its point, it must supply dramatic and apparent solutions for the vast slums of our largest city. If the demonstration cities program is to accomplish this goal, it must be given a vastly increased appropriation.

Notwithstanding these reservations, the cities and their liberal allies supported the legislation. The opposition to the proposal was predominantly anti-big city and anti-Negro in flavor since the bulk of the supplementary money would be spent in big-city ghettoes and would be accompanied by regulatory pressures for housing and related desegregation. The temper of the times was shown by the fact that Senator John Sparkman, chairman of the Senate Banking and Currency Committee and sponsor of all major housing legislation since 1949, declined to undertake the management of the bill in the Senate; he was facing a difficult campaign for reelection in Alabama against the opposition of Governor George Wallace and other reactionaries who considered him too soft on the issue of housing for Negroes and for the poor in general. Senator Paul Douglas, the long-time liberal who was next in seniority on the Senate committee, also stood aside on this issue; he too was confronted with a difficult (and ultimately unsuccessful) campaign for reelection in Illinois. It was left to Senator Edmund S. Muskie of Maine to shepherd the legislation through the Senate, a task which he performed with great skill.

The basic issues behind the opposition were seldom stated explicitly. For example, the National Association of Real Estate Boards, which was primarily motivated by its opposition to open housing, testified in the House of Representatives, as follows:

> The fundamental weakness in the bill is that it seeks solely by means of increased Federal grants to induce the cities to do that which they should have been doing . . .

Similarly, the minority report opposing the legislation in the Senate Banking and Currency Committee—filed by Republican Senators

Bennett, Tower, Thurmond, and Hickenlooper—justified their opposition in middle-class Calvinistic rhetoric. They attacked the bill as:

> an expansion of a faltering urban renewal program . . . Urban renewal was an enticing fantasy that preys on cities which could not afford all the luxury in a hurry that such a program offered. Much like the human failure of overindulgence at an attractive cafeteria counter . . .

It was left to Representative Paul A. Fino, presumably speaking on behalf of his predominantly white middle-class and lower-middle-class constituency in the Borough of the Bronx in New York City, to present the real issues boldly. In his minority views to the House Banking and Currency Committee, Congressman Fino said, in part:

> There is no doubt that the Federal Government can and will insist on schemes for "busing" and "pairing" and redrawing school district lines to achieve artificial integration . . . Then there is the requirement that a city plan work for economic and racial integraton. By this test, the Federal Government can insist that a city embark on a certain amount of rent supplement housing or build a certain amount of public housing in one-family income residential areas. . . .
> The demonstration cities bill is an ill-considered bill. The committee had pretty much agreed to toss out the program because of its poor structuring when the administration intervened with its usual closed mind and open bayonet . . . It is a very costly multi-billion dollar program. It would not be worth its cost even in the best of years. In its present raw and menacing form, set against the budget backdrop of the dollar-devouring quagmire of Vietnam, it is not even worth considering.

Notwithstanding this type of bombast and the underlying political pressures on members of Congress, particularly those with constituencies in suburban or rural areas, the strength of the White House was sufficient to secure the final enactment of the Demonstration Cities program, even though on an abbreviated two-year basis rather than the six years proposed by the President. There was a delay of more than three months in the House of Representatives because of uncertainties about the prospective voting alignment. However, the program survived a motion by Senator Tower in the Senate to strike out all grant funds; the vote was 27 in favor of the motion and 53 against, with 10 Republican Senators supporting the motion. Finally, on October 14, 1966, the House approved the Senate-passed version by a vote of 178 to 141.

CHAPTER 11

The Great Society and the Urban Crisis, 1966-68

The enactment of the Housing and Urban Development Act of 1965 and the Demonstration Cities and Metropolitan Development Act of 1966, along with anti-poverty and civil rights legislation, represented a massive effort by the Johnson Administration to cope with the growing urban crisis, accompanied by rising Negro unrest and violence. The fact that these measures became law, in the face of increasing disenchantment in Congress, was a tribute to the political pressure exerted by the Administration and especially by the President himself, together with the support of liberal forces in the field.

Over the short run at least, the effectiveness of these programs was nevertheless substantially frustrated by two overriding problems. The first was the skyrocketing economic impact of the war in Vietnam, over and above an increasing public disillusion with the war itself. The second was the reluctance of the Federal Government to reorder national priorities on a major scale in favor of the urban programs. For this, the responsibility was shared by Congress and the Administration.

The first major expansion in total national defense expenditures caused by the widening U.S. military involvement in Vietnam occurred in the Federal fiscal year ending June 30, 1966, when they rose by more than $7 billion. In the following fiscal year, there was a further massive jump of over $13 billion followed by another huge increase of $10.5 billion in the fiscal year ending June 30, 1968. The resulting large Federal deficits exerted strong inflationary pressures on the national economy. To counter these, the Johnson Administration and the Federal Reserve Board chose to follow a policy of so-called "credit restraint" and higher interest rates to channel excess funds into high interest rate obligations. The alternative would have been to institute credit controls and allocations, as was done during the Korean war.

As was the case in somewhat similar circumstances in 1957 and 1958 during the Eisenhower regimè, the chief sufferer from this policy was the private residential construction industry. Private residential builders rely almost entirely for their mortgage financing on funds deposited by individual savers in savings and loan associations, savings banks, and life insurance companies. With the flow of consumers' savings diverted largely from those institutions into higher interest-bearing obligations, the result was a drastic drying-up of the supply of funds for residential mortgages and an equally drastic decline in residential construction during the summer and fall of 1966. By October, 1966, the annual rate of construction starts of new housing had declined to 848,000 dwellings from the 1965 level of 1,451,000 units. For the year 1966 as a whole, only 1,142,000 units were started, the lowest level since 1946. In 1967, there was only a modest recovery to 1,268,000 dwellings. By contrast, the net capital funds secured by corporations from the sale of securities during 1966 were more than double the net amount secured in 1965.

The financial impact of the war in Vietnam on housing was felt in other ways through administrative actions. In the summer of 1966, in order to help relieve the critical slump in residential construction, Congress authorized the Federal National Mortgage Association (FNMA) to purchase $1 billion in mortgages on new lower-priced single-family homes. But the Bureau of the Budget, obviously acting with the concurrence of the President, impounded all but $250 million of this authorization as a step to limit the flow of Federal funds into the economy. Similarly, out of $450 million of FNMA funds authorized by purchase of 3-percent mortgages on rental and co-operative housing, the Bureau impounded all but $32.5 million.

The impact of the residential construction depression and of these kinds of administrative actions presumably were among the important political influences which caused the Democrats to lose 47 House seats and four Senate seats in the 1966 Congressional elections. However, the Democrats still retained control of the House of Representatives by a margin of 247 to 187 and of the Senate by 64 to 36. The reaction of liberal supporters of housing and urban development programs was well stated in a resolution adopted by the National Housing Conference on April 9, 1967:

> While the Vietnam conflict continues, we must protect our home front. It is neither sound nor equitable to throw the burden of domestic restrictions on the housing and urban development programs. We are at a time of crisis in housing. Today when the nation's need for housing is at its all-time peak, housing is at its lowest level of production in many years. We all know that our nation is experiencing an urban crisis with social unrest and violence in our cities. If we are to avoid increasing demonstrations and violence in our cities, we must take vigorous and immediate action to provide good homes and good neighborhoods for the ill-housed. We can no longer tolerate bad housing conditions which are at the heart of the urban crisis . . .
>
> The persistence of slum and blighted conditions constitutes a glaring contradiction to American resources and achievable American aspirations to establish a decent standard of living and a rewarding environment for all our population. As recent experience has shown, these large areas of blight, dilapidation and poverty are also breeding grounds in our cities for social disorders which are a blot on the image of American society, at home and in the world. . . .
>
> This grim picture will inevitably become grimmer unless there is a drastic realignment of national priorities. Such a realignment will require a re-thinking in depth of our Federal and local programs and activities and a massive upgrading of the Federal financial commitment for programs affecting the welfare of the vast majority of the American people. . . .
>
> The human needs of HUD programs have been given a lower priority in the budget than space and other programs. This is clear from the wholly inadequate level of all HUD programs when measured against needs affecting the welfare of the vast majority of the American people. The programs for housing and meeting our urban crisis should not be given a lower priority than the highway program, the space program, or putting a man on the moon . . .

The reality was that the total net expenditures of the Federal Government for all its programs related to community development and housing were substantially less than for each of the competing programs cited in the National Housing Conference resolution. In the Federal fiscal year 1966, the net Federal expenditures for community development and housing were $2.6 billion compared with $5.9 billion for space research and technology (of which $4.2 billion was for manned space flight) and $7.1 billion for commerce and transportation (of which $4 billion was for the highway program). The housing segment of the budget was also substantially under the agricultural segment of $3.7 billion. The same general relationship persisted in the 1967 fiscal year, with net expenditures for community development and housing actually declining slightly. (In these same two fiscal years, the net expenditures for national defense, including the war in Vietnam, were $56.9 billion and $70.1 billion, respectively.)

These disparate priorities in Federal expenditures for housing and related urban programs, on the one hand, and the other programs cited above were augmented by Congressional prejudices. In general, the legislative committees of Congress—in this field principally the Banking and Currency Committees of the two Houses—had majorities which supported progressive substantive legislation for housing and community development. But the Appropriations Committees, which control the purse strings and which are largely dominated by conservatives (especially in the House of Representatives), frequently display a cavalier attitude toward funding the substantive programs authorized by Congress.

This attitude was vividly illustrated by the appropriations actions on the rent supplement program. Enacted in August, 1965, the program received no appropriation in that calendar year and thus was inoperative. In May, 1966, annual rent supplement contracts of $12 million were finally approved by the Appropriations Committees, out of $30 million authorized by Congress. In September, 1966, $20 million was approved out of an authorization of $35 million for that fiscal year. Thus, out of $65 million in annual rent supplement contracts authorized by Congress for the first two years of this new program, the Appropriations Committees allowed only $32 million, or slightly less than half, to become operative, notwithstanding strong lobbying support from realtors, builders, and mortgage bankers in addition to liberal organizations. This represented the difference between about 72,000 and 35,000 homes for poverty families. The explanation of how the Appropriations Committees were able in this fashion to ride roughshod over the intent of Congress as a whole as expressed in enacted laws rests primarily on the Committees' power of financial life or death over myriads of projects of great political importance to individual members of Congress. Hence, members are usually reluctant to risk antagonizing the Appropriations Committees by sponsoring amendments on the floor to override the Committees' recommendations. This is particularly true in the House of Representatives.

In this case, while the Appropriations Committee reports made a bow to the overall Federal budgetary situation in justification of their drastic cuts in the rent supplement program, the underlying motivation appeared to be primarily racial and especially a desire to protect white suburban communities from incursions by housing projects to be occupied predominantly by low-income Negro families. The rent supplement law waives the usual requirement that any Federally-subsidized housing projects must be approved by the governing body of the locality in which it will be built. The intent of this provision, which survived despite extensive controversy, was to facilitate the development of housing for low-income families in suburban communities which officially would debar them. Notwithstanding this provision of Federal law, the House Appropriations Subcommittee handling HUD appropriations inserted language in the appropriations bill prohibiting the execution of a rent supplement contract for any project which had not been approved by the governing body of the locality involved. This clearly was legislation in an appropriations bill which, in theory, was prohibited under the rules of the House of Representatives. However, with the cooperation of the House Rules Committee, the House Appropriations Committee generally secured a rule for the consideration of its bills on the floor of the House which waived all points of order. So the subcommittee's gambit prevailed.

The bias of the subcommittee against the rent supplement program was further illustrated by restrictive language which it incorporated in its report. Evidently proceeding on the Calvinistic premise that the poor deserve only inadequate housing, the subcommittee declared that no dwelling covered by rent supplements could have more than one bathroom (regardless of the number of bedrooms), and that no project covered by rent supplements could have a swimming pool. In short, the subcommittee required that a housing development involving rent supplements be obsolete upon completion, in terms of contemporary housing standards. While these restrictions were not included in the appropriations bill itself, HUD interpreted them as legislative history which was equally binding as the statute itself.

Incidents such as these prompted the National Commission on Urban Problems to make the following observation, in its final report in December, 1968:

> In State legislatures and in the Congress itself there are strong indications that the old rural-city rivalry is being replaced by a rural/suburban-city rivalry. This new suburban and rural coalition until now has significantly limited the ability of urban legislators to change the nature of statutes and programs which affect the central city, and it also reinforces suburban exclusiveness, and the power blocs behind it. This reinforcement, in effect, exacts a subsidy from the central city by imprisoning low-income families and poor families in the central city and sharply limits the dispersion of low-income families to the suburbs.

In his characteristic fashion, President Johnson strove to put as good a face as possible on the sharpening dilemma of the mushrooming financial requirements of the war in Vietnam and the increasing requirements of the domestic programs of the Great Society, against the backdrop of mounting civil tension and unrest. In his state of the union message to Congress on January 10, 1967, he said:

> Our third objective is priorities—to move ahead on the priorities that we have established within the resources that are available.
>
> I wish, of course, that we could do all that should be done—and that we could do it now. But the nation has many commitments and responsibilities which make heavy demands upon our total resources. No administration would more eagerly utilize for these programs all the resources they require than the Administration that started them.
>
> So let us resolve, now to do all that we can, with what we have—knowing that it is far, far more than we have ever done before, and far, far less than our problems will ultimately require . . .

The President resorted to other techniques also to demonstrate his concern with the urban crisis. In January, 1967, he appointed the National Commission on Urban Problems under the chairmanship of former Senator Paul Douglas of Illinois, the long-time liberal who had been defeated in the 1966 elections by Charles H. Percy. The Commission was given a broad charter to investigate urban problems and to recommend improved programs, with particular emphasis on housing for low- and moderate-income families.

On March 14, 1967, President Johnson sent a special message to Congress on "urban and rural poverty." In asking for major expansion in the anti-poverty programs, he stated:

> It is difficult for most Americans to understand what it is to be desperately poor in today's affluent America. More than half our population was born after 1940. Less than half can remember the depression on the farms of the twenties, or the breadlines of the thirties . . . Yet for more than 31 million Americans, poverty is neither remote in time, nor removed in space. It is cruel and present reality. It makes choices for them. It determines their future prospects—despite our hope and belief that in America, opportunity has no bounds for any man.

Then came the eruption of racial violence in communities throughout the nation on a scale more massive than witnessed before during the troubled era of the Sixties. This was intrinsically the response of the Negro urban poor to the problems and frustrations of poverty and discrimination to which the President and his administration had been addressing themselves, even though inadequately. The most momentous and destructive of the riots in 1967 were in Newark, New Jersey, and in Detroit. However, the tensions and outbreaks were widespread throughout the country. Statistics compiled by the International City Managers' Association showed that there were 82 civil disorders in the United States in 1967, involving 17,306 arrests, 3,808 injuries, and 89 fatalities.

The political repercussions from the riots were intense and wide-ranging, and had a direct relationship to housing and other physical conditions in the ghettoes as well as to the overriding issues of poverty and discrimination. One of President Johnson's first reactions to the Detroit riot was to establish the National Advisory Commission on Civil Disorders, under the chairmanship of Otto Kerner, then Governor of Illinois, and with Mayor Lindsay of New York City as vice-chairman. In its report on March 1, 1968, after extensive investigations, the Commission observed:

> In nearly every disorder city surveyed, grievances relating to housing were important factors in the structure of Negro discontent.

The impact of the riots also penetrated the complacency of the national economic power structure. In August, 1967, an emergency session was convened in Washington to establish the Urban Coalition under the sponsorship of David Rockefeller, Henry Ford II, Andrew Heiskell of Time, Inc., and a roster of top industrial and banking executives. The organized labor establishment was also recruited in the persons of George Meany, Joseph Keenan, Walter Reuther, and others. Likewise the old-line Negro establishment was represented by Roy Wilkins of the NAACP, Whitney Young of the National Urban League, A. Phillip Randolph of the AFL-CIO, and their colleagues. The purpose was to organize concerted efforts by all these forces to relieve the problems of the ghettoes by action in Congress and in the cities.

In a related gesture, the major life insurance companies, which had largely stood on the sidelines in so far as financing new housing in the ghettoes was concerned, were persuaded by the President to enter into a joint commitment to make $1 billion in FHA-insured mortgage loans in those areas.

Writing for the National Housing Conference about that time on the growing recognition of the urban crisis impelled by the riots, I remarked:

> The inescapable fact is that this recognition did not spread through the broad public consciousness. It did not penetrate the complacency of the affluent society sufficiently to generate political action on a scale commensurate with the crisis.
>
> It is true that particularly over the past two years there were beginnings of break-throughs in the form of new programs focussed on the urban scene . . . Nevertheless, the inadequate scale of these programs and the difficulties encountered in securing Congressional funding of some of them indicated that the message of the urban crisis had not fully penetrated the veil of public and Congressional apathy.
>
> Now, in the aftermath of Newark and Detroit, there is evidence that this message is beginning to come through. . . . More profoundly, recognition of the reality and the threats of the urban crisis is finally having a major impact on powerful elements of the nation's private enterprise economy. In vivid contrast to the characteristic indifference and disclaimers of responsibility for solutions to the crucial problems of the cities, the array of private enterprise leadership which assembled for the emergency convocation of the

new urban coalition threw a hopeful light on the prospects for future support from the economic power structure of the nation.

The repercussions in Congress also were revealing. In the spring of 1967, the growing exasperation with urban problems in the House of Representatives was underlined when a majority callously laughed down a modest Administration proposal for special grants to help rid the slums and ghettoes of rats. Post Newark-Detroit, the House reversed itself and approved a comparable measure by a sizable margin. The new political pressures exerted by the Urban Coalition also were helpful in persuading the Senate to approve the full appropriation request for rent supplements and to restore a substantial portion of the House cuts in model-cities appropriations. Even though much of these increases was canceled out in conference with the House, the outcome represented some progress from the dim prospects earlier in the year.

Progressive elements in Congress also became restive with the Administration's lack of initiative in pressing for more far-reaching housing solutions in the face of the urban explosions in 1967. The official explanation for this inaction was that first priority must be given to securing adequate appropriations to fund the model cities and rent supplement programs. In the background, of course, was the overriding budgetary restraint imposed by the cost of the war in Vietnam.

Senator Charles Percy, the attractive Illinois Republican who had defeated Paul Douglas in 1966, moved part way into this vacuum by proposing a massive program of direct and indirect Federal subsidies to permit and stimulate home ownership by poor families. There were basic policy and technical defects in Senator Percy's original proposal as well as substantial overtones of political opportunism, not unrelated to his ambitions to be on the Republican Presidential ticket in 1968. These overtones were also reflected in the fact that all Republican Senators joined him as co-sponsors of his bill although many of them doubtless would have voted against the measure had it ever come to a vote on the floor of the Senate.

Nevertheless, the basic objectives of Senator Percy's proposal, which had long been advocated by the National Housing Conference and allied liberal organizations, had great merit as part of a more comprehensive housing approach and had great political appeal. Secretary Weaver of HUD overreacted to the political implications of

Senator Percy's gambit and attempted to destroy it by ridicule; Dr. Weaver's reaction also reflected his personal conviction that poverty families should not be burdened with the responsibilities of home ownership. However, the basic merit and political appeal of the Percy venture was not ignored by the Democratic leaders on housing legislation in Congress. In the Senate, John Sparkman, the astute and progressive chairman of the Banking and Currency Committee and of its Housing Subcommittee, took the initiative in calling extensive hearings on housing legislation during the summer of 1967. By skillful negotiation, he won unanimous agreement from his committee later that year on comprehensive legislative proposals which also incorporated Senator Percy's objective of assisting home ownership by lower-income families but on a workable basis.

In the House of Representatives, three Democratic members of the Housing Subcommittee jointly sponsored a bill which incorporated many of the recommendations of the National Housing Conference and its allied organizations. The bill—introduced by Representatives Thomas L. Ashley of Ohio, William S. Moorhead of Pennsylvania, and Henry S. Reuss of Wisconsin—would have substantially expanded the public housing and urban renewal authorizations and broadened the effectiveness of the programs for moderate-income families (including home ownership) by authorizing a sliding scale of subsidized interest rates, from zero to 3 percent, geared to the incomes of the occupants.

The silence of the Administration in the face of this Congressional activity in 1967 did not mean ignorance of the need for massive expansion of existing housing programs in order to help meet the urban crisis. There were studies in depth in process in HUD which were not made public under the restraints of the Vietnam budget. In fact, the annual report of HUD for the year 1967—not released until many months later—contained this significant but unfeatured paragraph:

> While housing statistics are not always precise, we know definitely that we will need, in the decade ending in 1978, somewhere around 26 million more housing units of all kinds. This involves all Americans, affluent and poor, and the demands of the market, the vagaries of the economy, and the stubborn obstacles of a financial marketplace that discriminates against housing when economic conditions

are toughest. Old practices and procedures will not suffice. New programs and readapting of old programs will be the only answer.

This, in a nutshell, was the position of the progressive forces in housing, but HUD's adherence to it was not disclosed in 1967.

What aggravated the situation was the dismal production record under the programs being operated by HUD for low- and moderate-income families which had the greatest pertinence to the urban crisis. A few examples are significant. Since President Kennedy took office in January, 1961, the actual construction starts of low-rent public housing ranged from a low of 22,400 dwellings in 1962 to a high of 33,400 units in 1967. Furthermore, in the three years 1965-67, well over half of the public housing started was especially designed units for elderly households, meaning that production for poor families with children was negligible. By the end of 1967, only 674,000 public housing units had been completed since the inception of the program in the Thirties. These units represented only 1.2 percent of the national supply of occupied housing at the end of 1967. In no year had the production of public housing even approached the annual rate of 135,000 units contemplated by the Housing Act of 1949.

The record for the program of 3-percent loans for housing for moderate-income families, while improving, was still far short of needs. In 1967, the starts of 23,660 units under this program were the highest since it was inaugurated in 1961 but still represented only 5 percent of the total starts of private multi-family housing in 1967. The rent supplement program and program for housing for moderate-income elderly households were not making any significant contribution to relieving the urban housing crisis.

There was no single simple explanation for this sorry showing: A good deal of the responsibility clearly rested with Congress and especially with its Appropriations Committees. Delays in appropriations, inadequate funding when appropriations were finally forthcoming, and arbitrary restrictions imposed by appropriations bills presented serious restraints on the development of low-rent public housing, particularly during the Fifties, and had prevented the rent supplement program from becoming an effective housing force. A sizeable share of the responsibility was in the local communities where neighborhood opposition to housing projects for poor families (meaning increasingly black families) created serious political problems in securing approval of housing sites. These prejudices were especially marked in most suburbs.

Part of the blame was on the shoulders of the Executive Office and the Bureau of the Budget, striving to hold down or cut domestic expenditures in the face of the skyrocketing costs of the war in Vietnam. The withholding of housing funds already authorized or appropriated, which has previously been referred to, was a major factor in restricting production for the low- and moderate-income markets where the needs were most acute. So was the practice of doling out funds on a quarterly basis, which effectively prevented forward planning by housing sponsors. Still another illustration was the refusal of the Administration to use the authority granted by Congress to participate up to 95 percent in construction loans for moderate-income housing even though the nonprofit sponsors of such housing were experiencing great difficulties in securing construction money from private lenders.

Finally, HUD itself was not without its share of the blame for the disappointing production record. While its staff was generally well-motivated, HUD's red tape and excessive bureaucratic procedures were the primary cause for interminable delays in approvals of urgently needed housing developments. For low-rent public housing, the typical time span between the start of planning and the actual start of construction was about three years, largely for these reasons. For moderate-income housing under the FHA's 3-percent interest rate programs, the typical time gap was 18 to 24 months. Furthermore, certain of HUD's administrative requirements seriously inhibited development in the high-cost inner-city areas. For example, by administrative fiat HUD refused to approve public housing projects whose overall costs, including land and site improvements, exceeded $20,000 per dwelling unit. This policy, primarily stemming from Secretary Weaver, made it virtually impossible to develop public housing for large families in the inner-city areas of New York, Boston, Philadelphia, Chicago, and other large or medium-sized cities, except on occasional vacant or cleared sites. As a related example, the mortgage ceilings imposed by HUD (well below those permitted by law) largely blocked the development of moderate-income housing in those same areas. Also, the financial restrictions imposed by HUD on private limited-dividend sponsors of moderate-income or rent supplement housing were substantially more stringent than those required of the sponsors of FHA-insured middle- or upper-middle-income housing. The result was that the mainstream of the private housing development industry, with a few notable exceptions, shunned the moderate-income and rent supplement field. It would have seemed that the realities of the urban crisis should have called for just the reverse of this policy.

The march of events began to force a revision in the Administration's covert policy of restriction on housing and community development. Violence continued to erupt throughout 1967. The Kerner Commission on Civil Disorders held extensive hearings during the fall of 1967 and early 1968. These hearings reemphasized the close relationship—which should have long been obvious—between discontent and violence in the ghettoes and the existence of slums, blight, and intolerable congestion. The political impact of these conclusions on the Administration was sharpened, of course, by the imminence of the 1968 Presidential elections.

President Johnson's first direct reaction was a move to improve performance under existing programs for housing and related programs and to expand their funding. He issued a directive to HUD requiring a reduction of at least 50 percent in the processing time for approval of applications from localities and private developers. And his proposed budget for the Federal fiscal year beginning July 1, 1968, recommended an increase in public housing starts to 85,000 dwellings from 51,000, an expansion in rent supplement starts to 35,000 units from 12,000, and an increase in Federally-assisted moderate-income housing to 90,000 units from 52,000. The President also ordered increased use of the "turnkey" method of producing public housing under which private developers acquired sites and constructed housing projects for sale to local authorities upon completion, thereby short-cutting much of the red tape involved in the development of conventional public housing projects.

The President's most important response, however, was in his proposal for new legislation in the form of the Housing and Urban Development Act of 1968. In a special message sent to Congress on February 22, the President finally embraced many of the short-term and long-term goals which had long been advocated by liberal organizations in order to meet the urban crisis. His message also recognized the depth of that crisis. He said, in part:

Today, America's cities are in crisis. This clear and urgent warning rises from the decay of decades—and is amplified by the harsh realities of the present . . .

We see the results dramatically in the great urban centers where millions live amid decaying buildings—with streets clogged with traffic; with air and water polluted by the soot and waste of industry which finds it much less expensive to move outside the city than to modernize within it; with crime rates rising so rapidly each year that more and more miles of city streets become unsafe after dark; with increasingly inadequate public service and a smaller and smaller tax base from which to raise the funds to improve them. . . .

With this Act, the Nation will set a far-reaching goal to meet a massive national need: the construction of 26 million new homes and apartments over the next ten years. Six million of these will finally replace the shameful substandard units of misery where more than 20 million Americans still live . . .

In specifics, the President requested legislation to establish new programs of Federal interest subsidies down to 1 percent for home ownership and rental and cooperative housing for moderate-income families, a major expansion in subsidies for low-rent public housing for the poor; a major expansion in subsidies for rent supplement housing for the poor; appropriations of $2.5 billion for the Model Cities program to be spread over a three-year period; additional appropriations of $1.9 billion for urban renewal; a new program of Federal guarantees to assure initial development financing for privately-sponsored new communities; increased appropriations for research and development in housing and for urban and metropolitan planning, and joint Federal-state-industry support for property insurance in inner-city areas. The President also called again for the enactment of fair housing legislation to prohibit discrimination in the sale, rental, or financing of all housing.

The President's special housing message was followed within a few days by the release of the final report of the National Advisory Commission on Civil Disorders. This was a strong, wide-ranging report, built on the basic premise that "our nation is moving toward two societies, one black, one white—separate and unequal" and ascribing much of the underlying responsibility for racial disorders to traditional white racism. The Kerner Commission's proposals for Federal action to meet the crisis went well beyond President Johnson's package of urban programs. The two were closest together on housing on the basis of the President's February 22 message. However, even here, the Commission proposed that 6 million housing units for low- and moderate-income families be built in five years, not ten as recommended by the President.

The President praised the Commission for its diligence; he did not endorse its report, neither did he reject it. As a portent of things to come, Richard M. Nixon, nearing the home-stretch of his campaign for the Republican nomination for President, commented that the Commission report "blames everybody for the riots except the perpetrators . . . Until we have order we can have no progress."

The Housing Subcommittees of both houses of Congress responded promptly to President Johnson's request for action on the Housing and Urban Development Act of 1968. Their response was also influenced by the political pressures generated by violence in the inner cities during a Presidential election year. In the Senate, since the Administration's proposal incorporated many of the new provisions adopted by the Banking and Currency Committee after its independent hearings and executive sessions in 1967, the bill had easy sailing. The Senate's acceptance of the bill also occurred against the background of the serious riots and destruction in Washington in the aftermath to the assassination of Dr. Martin Luther King in April. On May 28, the measure passed the Senate by the top-heavy majority of 67 to 4.

The same near-unanimity did not prevail in the House of Representatives. This was reflected in a lengthy minority report signed by nine Republican members of the Banking and Currency Committee which said, at one point:

> To date, the proposals of the Administration are only promises. The Administration's performance has not lived up to such promises in recent years and we object to any "brave" new programs, whether borrowed or dreamed, when they amount to a cruel hoax on the very section of the public which they are supposed to serve. It is time we stopped promising a brighter tomorrow when we cannot produce a streetlight today . . .

Nevertheless, the bill passed the House on July 10 by a vote of 205 to 114, with the House Republicans voting 111 to 63 in favor. After conference with the Senate, the Housing and Urban Development Act was sent to the White House and was signed by President Johnson on August 1 with great fanfare. The signing ceremony was held on the plaza of the monumental HUD building in Southwest Washington under a broiling August sun, with the Marine Band in its dress uniforms sweating out "Hail to the Chief" and the other traditional numbers, and with Vice President Hubert Humphrey basking in the reflected glory of the President's victory speech before the assembled Congressional leaders, Administration officials, and representatives of the private organizations which had supported the legislation. Senator Eugene J. McCarthy, still a competitor for the Democratic Presidential nomination, was not in evidence.

The 1968 Act was the high-water mark of Lyndon Johnson's remarkable record of success in securing important legislation on housing and community development from the Congress. The Act was, in truth, milestone legislation, not only for its substantive content but perhaps more significantly for its establishment of official national goals for the production of 26 million housing units over the coming decade, for producing 6 million dwellings for low- and moderate-income households in those ten years, and for eliminating all substandard housing during the same period. Realistically, there was the immediate question whether these fine goals would remain just that or were actually feasible of accomplishment. The overall production goal would require almost the doubling of the actual building rate in 1968 and most previous recent years and a ten-year total about equivalent to 50 percent of the aggregate national supply of occupied housing in 1968. The ten-year target of 6 million subsidized dwellings for low- and moderate-income households—or an average rate of 600,000 a year—contrasted with actual production of about 100,000 units in the fiscal year ended June 30, notwithstanding the intensive efforts of the Administration to step up that production.

The basic question was twofold: first, were the Administration and Congress prepared to give to housing the fiscal priority needed to finance this massive expansion through subsidies and allocations of private credit, and second, were the financial resources available in any event so long as the drain of Vietnam continued unabated? Notwithstanding the President's dramatic renunciation of renomina-

tion for the Presidency and his first tentative steps toward de-
escalation of the war, there was no major evidence of an improved
financing climate for housing even at the prevailing restricted scale.
Nor were there any signs of a major loosening of the restrictive attitude of the Appropriations Committees.

Nevertheless, in cold political terms, the programs and goals of
the 1968 Housing Act were good politics in a Presidential election
year, against the background of the urban crisis and violence in the
inner cities. For once, this lesson penetrated to a majority of the
Republican politicians, at least for the duration of the Presidential
campaign. This was reflected in the Congressional votes on the legislation and the large Republican majorities which supported it, even in
the House of Representatives. And, in vivid contrast to the Goldwater 1964 platform, which virtually ignored the urban crisis and
needs for housing, the 1968 Republican platform read as if pages
had been borrowed from Lyndon Johnson's messages. This was
largely the handiwork of Senator Hugh Scott of Pennsylvania, the
astute and moderate Minority Leader of the Senate, who was chairman of the platform subcommittee with jurisdiction over housing and
related matters. However, it clearly reflected a temporary consensus.
Here are some excerpts from the platform as adopted by the Republican National Convention in Miami Beach on August 6, 1968:

> We must bring about a national commitment to rebuild our urban
> and rural slum areas. . . .
> For today and tomorrow, there must be—and we pledge—a
> vigorous effort, nation-wide, to transform the blighted areas of
> cities into centers of opportunity and progress, culture and talent. . . .
> For tomorrow, new cities must be developed—and smaller cities
> with room to grow, expanded—to house and serve another 100
> million Americans by the turn of the century. . . .
> The need is critical. Millions of our people are suffering from
> expanding metropolitan blight—congestion, crime, polluted air and
> water, poor housing, inadequate educational, economic and recrea-
> tional opportunities. This continuing decay of urban centers—the
> deepening misery and limited opportunity of citizens living there—
> is intolerable in America. We promise effective, sustainable action
> enlisting new energies by the private sector and by governments
> at all levels. . . .
> Skyrocketing building costs and interest rates have crippled
> home building and threaten a housing crisis in the nation, endanger-

ing the prospect of a decent home and a suitable living environment for every family. We will vigorously implement the Republican-conceived homeownership program for lower income families and also the Republican-sponsored rent certificate program. Economic incentives will be developed to attract private industry and capital to the low-cost housing market. By reducing interest rates through responsible fiscal and monetary policy we will lower the cost of homeownership, and new technologies and programs will be developed to stimulate low-cost methods of housing rehabilitation.

In restrospect, these brave words make ironic reading in the light of what actually took place in housing in subsequent years.

The Republican platform strategy had the effect of neutralizing housing and community development as a major political issue in the 1968 Presidential campaign. The Democratic platform, of course, claimed justified credit for the major legislation which had been enacted under Kennedy and Johnson and promised future decisive progress in language at least as strong as in the Republican platform. Understandably, it was largely silent on the fiscal and budgetary restraints which had inhibited progress because of Administration policies growing out of the drain of the war in Vietnam and the ordering of priorities. However, as both major parties were in at least verbal agreement on general housing objectives, there was no major issue.

Under the march of events in late 1968, it is doubtful that housing would have been one of the decisive issues in the Presidential campaign even if there had been substantial differences in the public positions of the two parties on this matter. After the disastrous fiasco of the Democratic national convention in Chicago, the overriding issues and factors in the campaign were of a much different and more emotional character. Preeminent, of course, was the growing public disaffection with the war in Vietnam and the albatross carried by Hubert Humphrey by reason of his inability to repudiate Lyndon Johnson's primary responsibility for the escalation of the war. A related and important influence was the alienation of the young Democratic voters, especially those who had struggled valiantly for the nomination of Eugene McCarthy and whose support of Humphrey would have doubtless led to his election. Symbolic of this alienation was McCarthy's own brooding in the wings and his reluctant, half-hearted and last-minute endorsement of Hubert Humphrey. On the Republican side, the pervading issues were Richard Nixon's focus on law and order and his so-called Southern strategy of offering the carrot of relaxed desegregation policies to the Southern States. And then there was George Wallace's demagogic appeal to the hard-core Deep South and to the restless blue-collar white enclaves in the North. This was the climate which led to Richard Nixon's narrow minority victory in November. In these circumstances and in view of the demoralized Democratic party apparatus, it was remarkable that Hubert Humphrey and Edmund Muskie came as close as they did to winning the election.

The election results foretold a new ball game for housing and community development, notwithstanding the promises of the Republican platform. As if in anticipation of a Republican victory and a shift to the right on domestic social programs, the Congressional Appropriations Committees reverted to type and, one month before the election, gutted the program levels authorized by the Housing and Urban Development Act of 1968. The Senate Appropriations Sub-committee, headed by Senator Warren Magnuson of Washington, had attempted to meet most of the 1968's Act's funding levels. But, confronted by adamant House conferees, and himself involved in a close reelection campaign, Senator Magnuson capitulated. The result was that the initial funding of the new interest-subsidy programs for lower-income families was held to one-third the level authorized by the Act—$25 million each in annual subsidy contracts against $75 million. The buffeted rent supplement program received $30 million in annual subsidy contracts out of $108 million available. The Model Cities program was voted $312.5 million in supplemental grants out of $500 million authorized. Urban renewal was granted $1,065 million out of $1,750 million authorized.

In his swan-song messages to Congress in January, 1969, Lyndon Johnson, among many other things, called for full funding of the 1968 Housing Act programs and for increased appropriations in the coming Federal fiscal year. His final Economic Report to Congress also projected that the accomplishment of the objectives of the urban development programs would within three years require

Federal expenditures at an annual rate of $5.5 billion, double the amount called for in his final proposed budget.

In a cryptic farewell, President Johnson said:

> In my first budget message five years ago, I stated: "A government that is strong, a government that is solvent, a government that is compassionate is the kind of government that endures." I have sought to provide that kind of government as your President. With this budget, I leave that kind of government to my successor.

CHAPTER 12

Housing Under the Nixon Umbrella

The nation was several months into 1969 before it became possible to develop a clear reading of the position of the Nixon Administration on housing and community development. The supposition on the part of most observers was that President Nixon would be well to the right of Lyndon Johnson on these as well as on most other critical domestic issues. This supposition appeared to be supported by the so-called Southern strategy which had largely fashioned the President's narrow minority victory and by the conservative nature of his fiscal and credit policies which promised no relief for the credit crunch which was increasingly throttling the private housing industry. There also were reports of official skepticism concerning the validity of the ten-year goal of producing 26 million housing units which had been set by the 1968 Housing Act. This notwithstanding that the measure had been supported by large Republican majorities in both Houses of Congress and had in effect been endorsed by the 1968 Republican platform.

Mr. Nixon was receiving negative advice on this latter matter from a number of sources. One interesting source was Anthony Downs, an astute Chicago real estate analyst, who had been appointed by President Johnson to the National Commission on Urban Problems. Downs repudiated the Johnson Administration's housing goals as unrealistic and advised the President-elect to ignore them, seeking instead for "more realistic and more flexible" targets which would "reinforce the credibility of public authorities by producing results consistent with their official promises."

There were other political forces which led President Nixon to proceed cautiously on any overt repudiation of important domestic programs like housing. The most pervasive factor was that he was the first President in the twentieth century to face an opposition Congress from the outset of his first term. While the Republicans had gained seven seats in the Senate, the Democrats continued to control by a majority of 57 to 43. And the net Republican gain in the House of Representatives was only three seats, with the party division being 242 Democrats and 190 Republicans.

Another important influence was the strong support of the urban programs enacted durng the Kennedy-Johnson era on the part of the cities, labor, and the principal Negro organizations. While President Nixon had lost a majority of the votes in each of these segments in the 1968 election, the political balance in the nation was too delicate to justify dismissing this influence arbitrarily.

The nature of President Nixon's top appointments reflected a cautious balance. The strongest political figure was John N. Mitchell, the Attorney General, who had managed the President's campaign for the nomination and for the election. Mitchell was considered the author of the Southern strategy and the arranger of Spiro Agnew's nomination for Vice President as the minimum acceptable candidate to Senator Strom Thurmond and other Southern Republican leaders. Mitchell was also the principal architect of the new Administration's "law and order" policies. On the other hand, Mitchell had made his considerable fortune as bond counsel to municipalities and to local housing and renewal agencies. He therefore had had a major personal stake in urban programs. In fact, he had for a number of years been on the board of directors of the National Housing Conference and had supported the Conference's legislative efforts on behalf of housing and community development.

A key policy appointment was that of Arthur F. Burns as councillor to the President on the domestic economy. Dr. Burns had for three years been chairman of the Council of Economic Advisers in the first Eisenhower Administration and was considered a conservative but not a reactionary on fiscal and economic matters. From the standpoint of attitudes on housing and community development, there appeared to be significance in Dr. Burns's selection as his top assistant of Martin Anderson who in 1963 had authored *The Federal Bulldozer,* a demagogic attack on urban renewal, and who had been director of research for the Nixon Presidential campaign. The conservative bent of the Nixon appointments in the economic sphere was further evidenced by his selections of Paul N. McCracken, professor of economics at the University of Michigan, as chairman of the Council of Economic Advisers; David Kennedy, chairman and chief executive officer of Continental-Illinois Bank and Trust Company of Chicago, as Secretary of the Treasury; and Robert Mayo, a vice-president of Continental-Illinois, as Director of the Budget. McCracken had been a member of the Council of Economic Advisers during the latter years of the Eisenhower regime and thus was well-versed in restrictive economic policies.

This conservative flavor was partially offset by the President's surprise appointment of Daniel Patrick Moynihan as his Assistant for Urban Affairs. Moynihan, a somewhat flamboyant intellectual, had been Assistant Secretary of Labor in the Kennedy Administration and subsequently the director of the Harvard-MIT Joint Center for Urban Studies. He had angered the civil rights movement and the Negro organizations by his book attributing the social problems of the American Negro population primarily to broken families and the consequent matriarchal structure of Negro society. On the other hand, he saw the role of the Federal Government as central in dealing with the urban crisis and was an advocate of family subsistence allowances, government-guaranteed employment, and government-financed rebuilding of riot-torn areas.

President Nixon's selection for the Cabinet post most directly related to housing and community development—the Secretary of HUD—was definitely middle of the road. George Romney was, of course, the successful automobile manufacturer who had revitalized American Motors. He was also the successful Republican politician who had been a three-time Governor of Michigan, breaking the hold of Mennen ("Soapy") Williams and the Michigan Democratic organization. He was energetic, persuasive, and handsome. He was also inclined to shoot from the hip verbally, even though it was probably an oversimplification to say that he had sacrificed whatever chance he had for the 1968 Republican nomination by his famous blooper that he had been "brainwashed" by the American military apparatus during a visit to Vietnam. He was considered a moderate Republican and, after his withdrawal from the Presidential campaign, was aligned with Governor Nelson Rockefeller's ineffective bid for the Republican nomination.

Romney had been exposed to the urban crisis during his tour of office as Governor of Michigan and especially by the massive Detroit riots in 1967. After that event he had made a twenty-day inspection trip of slum areas throughout the country to sharpen his knowledge of those conditions and at the same time help his then Presidential ambitions. In the past, he had frequently called for a reordering of Federal budget priorities, with greater emphasis on urban problems and less on such things as highway beautification and space exploration. No doubt reflecting in part his Mormon background, he was also a staunch believer in the virtues of voluntary rather than governmental approaches to problem solving. Shortly after his nomination as Secretary of HUD, Romney was quoted by the *Wall Street Journal* as saying:

> I believe that the people of this country would respond in overwhelming numbers if their leaders asked them to give a "tithe of time" in constructive volunteer effort. Four hours—10 percent of a 40-hour week—spent in well-conceived volunteer effort at the local level could reshape America faster than Federal programs ever will.

In his opening gambits as Secretary of Housing and Urban Development, George Romney expressed skepticism about the feasibility of the housing goals set by the 1968 Housing Act and promised a major effort to apply industrial factory techniques to the production of housing. This was later officially christened "Operation Breakthrough." He also quickly tangled with the chiefs of the AFL-CIO on the allegedly obstructionist role played by organized labor in opposing the introduction of new techniques in the housing field.

The character of the other top appointments in HUD indicated that the Nixon Administration planned to follow a middle road in this field. For his Under Secretary, Romney selected Richard Van Dusen, a competent executive who had been a close associate during his years as Governor of Michigan. Since, for obvious reasons, the Nixon Administration was light on top Negro administrators, two of the key HUD positions at the Assistant Secretary level were given to blacks. Samuel Jackson was named to the new post of General

Assistant Secretary, which made him the third ranking HUD official, and was also assigned the responsibility for directing HUD's activities in metropolitan planning and development. Samuel Simmons was appointed Assistant Secretary for Fair Housing to administer the Fair Housing Act of 1968.

For the important post of Assistant Secretary for Renewal and Housing Assistance, the White House selected Lawrence Cox who for more than twenty years had been the executive director of the highly successful urban renewal and public housing program in Norfolk, Virginia. Cox had a national reputation in these fields and was highly regarded by the professionals. He also was a long-time business and personal friend of Attorney General Mitchell; it was generally assumed that Mitchell was primarily responsible for his selection. Floyd Hyde, the progressive Republican mayor of Fresno, California, was named the Assistant Secretary to administer the controversial Model Cities program. As Mayor, Hyde had strongly supported the Model Cities and urban renewal programs in Fresno. He also had been active and well-regarded in the U.S. Conference of Mayors and the National League of Cities, which generally were weak spots for the Nixon Administration. After extended delays occasioned by difficulties in finding a suitable candidate who would be free of conflicts of interest, Eugene Gulledge, a successful North Carolina builder and the current president of the National Association of Home Builders, was selected as Assistant Secretary for Mortgage Credit and FHA Commissioner. Aside from his experience and ability, Gulledge's appointment was interpreted as a gesture to placate the home builders; predominantly Republican in politics, the builders were bitterly disillusioned by the near-disastrous slump in private residential construction brought on by the fiscal and monetary policies of the Administration and the Federal Reserve Board.

The new General Counsel of HUD was strictly a White House selection. Sherman Unger was a youngish, shrewd, and somewhat brash attorney from Cincinnati with no experience in housing law but with a strong record of support for President Nixon in the 1968 campaign and previously. Unger had no hesitancy in announcing that he was the President's man in HUD with the assignment to keep HUD on a straight path in accordance with White House policies. At a later date, Harold Finger, who had held top posts with NASA for many years, was appointed Assistant Secretary for Research and Technology with particular reference to Operation Breakthrough.

The new top team in HUD was generally competent and well motivated. The question was where HUD could go, given the cross-currents within the Nixon Administration and the budgetary stringencies imposed by the continuing war in Vietnam.

The first test of the new Administration's actual position on the HUD program came with its appropriations requests, both for the remainder of the 1969 Federal fiscal year and for its revisions in the proposed budget for the coming fiscal year which had been bequeathed it by Lyndon Johnson. Of particular moment was its stance on the new interest subsidy housing program for moderate-income families, on urban renewal, on public housing, and on the Model Cities program.

On these issues, the Administration's position was mixed. For the interest-subsidy programs, the Administration requested full funding of the amounts authorized by the 1968 Housing Act, both to restore the two-thirds cut for the first year imposed by the Appropriations Committees in the fall of 1968 and for the larger sums authorized for the second year. (The Appropriations Committees in 1970 approved considerably less than these requests, thereby displaying a cool bipartisan attitude in their propensity to cut appropriations for housing authorized by their colleagues in Congress.) The appropriation for public housing subsidies survived intact, mainly because public housing was the one remaining HUD program where the legislative authorization was in the form of contract authority which Congress was obligated to honor through subsequent appropriations. However, the Administration refused to request appropriations for the special grants authorized by the 1968 Act for social and counseling services for public housing tenants. (The lack of such service had long been a prime point of criticism of the public housing program.)

In the case of urban renewal, the Administration rode with an inadequate appropriations request of $1 billion for the fiscal year beginning July 1, 1969, which was $687.5 million less than the outstanding authorizations. It did, however, point out that its request was only 6 percent below the urban renewal appropriations for the preceding fiscal year, enacted under the Johnson Administration. The inadequacy of the request was clearly shown by HUD's admission that it held $2.1 billion in unfunded renewal applications from cities and that new applications were being received at a monthly rate of about $200 million.

With the Model Cities program, there had been a serious internal dispute about its standing within the Nixon Administration's scheme of things. Along with the equally controversial anti-poverty program, Model Cities carried the clear hallmark of Lyndon Johnson's Great Society and there was an inclination on the part of some at the White House and at HUD to scrap it. The *Washington Post* reported that the program was preserved only after an hour-long appeal by Assistant Secretary Floyd Hyde before the President's Urban Affairs Council. The outcome was a Presidential request for continued funding of the program in the 1970 fiscal year but at a reduced level of $675 million as against $750 million recommended by President Johnson.

A second test of the Administration's actual stance on housing and community development was whether it would reconcile its position with the ten-year housing goals established by the 1968 Act or would in effect repudiate those goals as unfeasible. George Romney was compelled to give some answers when he was called to testify on this specific question in May, 1969, before the Housing Subcommittee of the House Banking and Currency Committee. His gingerly and somewhat grudging acceptance of the goals was presented in these words:

> In 1949, the Congress declared "the goal of a decent home and a suitable living environment for every American family." Last year, the Congress sought to quantify this goal by asserting that it can be substantially achieved within the next decade by the construction or rehabilitation of twenty-six million housing units, six million of these for low and moderate income families.
>
> I accept these goals: not as an engineer's measure, but as a reasonable expression of our national need by a knowledgeable and humane Congress which sought to give some definite expression to the ends we seek in housing.
>
> In accepting these goals, however, I am not prepared to endorse production schedules forecast by others in the past. Nor am I prepared to make predictions of my own.

As an ironic footnote to this less than enthusiastic statement, HUD released a statement a few months later by its top expert on economic and market analysis declaring that "estimates of 26 million new housing units as the national requirement in the next decade are proving sound, and may even be a little conservative."

The third test of the Nixon Administration's true direction in housing was to be what, if anything, it would do to relieve the growing recession in private residential construction. In truth, the credit and monetary actions taken by the Nixon Administration, in conjunction with the Federal Reserve Board, were a repeat of the actions during 1966 and 1967 under the Johnson Administration except that the 1969 actions resulted in much higher rates of mortgage interest. Again, the main weight of the tight money policy fell on the private housing industry.

In its first major action on housing, the Administration in January exercised its authority to increase the interest rate of FHA-insured mortgages and GI loans to 7½ percent. This was supposed to reduce the discounts on such loans, i.e., the difference between the principal amount of the loan and the amount which lenders would actually advance on the loan. Instead, within a few weeks discounts had returned close to their previous levels notwithstanding the substantially higher rates of interest. While the absolute shortage of mortgage funds was not as severe as in 1966, the exorbitant cost of mortgage money was pricing an increasing proportion of potential buyers out of the market. As a result, the rate of private home building, already at least one-third less than the rate contemplated by the 1968 Housing Act, declined by 25 percent between January and November 1969.

All this was supposed to be anti-inflationary even though paradoxically the rise in the cost of mortgage money and the decrease in production were prime causes of the inflation in the housing element of the cost of living. This paradox was recognized by Secretary Romney in his testimony before the Housing Subcommittee, previously referred to. He said:

> In housing, as a matter of fact, the inflationary cycle is especially vicious. Inflation raises costs of new housing. It prices would-be home owners out of the market. It cuts builders' production. Such lowered production comes at a time when we already have a housing shortage in many areas with abnormally low vacancy rates. This shortage of supply further inflates the market prices of what is already available for sale or for rent. So inflation engenders inflation. And costs and prices rise again. Furthermore, inflation

makes mortgages, which are long-term fixed-income securities, unattractive to investors. Thus it not only forces interest rates up, but it also dries up the supply of money for housing.

But the only solutions offered by Secretary Romney for this dismal set of problems were, in effect, to grin and bear it until such time as the Nixon Administration's restrictive budgetary and fiscal policies checked the inflationary trend:

> If the Administration and Congress press firmly ahead on controlling inflation, and if Congress concurs in the repeal of the 7 percent investment tax credit, I think we can look forward quite hopefully to some increase in the flow of funds into the mortgage market and a gradual easing of what we all recognize are onerously high rates for these funds.

There were positive steps which the Nixon Administration could have taken in 1969 to expand the flow of funds into housing, if it had so desired. One was to make aggressive use of the more than $1 billion in special assistance mortgage purchase funds which had been made available by Congress to support housing production under the new interest subsidy and rent supplement programs and other housing programs aimed at the moderate and middle-income housing markets. In conjunction with the large resources of the Federal National Mortgage Association (which had become a quasi-private institution) such action would have generated substantial funds in the segments of the housing market where the needs were most acute. The technique would have been for the General National Mortgage Association, using special assistance funds, to purchase such mortgages at par and subsequently sell them to FNMA at whatever the market rates were, absorbing any discounts out of its own funds. In this manner, GNMA could have turned over its $1 billion of special assistance money rapidly and could have generated a much greater volume of par mortgage financing, at little cost to the Federal Treasury. But Sherman Unger ruled that HUD lacked the legal authority to undertake this procedure, even though the Congressional authors of the 1968 Housing Act were of a contrary opinion.

Another important step which the Nixon Administration could have taken in 1969 was to place in operation a provision of the 1968 Act authorizing FNMA to sell bond-type securities backed by FHA-insured or VA-guaranteed mortgages and further fully guaranteed as to principle and interest by GNMA. The prime purpose of this provision was to tap the vast and growing financial resources of pension funds and private trusts. In most instances, the institutions administering these funds were uninterested in making direct mortgage investments even where the mortgages were fully insured or guranteed by the Federal Government. The new provision would offer these institutions a coupon-clipping type of obligation, comparable to the highest-grade corporation bonds, and with the further security of a double Federal guarantee. Hopefully, this would lead to a much larger, even if indirect, participation by these institutions in housing finance and thereby lessen the almost total reliance of the housing industry on savings institutions, subject as they were to the vagaries of Federal credit policies. But the Treasury Department balked and successfully blocked the initiation of the new provision on the argument that the new guaranteed securities would be competitive in the private bond market with direct Treasury obligations.

Still another step which the Nixon Administration could have taken would have been to apply pressure on the Federal Reserve Board, publicly and privately, to institute measures increasing the flow of funds into the savings institutions responsible for most housing finance. This, the Administration did not do. It appeared clear that the Administration generally saw eye-to-eye with the Federal Reserve Board on the policies which threw the brunt of the credit squeeze on the sources of residential mortgages rather than on the market for new corporation security issues.

It was also clear that these matters of credit policies and priorities were largely beyond the control of Secretary Romney. It was likewise clear that his primary personal interests were wrapped up in Operation Breakthrough. This was entirely understandable in view of his successful manufacturing background and his interest in production. Aside from the Madison Avenue PR connotations of its title, the primary objective of Operation Breakthrough, namely to introduce the techniques of factory assembly-line manufacturing into the production of housing, was praiseworthy. A related important objective was to attract large established industrial concerns into the factory production of housing, in addition to stimulating the establishment or expansion of smaller firms. In view of the essentiality of achieving much greater housing production capacity, this was a fruitful goal, if it could be achieved.

George Romney described the program as follows:

> Breakthrough is concerned with innovative technology in housing production, but it is really much more than that. What we are trying to do is focus not only technical ingenuity but the whole complex of modern industrial management on each stage of the problem: the identification of markets; the identification and more effective use of available land; the design of the product and its environmental situation; its production; and its financing and distribution to the consumer.

There were numerous obstacles confronting Operation Breakthrough. First, it had yet to be conclusively demonstrated that there were actual savings in costs of the physical dwelling from the use of factory-produced modules or panels as compared with the most efficient on-site conventional building methods. It did appear definite, however, that there were sizable savings in erection time from the use of factory-made components. Again, there was only $15 million available in Federal research and development funds for the initial participants in the program, a drop in the bucket as compared with the vast sums available for military or space programs.

Of at least equal significance was the fact that factory-produced housing would face the same inflated land costs and the same inflated financing costs which were plaguing the conventional home building industry. The average market price of lots for new FHA-insured single-family homes had quadrupled between 1950 and 1968. There had also been a sharp rise in the cost of construction money to the builder and of mortgage money to the home buyer which had risen by about one-third within a few years. There was nothing in the Operation Breakthrough formula which by itself could cope with these basic economic factors.

Other problems confronting the program included outmoded building codes which, in some localities, would bar the use of factory-built modules or components as well as restrictive zoning regulations which in many suburban communities were designed to exclude housing for low- or moderate-income families. On these problems, the HUD tactic was to seek the cooperation of state and local governments in removing such barriers, with the implied threat of seeking legislative solutions if cooperation was not forthcoming. There was also the question of whether the AFL Building Trades unions would cooperate with the erection of factory-built housing or might strike such projects. Traditionally, the building trades unions had opposed factory-produced housing for obvious reasons of the job security of their members. However, there were an increasing number of instances in which unions had entered into contracts with industrial housing producers, covering both the factory workers and on-site labor for erection and site preparation.

In any case, Operation Breakthrough did not offer any immediate relief to the housing crisis. Secretary Romney conceded that Operation Breakthrough, if successful, could not be expected to add materially to volume housing production for at least two years. In the meantime, where were the solutions for the critical housing problems facing the nation, and especially the cities?

The Nixon Administration had no new solutions to offer nor, as pointed out previously, was it willing to make use of some partial solutions already available in relieving the credit stringency for housing. The Administration did propose certain amendments to the housing statutes which were generally technical in character, with two exceptions. These exceptions were indicative of a negative attitude toward the housing crisis. The first, rather than proposing increased Federal support to relieve the mortgage crisis, requested that Congress rescind the $500-million additional mortgage-purchase authority which it had provided in the 1968 Act. The second recommended that the future volume of appropriations for the basic housing and urban development programs not be predicated on specific Congressional authorizations but simply on "such sums as may be necessary." This would have turned over the determination of future program levels to the tender mercies of the Bureau of the Budget and the Congressional Appropriations Committees. As I commented in testimony before the Housing Subcommittees of the two Houses: "We believe such language would liquidate the basic responsibility of the legislative committees of the Congress to determine program goals, standards and desirable volumes."

It quickly became crystal-clear that the legislative committees of Congress had no intention of presiding over the liquidation of their responsibilities. Both Housing Subcommittees conducted hearings in July, 1969; their scope ran well beyond the limited and negative amendments proposed by the Administration. There was particular focus on the need for increased funding of the basic programs and for measures to increase the flow of mortgage credit.

The legislation which resulted from these hearings was remarkable for its scope (unsolicited by the Administration) and for its bipartisan support. The Republican legislators, it appeared, had also been hearing from home on the housing recession. In the Senate, the legislation passed without objection. In the House, it was approved 35 to 0 in the Banking and Currency Committee and passed on the floor of the House by the amazing vote of 339 to 9.

While the Housing and Urban Development Act of 1969 did not strike any important new ground, it greatly enlarged the funds available or authorized for existing programs. Rather than rescind the $500-million special mortgage-purchase authority, as requested by the Administration, it increased that authority by $1.5 billion. To overcome HUD's legal objections, the law specifically authorized GNMA to purchase mortgages at par with special assistance funds and resell them to FNMA or others at whatever the market rate was. Authorizations for interest subsidies on homes and rental properties for lower-income families were increased by $25 million each and both programs were extended through the fiscal year beginning July 1, 1971, at annual rates of $170 million. The urban renewal authorization was increased by $1.7 billion effective July 1, 1970. There was an increase of $75 million in annual subsidies for low-rent public housing over and above $150 million already available for the year. Senator Edward W. Brooke of Massachusetts, a liberal Republican and the only Negro in the Senate, successfully sponsored an amendment limiting rents in public housing projects to a maximum of 25 percent of annual family incomes and providing additional subsidies to accomplish this objective. Under the pressures of rising maintenance and operating costs, many local housing authorities had had to raise their minimum rents to levels representing substantially more than 25 percent of the incomes of the poorer families. Again, whereas the Administration proposed to phase out the program of direct 3-percent Federal loans for housing for moderate-income elderly households, the 1969 Act voted an additional authorization of $150 million for this program and the committee reports warned HUD against terminating it.

The committee reports of both Houses also strongly criticized, in substantially identical language, the Administration's failure to put into operation the authority voted in the 1968 Act for FNMA to sell in the private market bond-type securities guaranteed by GMNA. The Senate report stated:

> The committee has been quite disturbed over the long delay, over one year, in the implementation of this very promising program to attract new sources of investment in the mortgage market. Events over the past year leading to a tightening of mortgage credit have demonstrated all too vividly the need for such additional methods to attract investment in mortgages. . . .
>
> It has been reported to the committee that one barrier to implementation has been and still is the reluctance of the Treasury Deparment to permit a number of issuers to come to the market with Federally guaranteed securities. Treasury is reportedly doubtful of the propriety of using the full faith and credit of the United States in this manner. It is also reluctant because of possible competition of such fully guaranteed securities with its own borrowings. The committee feels that the Congress, not the Treasury, should decide such matters of national policy; Congress in this case has made such a decision. We call upon the Administration to remove this extralegal roadblock to the program so that, in these most trying times, the housing market may have access to the flow of capital this program would allow.

While Congress was thus asserting its independent initiative in the Housing and Urban Development Act of 1969, there were other important cross-currents. George Romney, reacting to pressures from the urban areas and also expressing his long-held views, had been making no secret of his hopes and plans for obtaining a higher priority for HUD programs once the budgetary drain of the war in Vietnam was eased. (For example, in a statement extolling the first moon landing, Romney declared that the nation's next top priority should be meeting the urban housing crisis.)

But this was not the view of Daniel Patrick Moynihan, the President's urban affairs adviser, or of the President's Council of Economic Advisers. After a meeting of the President's Urban Affairs Council late in August, 1969, Moynihan dismissed a previous Treasury estimate that $22.9 billion in extra Federal funds would be available for spending on domestic programs within eighteen months after the end of the war in Vietnam. Referring to an analysis of this estimate made by the Council of Economic Advisers, Moynihan declared:

"Clearly, the conclusion of the analysis is that the so-called peace an growth 'dividends' policy forecast is not realistic." He went on t say that it "just isn't going to happen that the Federal governmen will suddenly be able to pour billions more into urban relief an other domestic priorities" and that in a post-Vietnam situation th military budget could well be higher rather than lower than it ha been.

Diametrically opposed to this conclusion was the implication of significant report by the National Committee on Urban Growt Policy. This was a bipartisan group headed by former Representativ Albert Rains and made up of Congressional leaders, the heads of th municipal and county government organizations and co-sponsored b Urban America. The conclusions of this report were that massive bu well-planned programs of urban growth were required to meet th physical crisis of the cities, to accommodate the anticipated populatio growth of 100 million by the end of the century, to overcom suburban sprawl, and to reverse the collapse of rural communities All of this spelt very large Federal expenditures.

In the midst of the drastically worsening conditions in the privat housing industry, a report was issued in September, 1969, by the Com mission on Mortgage Interest Rates. The commission was a bipartisa group authorized by Congress in 1968 and consisting of ten member of Congress and five representatives of the public, appointed b President Johnson. The commission's report stated bluntly that "th Federal Government should recognize more fully that it bears the major responsibility for assuring that national housing goals are realized—and act accordingly." The commission recommended, among other things, that legislation be enacted channeling a portion of Social Security reserves and of other Federal trust funds into housing obligations fully guaranteed by the Federal Government and further that the Federal Reserve Board take steps to expand the flow of credit to mortgage lending institutions specifically for housing finance purposes. These were measures which were being strongly advocated by the National Housing Conference and the National Association of Home Builders, among other organizations with a direct stake in housing.

At hearings before the Senate Banking and Currency Committee on the report, the response of Administration spokesmen was to repeat a refrain which could be paraphrased as: "We deplore the recession in housing production but we strongly oppose any positive steps to overcome it." Here are some examples:

> *Undersecretary of the Treasury Paul Volcker:* "A second recommendation of the Commission which should be of concern to all of us is that the Federal trust funds be invested, at least in part, in special housing bonds. This procedure would simply be a subterfuge for, and have the same net effect of, a direct Congressional appropriation to purchase the bonds . . . In expressing the Treasury's concern over these particular proposals, I want also to emphasize our recognition of the large challenge before us in moving toward our housing goals."
>
> *Senator Proxmire of Wisconsin* (questioning William McChesney Martin, chairman of the Federal Reserve Board, on financing to meet national housing goals): "I am afraid that certainly at least this 20 million area is going to have an impossible task, no matter how determined Congress is, if the Federal Reserve and the Treasury insist on following policies which may have a marginal benefit to housing here and there, but which by and large their main thrust is to depress it."
>
> *Mr. Martin:* "As long as we are going to overspend and not have any budgetary surplus, there will be some things that will have to be reduced, you are going to have to take it away from somebody else. You are going to take it away from small business, or some other activity."

During the fall of 1969, the main political emphasis of the Nixon Administration in Congress was not on the relief of domestic problems but rather was to defeat the Senate attempt to block the ABM missile program, where the Administration prevailed by a single vote, and to secure Senate confirmation of Judge Clement Haynsworth as a Justice of the Supreme Court, where the Administration was decisively defeated. But the domestic problems such as housing would not go away.

As one example, on November 20, 1969, Representative Carl Albert of Oklahoma, the Democratic Majority Leader, told the House:

> The economic policies of the Administration, reflected in housing construction statistics, are placing this country in dire peril of recession. Current tight money policies are a carbon copy of those pursued in 1957 under Secretary of the Treasury George Humphrey. Then, as now, we experienced a sharp decline in housing

construction. The economic ill health foisted on the housing industry by a Republican Administration then fed back into the general economy and resulted in the 1958 recession, our sharpest post World War II economic setback.

The disillusion with the state of domestic affairs and the Administration's role or lack of role was dramatically illustrated by a speech on December 9, 1969, before the National Press Club by John W. Gardner, the chairman of the Urban Coalition Action Council. Gardner, who had been Secretary of Health, Education and Welfare during part of the Johnson Administration, was a progressive Republican; previously during the Nixon Administration, he had avoided public criticism of its policies and had tried to influence those policies from within working from the prestigious private enterprise sponsorship of the Urban Coalition. Before the Press Club, however, he spoke scathingly:

> With a few notable exceptions, there has been a failure of leadership . . . We have had failures of leadership before. But rarely have we had the widespread distrust of our own institutions that we see today. And that distrust is not limited to radicals. Ask shopkeepers, housewives, young executives or insurance salesmen what concerns them. If you travel around the country as I do more or less continuously, you will find that there is a deep and pervasive feeling among all segments of the populace that "things aren't working"——and Washington is given a major share of the blame. When the great majority of Americans share that uneasiness, when a growing number are losing all confidence in our society, when the problems themselves are terrifyingly real, then it is immoral for our national leaders—in the Congress and the Executive Branch—to temporize. It is indecent for them to let us imagine that we can solve our problems without money or that we cannot afford to tackle them. It is criminal for either Republicans or Democrats to put politics before the nation's future. . . .
>
> We are not—and should not become—blind followers of the leader. But only the President's clearly-expressed concern and clearly-stated priorities can mobilize the Federal apparatus, encourage Congress to shake off its lethargy, and enable leaders in other sectors of American life to move decisively.
>
> On the domestic front the President must say more explicitly—and with greater urgency—what he conceives to be an appropriate strategy for dealing with the dilemmas of the cities, with equality of opportunity, with the environment and with other problems that are wracking the nation.

Not only must he propose social programs adequate to our need, but when the legislation goes to Congress he must fight as hard for it as he fought for the ABM and Judge Haynsworth . . .

For housing and community development, the Administration's response to the growing pressures was a mixture of verbal sympathy and negative action. On the latter score, the Administration made use of its new authority by raising the maximum interest rate on FHA-insured mortgages and GI home loans to 8½ percent; once again this action failed to expand the flow of credit into housing and had the effect of increasing further the inflation in housing costs and of pricing additional households out of the housing market. Likewise, notwithstanding a HUD projection that the present and anticipated demand for urban renewal funds in 1970 would be $3.8 billion, the Administration persisted in holding its appropriation request to $1 billion.

From the standpoint of verbal sympathy for the plight of housing, the Administration became effusive. At a press conference on January 8, George Romney conceded that "the over-all housing shortage has greatly increased and is the worst since World War II." He added: "Success in programs needed to meet national housing needs can be the principal stimulant of future sound economic growth when inflation has been curbed. Such success also can provide the new jobs needed when our involvement in Vietnam is over. Our biggest under-developed domestic market is housing."

Later in January, Secretary Romney encountered the embittered home builders at their annual convention in Houston. The climate was typified by the statement of Louis R. Barba, the national president of the builders' association: "There is a total lack of concern for housing in Washington today. In the absence of any policy changes at the Federal level, the outlook is dismal and getting worse."

In response, Romney could only concede that conditions were bad and were continuing to deteriorate: "The present housing shortage is grave, and the immediate outlook is not encouraging. . . . Housing is bearing far more than its share of the burden of fighting inflation." But his proffered solution was in essence a statement of resolution that housing must receive a higher national priority and that housing production must be increased.

With private residential construction dropping in January, 1970, to an annual rate of little more than 1 million dwellings, a decrease of one-third from 1968, President Nixon likewise felt impelled to issue verbal reassurances. Describing housing as in "a crisis situation," the President maintained that his Administration "will take every possible step to solve this most consistent problem with the over-riding need to contain inflation." He went on to say: "Some needed Federal programs simply will have to be postponed so that we live within our means. The need to regain early control over inflation is paramount and voluntary steps to restrain unnecessary spending can play a vital role. The decline in housing production must and will be stopped. The private sector and all levels of government must take the steps necessary to assure that the nation's housing needs are met."

President Nixon's budget message to Congress on February 2 and the accompanying Economic Report of the President were strangely silent on the "crisis" in the housing industry and on the impact of the growing housing shortage. The budget did request full appropriations for interest subsidies for housing for lower-income families. It also acceded finally to the urgent Congressional requests for the use of available governmental guarantees to provide for the mortgage financing of interest-subsidized housing and to begin to tap new capital sources for residential construction. But it did not signal any decisive reordering of national financial priorities in order to meet national housing goals. Furthermore, in the critical area of urban renewal, the budget request was kept at $1 billion, notwithstanding authorization already voted by Congress for an additional $1.3 billion and notwithstanding a projection by George Romney that total demand for urban renewal funds from the more than 1,000 communities participating in the program would total about $3.8 billion in 1970.

The political cross-currents on the responsibility for the housing and urban crisis ran strongly during the winter and spring of 1970. In the absence of any positive action by the Nixon Administration, Congress again seized the initiative and introduced proposed emergency legislation to force a sharp expansion of funds into residential financing from sources such as the Federal Reserve Board, governmental trust funds, and pension funds. In the House of Representatives, the leadership in this move was taken by Chairman Wright Patman of the Banking and Currency Committee and by Mrs.

Leonor Kretzer Sullivan, a long-time Representative from St. Louis. The House Committee held hearings through February. The first witness was Mayor John V. Lindsay of New York City who declared that the Administration's tight money policies were threatening the right of every American to a "decent home in a suitable living environment" and "have bled New York of the resources to build" needed housing. Mayor Lindsay acknowledged that "it is important to fight inflation." It should be fought, he continued, "by cutting military waste, slowing down our space program, reducing environmentally dangerous highway building, and, if necessary by careful controls in the wage and price area."

Mayor Joseph L. Alioto of San Francisco told the Committee: "The housing crisis is almost without hope of improvement. This is what people are beginning to think."

Louis R. Barba, president of the National Association of Home Builders, testified:

> I cannot overemphasize my alarm and frustration with the current situation. It is appalling to note that the housing and mortgage finance situation continues to deteriorate and the industry drifts towards irreparable damage even though the Congress has responded to the current crisis with significant legislation. . . . It is almost beyond belief that we can allow an industry that has proven to be a great national resource aimed at solving a basic human need for the country to be crippled so seriously.

In my testimony before that Senate Committee on behalf of the National Housing Conference, I remarked:

> It is ironic and tragic to see the housing economy once again become the football of fiscal and credit policies. . . . It is clear that the national policies of severe credit restraint have borne much more heavily on the housing industry than on any other major segment of the American economy. This means that millions of American families in need of housing are being denied the opportunity to fulfill those needs and, under current policy, have little prospect for a better situation in the future. . . . Yet most of the substantive proposals for relief of this fiscal crisis and for providing the priority position in the allocation of financial resources necessary to achieve the established housing goals for the nation are being rejected out of hand as inflationary by the fiscal authorities

of the Federal Government, particularly the Federal Reserve Board, the Treasury Department, the Bureau of the Budget and the Council of Economic Advisors.

This was the tenor of most of the extensive testimony on the housing credit emergency before the Senate and House Committees in February and early March, 1970. Secretary George Romney was as blunt as any in describing the severity of the crisis even though inhibited by Administration policies in prescribing solutions. In his appearance before the Senate Committee, Romney pointed out that the median sales price of a new home had increased to $27,000 and estimated that an annual income of close to $14,000 was necessary to afford to purchase and carry a new home at this price. He said: "Fewer than one family in five has this high an income. By contrast, the median-priced home five years ago could have been afforded by two families in five." He added:

> I want to emphasize that this rising cost of housing cannot and should not be pinned on any single element. Costs of money, land, construction, labor, materials, taxes, insurance maintenance and repair are all up—and significantly. The rising cost of money has hurt most however. Its cost—both for construction and permanent financing—has risen by an exorbitant and unwarranted 15-25 percent during the past year to the highest levels in a century.

Still, the fiscal authorities of the Federal Government stood fast against granting a financial priority to housing sufficient to solve the crisis. Dr. Arthur F. Burns, who had become chairman of the Federal Reserve Board, told the House Banking and Currency Committee: "We do not favor tapping Federal Reserve Credit for the support of a restructuring of credit flows, no matter how worthwhile the immediate objective may be. Special purpose lending by the Federal Reserve for housing would be likely to lead to demands for other types of special lending as well." And Paul McCracken, the chairman of the Council of Economic Advisers, said to the same body: "The demand for additional housing is to some extent postponable. . . . What is required is not only to put more money into housing but also to take some money out of something else." The remarks by Dr. Burns and Dr. McCracken were prefaced and followed by bows to the urgency of housing needs, but their message remained clear.

The Nixon Administration had taken a few steps to improve the flow of funds for private housing. Under Congressional pressure, it was finally moving to the sale of Federally-guaranteed bonds backed by FHA-insured mortgages and GI loans. The Administration also recommended legislation authorizing a $250-million subsidy to the Federal Home Bank Board to permit a reduction in the interest rate charged on advances to savings and loan associations and establishing a secondary market for conventional home mortgages through the Federal National Mortgage Association and a new Federal Home Loan Mortgage Corporation. These proposals were incorporated in the emergency legislation which was being shaped by the Congressional committees.

Notwithstanding the adamant opposition of the Federal Reserve Board and the other Federal fiscal authorities, there was growing sentiment in Congress, however, for much stronger financial measures establishing a strong priority for housing by requiring participation in housing finance by the Board and by pension funds. In the Senate, the principal measure along these lines was sponsored by Senator Proxmire of Wisconsin; it would have required the Federal Reserve Board to make loans of $3 billion a year at no more than 6 percent interest to the Federal Home Loan Bank System, which in turn would advance these funds to savings and loan associations for the purpose of making home mortgages at not to exceed 7 percent. (This would have been 2 to 2½ percent below the going rate for home mortgages.) A generally similar measure was being pressed in the House by Congresswoman Sullivan and by Congressman William A. Barrett of Pennsylvania, chairman of the Housing Subcommittee. Chairman Wright Patman of the House Banking and Currency Committee was pushing a bill to require pension funds to make massive contributions to a housing development bank.

When the Proxmire proposal was incorporated in the emergency bill by the Senate Banking and Currency Committee on a 9-to-6 vote, the White House reacted with alarm. President Nixon wrote to the leaders of the Senate implying a Presidential veto of the entire measure if the Proxmire provision were not deleted. This stand placed the President in a contradictory position on the question of priorities for housing. On April 1, 1970, in releasing the second annual report on national housing goals (required by the 1968 Act), the President described the goal of 26 million dwellings in ten years as "a reasonable expression of the magnitude of overall needs" and as "consistent with other urgent claims on our productive resources. This volume of housing can be produced if we follow appropriate policies." The President went on to say:

> Meeting the goals will however, require that both the executive and the Congress—and, in a broader sense, the whole nation—accord to the national housing effort the appropriate and necessary priority among the nation's domestic concerns. If this conviction of urgency and sense of priority are wanting, the prospects for success will be meager indeed.

However, this conviction of urgency and sense of priority were evidently blunted when confronted by an actual proposal to give housing priority access to Federal Reserve funds. The President characterized the proposals as "an intolerable invasion of the Federal Reserve" and he asked: "If housing is to be so favored, how could other sectors like small business and state and local government be denied?"

The implied threat of a veto was sufficient to kill the Proxmire move, at last for the time being. In due course, the Emergency Home Finance Act of 1970 was approved by Congress. As passed, the law contained a compromise program intended to preserve the Proxmire objective of a 7-percent interest rate on housing for middle-income families through interest subsidies. The Act authorized subsidies of $105 million a year for three years, sufficient to subsidize about 300,000 dwellings a year. The President signed the bill but, in effect, pigeonholed the Proxmire compromise by refraining from requesting the appropriations necessary to place it in motion.

The political contest between Congress and the Nixon Administration on housing and community development now entered the area of long-range legislation as well as the area of adequate funding of existing programs to meet the rapidly expanding needs generated by the urban crisis. HUD, after lengthy clearances within the White House and the Bureau of the Budget, presented a voluminous bill which was largely limited to consolidating, simplifying, and making more uniform the provision of existing Federally-assisted housing programs. The bill contained no major new proposals for meeting the physical needs of the urban crisis.

The HUD legislation drew a less than enthusiastic reaction from the Congressional committees or from the organizations with a direct stake in housing and community development, Mayor Hugh C. Curran of Bridgeport, speaking for the U.S. Conference of Mayors and the National League of Cities, referred to the drastic under-funding of urban programs and commented: "In the face of these pressing demands, we find it rather difficult to concentrate on a proposal by HUD whose primary emphasis is restructuring of present housing programs." The AFL-CIO dismissed the proposal as merely "tidying up" the various housing programs now on the books rather than meeting the nation's "housing crisis."

The National Housing Conference supported in principle the objectives of simplifying the many Federal housing programs but declared that "as introduced, we believe the bill would produce inequities and would present serious roadblocks to the effective functioning of these programs"; the NHC presented 18 detailed amendments to correct these defects, including a HUD formula which would have resulted in widespread rent increases for tenants in public housing and moderate income projects. Mayor Lindsay of New York City characterized the HUD bill as "a step backward" and as posing "a serious threat to the validity of our existing housing programs by narrowing rather than expanding their scope." He added: "There is an urgent need to enlarge the range of eligibility for publicly-assisted housing because fewer and fewer of our moderate and middle income families can afford the market price of decent housing."

The HUD bill contained no provisions for urgently needed money expansions for urban programs but instead repeated its tactical error of 1969 by proposing that the legislative committees surrender their responsibility for setting desired program levels to the Bureau of the Budget and the appropriations committees. By contrast, the involved organizations like the National Housing Conference and the U.S. Conference of Mayors made specific recommendations for large increases in authorizations for all the basic urban programs.

In these circumstances, the Congressional committees largely ignored the HUD proposals and determined to fashion their own legislation on their own initiative, as they had done in 1969. This legislation was to include a far-reaching new program on urban growth and new community development. Drawing largely on the recommendations of the National Committee on Urban Growth Policy and on extensive hearings, these provisions were aimed at meeting the oncoming problems created by massive population growth over the balance of the twentieth century. The broad purposes of the legislation were to extend broad-scale Federal financial aid to public or private development corporations for the development of new cities or the expansion of existing small towns, both on a well-planned and largely self-contained basis, and also to give a boost to the revitalization of obsolete and blighted central city areas largely through liberalized urban renewal techniques for the redevelopment of obsolete or underutilized nonresidential structures. The sponsors of this new venture were Representative Thomas L. Ashley of Toledo in the House and Senators Sparkman and Muskie in the Senate.

The rationale for these new proposals was summarized in the report of the House Banking and Currency Committee:

> In the view of many experts, the United States is likely to experience a population increase of about 75 million people during the remainder of this century. If present patterns of urban development continue, this population increase will contribute additional impetus to the marked deterioration in the quality of life which has come with past disorderly urban sprawl. Among the results which may be expected are wasteful and inefficient uses of our land resources, including increased air and water pollution; inefficiencies in public facilities and services; and the failure to make use of resources of the Nation's smaller cities and towns.
>
> Unless concerted action is taken now to plan for urban growth on a national scale, the future will bring lessened employment and business opportunities for the residents of central cities and of the ability of such cities to retain a tax base necessary to support vital public services; further separation of people within metropolitan areas on the basis of income and race; further increases in the distances between the places where people live, work, and seek recreation; decreased effectiveness of urban transportation; and lessened opportunities for the home-building industry to provide good housing.

The Congressional initiative on this issue provided a significant contrast in attitudes between the Democratc leadership in Congress and the Nixon Administration. HUD, too, had been preparing legislative proposals on urban growth, even though on a less ambitious scale than the Congressional proposals. But, on June 6, 1970, the *New York Times* reported as follows:

Washington, June 6—The White House has overruled plans by the Department of Housing and Urban Development to send to Congress this year comprehensive legislation to assist in the creation of new cities.

Authoritative sources said proposals drafted by the Department after months of research had been laid aside because they would require new spending commitments at a time when the Administration was trying to control inflation with a tight budget.

Further development soon accentuated this contrast in attitudes on housing and community development. While the legislative committees continued their work on the Housing and Urban Development Act of 1970, which would also involve large increases in funds for the basic existing programs, the House Appropriations Committee was considering the Administration's restricted budget for these activities in the fiscal year beginning July 1, 1970. The House Committee made no effort to increase this budget, which included only $1 billion for urban renewal (as against Congressional authorizations of $2.3 billion) and only $150 million for water and sewer grants. On the floor of the House, in response to pleas from hard-pressed communities, the appropriation for water and sewer grants was increased to $500 million.

In the Senate, there was concerted pressure from mayors and allied organizations to increase the urban renewal appropriation. As a result, an amendment was adopted by a large majority increasing the appropriation to $1.7 billion. In the ensuing conference with the House, the urban renewal appropriation was compromised at $1.35 billion and the water and sewer amount was kept at $500 million. This was the bill which was sent to the White House.

But President Nixon said no. In vetoing the HUD bill on August 11 because of the increase in the urban renewal and water and sewer appropriations, the President asserted that he was "mindful of the urgent needs of our cities" but added:

> I am vetoing this bill because it helps drive up the cost of living, harming the people it is most designed to help. This kind of excessive spending would also help cause the kind of huge deficits that drive up interest rates, which would make it impossible to speed the recovery of the housing industry . . .

The facts were that the increases in the HUD appropriations

would have had zero impact on actual Federal expenditures in the current fiscal year, because of the lead times involved. However, the increases would have been helpful to communities in providing a base for future projects.

The press interpreted the President's veto of the HUD bill and his simultaneous veto of the Office of Education appropriation bill as a political gesture designed to foster his image as defender of the dollar and opponent of inflation. His political gamble was 50 percent successful. The veto of the education bill was overridden on August 13 in the House of Representatives by a vote of 289 to 114, with 77 Republicans deserting the President on this issue. But the veto of the HUD bill was sustained through a revival of the traditional Republican-conservative-Southern Democratic coalition. Only 22 Republicans voted to override the HUD veto, while 155 voted to sustain it. George Mahon, the conservative Texan chairman of the House Appropriations Committee, repudiated the Democratic leadership on this vote and led 39 other Southern Democrats to support the veto.

This setback on appropriations did not deter the Congressional legislative committees from proceeding with their work on the Housing and Urban Development Act of 1970. On September 21, the Senate Banking and Currency Committee unanimously reported a comprehensive measure, incorporating the urban growth proposal as well as major expansion in funding authorizations and perfecting amendments for the basic existing programs such as urban renewal, low-rent public housing, and the various subsidy programs for privately-sponsored housing for moderate- and low-income families. Under the skillful floor management and leadership of Senator John Sparkman, the Senate approved the bill on September 23 by an unprecedented majority of 59 to 2. In the House, the Banking and Currency Committee reported a companion bill on October 5 which in certain respects went beyond the Senate bill in liberality. The vote in the committee was 24 to 4, although 11 of the committee Republicans joined in a minority report critical of certain of the provisions of the measure, including the amounts of authorizations. With the recess of Congress for the elections fast approaching, floor action in the House was deferred until after the elections.

During the hectic off-year Congressional campaign of 1970, the overriding issue was the frantic effort by President Nixon and Vice

President Agnew to paint the Democrats as soft on violence, campus unrest, and law and order, and the efforts of the Democrats to rebut these allegations. There were, however, underlying economic issues which turned out to be more influential in the final election results than the scare tactics of the Republican leadership. These issues included the acute housing shortage and inflated mortgage interest rates, along with unemployment and the rising cost of living. The failure of the Nixon-Agnew gambit to alter the power balance in Congress and the sweeping Democratic gains at the state level appeared to place the cause of housing and community development in a somewhat stronger political position.

The unanswered question was whether the Nixon Administration, with the 1972 Presidential campaign in the offing, would adjust its restrictive policies so as to accommodate the acute needs for housing and development in the urban areas and metropolitan districts.

When Congress reconvened after the elections, the Appropriations Committee fashioned a compromise appropriation bill cutting the increase in appropriation for urban renewal and water and sewer grants above the budget to $200 million each. This bill was ultimately signed by President Nixon. However, using his executive powers, the President promptly ordered HUD not to use any of the increased appropriations during the fiscal year for which they were voted. This action became a point of high controversy in the incoming Congress on the grounds that it represented in effect a "line item" veto of portions of legislation, which is prohibited by the Constitution.

On the Housing and Urban Development Act, the House of Representatives adopted a compromise bill which followed generally the provisions of the Senate-passed measure. The bill was sent to the White House just before Christmas. The President waited until the last minute before signing it on December 31, 1970—without comment.

CHAPTER 13

A Prognosis of Housing Politics, 1970-90

Since 1933, when the Federal Government first began to assume a major role in the national housing scene, a chart of progress in meeting the nation's housing needs would show a succession of peaks and valleys. As described in the preceding chapters of this book, these fluctuations have had their origin in part in the varying political alignments in Congress. They have reflected the attitudes and objectives of the six Presidential administrations which have presided over the nation since that year. They have been profoundly affected by the economic consequences of United States' involvement in three international conflicts: World War II, the Korean war, and the undeclared war in Indochina. They have related to the growing urban crisis in the country, the social tensions, and the accompanying racial divisions.

An assessment of the future outlook for housing and related necessities in the United States must start with a basic question: After four decades of effort, what, on balance, has been the net accomplishment?

It is quite possible to present a negative and pessimistic answer to this question:

- The nation currently has the most severe housing shortage since immediately after World War II, a shortage affecting not only the poor and the racially disadvantaged but also the middle class.
- The national goal of "a decent home in a suitable living environ-

ment for every American family" which was first legislated in 1949 and strongly reaffirmed by Congress in 1968 is still far from accomplishment, after 25 years.

- The central cities are becoming ghettoes for blacks, other minorities, and other poor. The cities are collapsing from physical decay, increasing crime, and unbearable financial strains.
- The middle-class whites continue to migrate to the suburbs, in flight from the blight, crime, and racial tensions of the central city. In turn, they are creating middle-class suburban ghettoes, marked by sprawl, incipient congestion, and disregard for the environment.

These pessimistic judgments can readily be substantiated. On the positive side of the record, however, there are factors which, in the opinion of this writer, are of greater significance for the future:

- Throughout the political vicissitudes since 1933, the principle of ultimate Federal responsibility for the housing welfare of the American people has survived. This has included three terms under conservative Republican Presidents and three wars. Presently, the principle is surviving notwithstanding President Nixon's open repudiation of it.
- While the goal of satisfactory housing for all Americans is still far from achieved, there had been rather impressive progress in expanding housing production for moderate- and low-income households until the imposition of the freeze on HUD subsidies in January, 1973. In fiscal year 1971, a total of almost 400,000 dwellings were placed in construction with Federal subsidies from HUD, ranging from low-rent public housing to developments for moderate-income families. This represented about one-third of total residential construction and was by far the largest level ever reached under the Federal subsidy programs; it occurred despite acute stringencies in the housing finance market. In fiscal year 1972, the total commitments made by HUD totaled 453,000 units.
- In recent years, Congressional votes on crucial housing and community development issues have pointed to an emerging positive majority, in the House of Representatives as well as in the Senate.
- There is beginning evidence of a reordering of Federal spending priorities in favor of urgent domestic civilian programs as against the Pentagon and the space program. This trend is obviously more conspicuous in Congress than in the Nixon Administration. Housing and community development prgorams are in the forefront of this emerging sentiment.

• The problem of adequate housing and the plight of urban areas have gained wide public recognition which should lead eventually to more effective political action. This recognition is beginning to spill over into suburban communities.

The political forces which will shape housing and community development activities over the coming two decades and the Federal involvement therein stem mainly from three points of reference: first, public demands and sentiments; second, the impact of the latter on Congressional political alignments, and, third, the attitude, response and leadership of the Executive Branch of the Federal Government.

The broad public attitudes on housing and community development reflect in part the deep current divisions within American society. Still, there is in a sense a common bond of adversity shared on housing problems among the classes, except the most affluent. The severe mortgage credit crunch in 1969 and 1970, the inflation in interest rates and in construction costs and sales prices, and the sharp decline in private residential building bore heavily against middle- and lower-middle-class families. So does the impact of the acute housing shortage. This trend persists under the more pronounced inflationary influences of the Seventies.

Another illustration: The biggest population gainers during the Sixties were the suburbs within metropolitan areas, resulting largely from migration from the central cities by middle-class white families. It was widely anticipated that this suburban population would be predominantly conservative and hence Republican in its politics. Yet, the suburbs have rapidly developed urban problems of their own— congestion, blight, pollution, inadequate public utilities, schools and recreation areas, rising crime rates, and rising local taxes. It is therefore unrealistic to assume that the suburbs will remain large political enclaves by themselves, immune from the urban pressures which will generate demands for increased Federal aid, including housing and community development. Granted, the suburbs, in the main, are still a strong bastion against the infiltration of housing for low-income families, meaning primarily low-income blacks. This position was reinforced by the split decision of the Supreme Court on April 26, 1971, upholding the constitutionality of State laws permitting a referendum to block construction of low-rent housing for the poor.

However, it is difficult to conceive how these exclusionary policies can long survive in the face of pressures from the central cities and of the suburbs' own demands for other Federal urban aids. These trends in public political thinking obviously will have a major impact on alignments in Congress. During most of the time span covered by this book, there generally has been a comfortable majority in the Senate favorable to liberal housing and community development legislation. In the House of Representatives, however, the balance of power for most of this period has been held by a coalition of Republican and Democratic representatives from rural districts, the Democrats in this group being almost entirely from the Deep South. This coalition was responsible for the many close votes and occasional defeats in the House on critical housing and community development issues as well as other important urban matters. In recent years, however, the strength of this coalition has been diminishing. This has reflected in part the increasing political pressures for solutions for critical urban and metropolitan problems and a trade-off of urban votes on matters important to the rural bloc in return for rural support or lessened opposition on issues important to the urban and suburban blocs. But it also reflects a shrinkage in the actual number of rural members in the House. This has resulted from the continued population flow from the rural areas into the metropolitan areas and from the impact of the Supreme Court's "one man-one vote" rule on Congressional redistricting.

A significant analysis of this trend by Professor Richard Lehne of Rutgers University projected that the redistricting resulting from the 1970 Census of Population as well as previous redistricting on the basis of the Supreme Court's decision would result in a decrease of 37 seats in the House for rural districts just since 1966 and an increase of the same number in the number of seats from predominantly suburban districts within metropolitan areas.

His projected alignment of seats for the House was 129 predominantly suburban districts, 100 central city districts, and 144 rural districts, with 62 districts mixed. Professor Lehne's analysis of voting patterns by Representatives from suburban districts in 1967-68 also showed a much closer correlation with the votes of central city Representatives than with rural Representatives. Accompanying this trend, the number of Democratic Representatives from outside the Deep South has overtaken the number of Republican Representatives, rising to 176 Democrats against 153 Republicans in the 1970 elections. On the other hand, the increase in Republican Representatives from the Deep South has primarily been a trade-off of conservative Republicans for conservative Democrats.

The answer to the third basic question on future political alignments on housing—the attitude, response, and leadership of the Executive Branch—is more complex. This reflects in large degree the complicated political motivations of the Nixon Administration.

President Nixon's State of the Union Message to Congress on January 22, 1971, gave significant glimpses of his view of future urban and metropolitan policies and their relationship to his efforts to secure reelection. Here are a few samples:

> Let's face it. Most Americans today are simply fed up with government at all levels. They will not—and should not—continue to tolerate the gap between promise and performance. . . .
> The time has come to reverse the flow of power and resources from the states and communities to Washington, and start power and resources flowing back from Washington to the states and communities and, more important, to the people, all across America. . . .
> Local government is the government closest to the people and more responsive to the individual person; it is people's government in a far more intimate way than the Government in Washington can ever be . . .
> But above all, what this Congress can be remembered for is opening the way to a new American revolution—a peaceful revolution in which power was turned back to the people—in which government at all levels was refreshed and renewed, and made truly responsive. This can be a revolution as profound, as far-reaching, as exciting as that first revolution almost 200 years ago.

While the rhetoric was different, the President's position in essence is a return to the classic conservative Republican stance in the twentieth century. This was that on domestic economic and social issues the Federal Government should be in a weak position and that governmental power should on these matters be fragmented among state and local governments, which would be more readily manageable by the private power centers. During the earlier decades of the century, this had been promoted under the banner of "states' rights." President Nixon was presenting the principle as "a new American revolution." It was, in fact, more in the nature of a counterrevolution since, if successful, it would overthrow the basic concept of primary Federal responsibility on social and economic issues affecting the general welfare which had been established under the New Deal and since continued. President Eisenhower had made a modest effort to shift some powers back to the states but without significant results.

President Nixon's approach did take into account some of the realities of the 1970s. While the core of his "new revolution" was revenue sharing with state and local governments, his initial proposal would divert only a little more than 2 percent of total Federal receipts to "general" revenue sharing. Nor did he propose any relinquishment of Federal tax sources to state and local governments. The largest financial heft of his proposals would be through "special" revenue sharing under which a number of existing Federal grant-in-aid programs would be terminated and merged into six broad-purpose funds, under which decisions regarding their use would be made by the State and local governments. The total initial Federal funds allocated to these six programs would be $11 billion, representing the existing funding of the programs to be terminated. In the case of housing and community development, the President's proposals did not involve the existing subsidized housing programs but proposed terminating the urban renewal, model cities, water and sewer grant, and rehabilitation loan programs—all bearing the hallmark of Democratic Administrations—and their consolidation in a single community development fund to be spread among the communities for use at their discretion. The initial annual level of funding requested —$2 billion—was substantially less than existing demands from communities and Congressional authorizations.

There has been much speculation on the immediate political motivations underlying President Nixon's proposals. In general, the critical consensus views his strategy in these terms: his failure to carry the big cities in 1968 and his bias against most existing Federally supported urban programs; his political weakness within the growing black minority; his attempt to strengthen his political base within the middle- and lower-middle income classes—North as well as South—by curtailing central city programs and by whittling away at the enforcement of civil rights laws for education and for "open" housing in the suburbs; and his conviction that the potential base for future Republican majorities lie with the State and local governments notwithstanding the extensive Democratic gains in the 1970 state elections and the predominant Democratic control of the large urban centers.

The actual 1972 voting patterns were a mixed bag but clearly not a public decision to return to the pre-FDR allocation of political power. On the one hand, the President's unprecedented pluralities in both the popular vote and the electoral college were clearly a repudiation by "Middle America" of Senator McGovern's tentative move to the left. On the other hand, the President's inability to win control of Congress or even make substantial gains indicated that a majority of the American people were not prepared to follow the President in his rightist so-called revolution.

An incisive comment on the President's strategy appeared in the *Wall Street Journal,* February 11, 1971. Under the heading "The Politics of Nixon's 'Revolution,' " Monroe W. Karmin, the *Journal's* Washington urban affairs specialist, wrote:

> Though details of the strategy are still to be penciled in, the potential beneficiaries of Mr. Nixon's proposed "peaceful revolution in which power will be turned back to the people" seem obvious. They will be "Nixon people"—people who voted for him in the past, plus those considered open to voting for him in the future. They are suburban people and rural people and Rocky Mountain people; they are middle-class people and upper middle-class people; they are white people. They are not Democratic Party people in the teeming central cities of the industrialized states. . . . In a sentence, the "urban crisis" in terms of the priority treament of the Kennedy-Johnson era, is over.

The Nixon Administration's bias against the existing Federal urban programs was conspicuous in his special message to Congress on the proposed Special Revenue Sharing for Urban Community Development. In fact, the extravagance of his language supporting this proposal might be considered as verbal overkill since it could easily be construed as calling for a vast expansion in Federal urban aid, which clearly was not his intent:

> As the size of Federal progrems for renewing our cities has grown in recent years, so has the evidence of their basic defects. Plagued by delay and duplication, by waste and rigidity, by inconsistency and irrationality, Federal grant-in-aid programs for urban develop-

ment have simply not achieved the purposes for which they were established. . . .

On every hand we see the results of this failure: a sorely inadequate supply of housing and community facilities, vast wastelands of vacant and decaying buildings, acre upon acre of valuable urban renewal land lying empty and fallow, and an estimated 24 million Americans still living in substandard housing. Many of our central cities—once symbols of vitality and opportunity—have now become places of disillusion and decay. As many suburban neighborhoods have grown older, they, too, have begun to deteriorate and to take on the problems of the central cities. Even some of the newest suburban subdivisions, planned and developed in a shortsighted, haphazard manner, are not prepared to provide essential public services to their growing populations. They are already on their way to becoming the slums of tomorrow. . . .

Lest the inference be drawn from his grim description of urban problems that he was advocating greater Federal aids to urban areas, the President covered his position in this manner:

If only we appropriate more funds, we are often told, then everything will be all right. How long will it take us to learn the danger of such thinking? More money will never compensate for ineffective programs.

This, in the face of the clear fact that the principal problem limiting Federal housing and community development over the years has been chronic underfunding.

There were also important issues of principle and policy at stake, involving the basic question of Federal responsibility for the general welfare. With regard to the proposed Special Revenue Sharing for Urban Community Development, this concern was well stated by Milton Semer, former general counsel of the Housing and Home Finance Agency, former special counsel to President Johnson and then active in Senator Muskie's incipient campaign for the Democratic Presidential nomination. In a keynote speech before the annual convention of the National Housing Conference in March, 1971, Semer warned that the revenue sharing plan would "reverse the history of the last half century":

It would declare that the general character of urban growth, and the health and vitality of our urban communities, has ceased to be a matter of national concern and is to be considered in the future as a matter solely for random local decision. Does the Administration really mean to say that there should no longer be a national involvement in policies for urban growth and development?

The membership of the National Housing Conference adopted a resolution opposing the special revenue sharing plan for urban community development on similar grounds:

> NHC believes that Federal grants should provide incentives to promote national programs and objectives relating to housing and community development. . . . We are deeply concerned that many of these programs—with their emphasis on serving the underprivileged and racial minorities—would be prejudiced by the proposed consolidation of the categorical programs into a single community development grant program under which each local government would determine which activity it elects to pursue.

Most of the public interest organizations—labor, professional, women's, and church groups—have followed the line of the National Housing Conference on revenue sharing. The U.S. Conference of Mayors and the National League of Cities, whose municipal members are mostly in desperate financial straits, have been lured by President Nixon's general revenue sharing proposal but are predominantly skeptical of the benefits to them of the special revenue sharing programs as compared with the existing categorical grant-in-aid programs if adequately funded.

The political experience in Congress and in the field in 1971 and 1972 did not disclose any strong support for the President's proposed "revolution." In housing and community development, the pressures from the field continued to be for adequate funding of ongoing programs rather than on the abandonment of those programs. These local pressures were, in fact, largely responsible for the expansion in subsidized housing production within the limits of available authorizations. This expansion evoked an ambivalent reaction in the Administration. George Romney, production-oriented throughout his career, was inclined to claim credit for the production gains whereas the Office of Management and Budget, dedicated to the abandonment of the programs, took a dim view and sharply curtailed the staff appropriations for their administration. (This made maladministra-

tion inevitable and permitted OMB and HUD to point to the resulting abuses as evidence of defects in the underlying Federal housing
statutes.)

The acid test of the housing aspects of the Nixon "revolution" has
followed Nixon's landslide reelection in 1972. This persuaded the
White House that the political alignment finally made it feasible to
liquidate Federal housing and related, programs once and for all.

This in effect is what the Nixon Administration undertook to do
in January, 1973, when it arbitrarily and brutally suspended or terminated all the housing programs involving Federal subsidies, notwithstanding continuing needs and demands from the communities
for the expansion and continuation of these programs. The official
explanation from the White House and the new regime at HUD was
that the weaknesses and failures of the programs justified a suspension of activity for sixteen months while the Administration studied
new solutions. (In truth, to the extent that failures had occurred
they reflected primarily failures of administration by HUD if not
deliberate policy of OMB.)

The arbitrary freeze on housing programs for moderate- and low-
income families caused a great outcry from the cities, from labor,
and from the majority of Democratic leaders in Congress. But
Nixon's silent majority was silent on this issue, too. The erosion of
the President's political standing on Capitol Hill because of the
Watergate scandals made it highly doubtful that the President's proposed negative program on housing could command anything like a
majority in Congress.

On the other hand, the political trends which presage greater
strength for urban and metropolitan programs in Congress have already been cited. The acute housing shortage is a reality in most
urban and suburban areas throughout the country, affecting all
classes. Current upward pressures on the private mortgage market
promise no real easing for the middle classes. The lag in correction
of substandard housing conditions continues to aggravate social tensions, and not just in the big cities. The financial strain on the major
cities is at the breaking point and this strain is migrating to the
suburbs along with other urban-type problems.

All this points to increasing political pressure for more extensive
and massive Federal aid for housing and related community devel-

opment, along with education, health care, pollution correction, welfare, and other critical urban and metropolitan issues. Add to this the impact of population expansion over the next two decades. While the rate of population growth in the United States has subsided and probably will continue to subside, the present age composition of the population makes further expansion inevitable over the next two decades and a type of expansion which will exert maximum pressure for a massive increase in the housing supply. Projections by George H. Brown, former director of the U.S. Census Bureau, are that of a total expected population increase of 36 million persons between 1970 and 1985, 28 million will be in the age brackets between 20 and 45, precisely the age range which will demand housing. And not all of them will be affluent.

The Census Bureau also estimates that by 1985 almost one-half of the total U.S. population will be living in suburban areas as compared with about one-third in 1970. It is also projected that the black proportion of central city population will grow to one-third from one-fifth. Translated into political terms, this means that the suburban bloc combined with the central city bloc, both sharing urgent needs for housing and related urban facilities and services and requiring extensive Federal aid, should have decisive political control in Congress and in the legislatures of most states.

Can the nation afford to reach a full housing economy? The answer is clearly yes, if the political force of the American public and its response in Congress and in the Executive Branch of the Government insist on policies assuring a reasonable priority. If the 1971 projections of the Council of Economic Advisers are used as a base and if Federal policies allocate to housing a share of the national gross product midway between the low of 3.4 percent in 1969 and the high of 6.1 percent in 1955, there would be $60 billion available for housing development by 1975, sufficient for 3 million new houses a year.

My prediction is that the political forces of the future will insist on at least this much.